CONQUERING THE PACIFIC

An Unknown Mariner and the Final Great Voyage of the Age of Discovery

ANDRÉS RESÉNDEZ

HOUGHTON MIFFLIN HARCOURT

BOSTON | NEW YORK

2021

hmhbooks.com

Title page map courtesy of the John Carter Brown Library, Brown University.
All other maps by Mapping Specialists, Ltd.

Library of Congress Cataloging-in-Publication Data
Names: Reséndez, Andrés, author.
Title: Conquering the Pacific : an unknown mariner and the final great voyage of the
Age of Discovery / Andrés Reséndez.
Other titles: Unknown mariner and the final great voyage of the Age of Discovery
Description: Boston : Houghton Mifflin Harcourt, 2021. |
Includes bibliographical references and index.
Identifiers: LCCN 2021004112 (print) | LCCN 2021004113 (ebook) |
ISBN 9781328515971 (hardcover) | ISBN 9780358676348 |
ISBN 9780358638339 | ISBN 9781328517364 (ebook)
Subjects: LCSH: Legazpi, Miguel López de, 1510?–1572 — Friends and associates. |
Martín, Lope. | Pilots and pilotage — Biography. | Philippines — Discovery and
exploration — Spanish. | Pacific Ocean — Discovery and exploration — Spanish. |
Explorers — Spain — Biography. | Barra de Navidad (Mexico) — History, Naval. |
BISAC: HISTORY / Europe / Spain & Portugal | HISTORY / Expeditions & Discoveries
Classification: LCC DS674.9.L4 R47 2021 (print) | LCC DS674.9.L4 (ebook) |
DDC 959.9/01092 [B] — dc23
LC record available at https://lccn.loc.gov/2021004112
LC ebook record available at https://lccn.loc.gov/2021004113

Book design by Chloe Foster

Printed in the United States of America

1 2021

4500832111

Most people realize the sea covers two thirds of the planet, but few take the time to understand even a gallon of it. Watch what happens when you try to explain something as basic as the tides, that the suction of the moon and the sun creates a bulge across the ocean that turns into a slow and sneaky yet massive wave that covers our salty beaches twice a day. People look at you as if you're making it up as you go.

—Jim Lynch, *The Highest Tide*, 2006

The voyage from the Philippines to America may be said to be the most dreadful and longest of any in the world. The ocean to be crossed is vast, almost half of the terraqueous globe, with the wind always in front, terrible tempests, one on the back of another, and mortal diseases in a voyage lasting seven or eight months, sometimes in higher and lower altitudes, in cold, temperate, and hot weather. It is enough to destroy a man of steel.

—Giovanni Francesco Gemelli Careri, *Giro del Mondo*
(Voyage Around the World), 1699

Lord my God, You are very great . . . You make the clouds your chariot, and you walk upon the wings of the winds.

—Psalm 104:1–3

NOVA ALBION *Terra sub latitudine 42 adc*
est frigida, etiam media æstate, ut F. Drucus pre inge
frigore, in Austr. reverti coactus sit, mense Junio
Incolæ idololatræ sunt, corporum factis lacerationi-
bus & crebris sacrificijs in montibus utuntur.

De este Cobo Mendocino Hasta el Estrecho de Anian esta por Descubrir

NOVA ALBION

y.as de Armenio.
vicas de Plata

Cuimpango.
Maior Rica
de Oro y Plata

Dos hermanas
alalexio
S.Ieronimo
Martieres

Tropicus

Vulcan

MARE

PA

S Bartolome
B. de Villabos

Stades Pablo

Las desa
Praechadas
Y de Paxaros

Y.llos Reies
Barbudos
Y. de don alonso
de Arvellano

CVM

alvedores
Miracemvas

dos Vecinos
Nadadores

CIRCVLVS

Y de

Canana
Labvriada

R. de S.pvsE

May de N.a señora
Bolcan
La redonda

B. Segundos

Baxos de
candelaria

Las Ranas
Malaita
Malay

Nombr
The

Contents

Contents

List of Illustrations

List of Maps

CONQUERING THE PACIFIC

Preface

$\mathcal{S}$een from a satellite above the Pacific Ocean, Earth appears as a magnificent ball of indigo. The continental lands recede to the edges, as if about to slip to the far side. What remains in view is an immense span of blue interrupted only by minuscule specks of land. All of us have looked at satellite images of the Pacific. Yet we are utterly incapable of comprehending its vastness: so large that all the continents and islands would fit within it, and so deep that it holds almost exactly half of the water contained in all the world's oceans. Such comparisons, impressive as they may be, are still on an alien scale, so here is a more human attempt at understanding: if we were to drop an average swimmer in the middle of the Pacific, she would need three months without ever stopping just to reach the closest continental shore. Without swimming and left only to the currents, the trip would take a lot longer. A fisherman swept off the coast of Mexico on a boat with a faulty motor spent nearly fourteen months adrift in 2012–2014 before washing up in the Marshall Islands, three-fifths of the way across the Pacific. Buoys with transmitters deployed by scientists near Hawaiʻi bobbed and drifted for a year before some of them began washing up in the Philippines. Of course, the stranded fisherman and the scientific buoys covered only portions of the Pacific. Anyone actually contemplating crossing it from one continental shore to the other—like the explorers in this book—would have to double these times: six months of around-the-clock swimming or close to two years of free-floating coupled with unbelievable luck.[1]

We tend to think of the Pacific as just another ocean, like the Indian or the Atlantic. In fact, it is different, as Erasmus Darwin—Charles's grandfather—noticed in 1791. He believed that the South Sea, as it was often called, was nothing less than the hole left behind after the Moon had split from Earth. Erasmus was a scientist, but rather than attempting to prove this audacious theory, he bequeathed it to posterity in a poem:

Gnomes! How you gazed!
When from her wounded side,
Where now the South-Sea heaves its waste of tide,
Rose on swift wheels the Moon's refulgent car.[2]

Nearly a century would pass before another Darwin—George Howard Darwin, Erasmus's great-grandson and Charles's son—would take the bait. George studied the Moon's orbit and developed a set of equations that described the history of the Moon's rotations around Earth. Running his model as far back as it would go, the younger Darwin estimated that the Moon had once orbited a mere six thousand miles away from our planet. This had occurred fifty-four million years ago "or before," according to his calculations, a time when the Earth and the Moon may still have been in a molten state and, as he put it, "formed parts of a common mass." The inescapable conclusion was that the Moon had been flung off from Earth in the distant past.[3]

George Darwin's contemporaries were enthralled. In a letter to the editor of *Nature* in 1882, geologist Osmond Fisher praised the younger Darwin's efforts and offered some additional thoughts. The Moon's separation from Earth must have been so sudden, Fisher reasoned, "that a great but shallow hole must consequently have been formed, whose centre would have been on or near the equator." Fisher's addendum gained acceptance, and thus was born the idea of the Pacific as "the scar" left after the Moon separated. The fission theory, as this explanation became known more formally, remained popular at least through the 1930s. The men and women of that generation believed that an ancient planetary event accounted for the immensity of the Pacific.[4]

Modern geology has provided an alternative explanation for how the vast Pacific came to be that is just as fantastical in its own way. Scientists have now established that Earth is much older than previously thought, around 4.5 billion years. During this time our planet has undergone dramatic changes in the arrangement of its continents and oceans. The latest configuration is the most relevant. Three hundred million years ago, all lands on Earth were fused together in a supercontinent known as Pangea ("all-earth" in Greek), while the rest of the planet consisted of a vast region of water referred to as Panthalassa (all-ocean) or sometimes Pre-Pacific. A German meteorologist named Alfred Wegener first came to this elegant vision of our planet after merely staring at a map and noticing how the contours of different continents fit so neatly together, as if they were pieces of the same jigsaw puzzle. "Does not the east coast of South America fit exactly with the west coast of Africa as if they had formerly been joined?" he wrote excitedly to his fiancée in 1910.[5]

Over the course of five years, Wegener built his case. He identified species like marsupials that live in Australasia and South America to show that an ancient land connection was the only reason for this curious distribution. He also enlisted the fossil record to his cause, observing how skeletal remains of Mesosaurus — an enormous lizard that lived some 280 million years ago — had turned up only in southern Africa and eastern South America, indicating once again that these two lands had been joined together in the distant past. Most persuasively perhaps, Wegener showed that the Appalachian Mountains of North America formed a single geological system with the Caledonian Mountains of Scandinavia and the British Isles. According to the theory that he advanced in *The Origin of Continents and Oceans,* first published in 1915, these were "fragments of the edges of the separating blocks, whose detachment is easily understandable in just such a region of tectonic disturbance."[6]

Unfortunately, Wegener came up against a scholarly establishment unreceptive to the idea of wandering continents. At the University of Cambridge, physical geographer Philip Lake chastised Wegener for not seeking truth but advocating a cause that was "blind to every fact and argument that tells against it." Paleontologist Edward Wilber Berry of Johns Hopkins University was harsher. "My principal objection to the Wegener hypothesis rests on the author's method," Berry declared at a meeting in 1926. "It takes the familiar course of an initial idea, a selective search through the literature for corroborative evidence, ignoring most of the facts that are opposed to the idea, and ending in a state of auto-intoxication in which the subjective idea comes to be considered as an objective fact." Wegener's continental drift—the precursor to the modern theory of plate tectonics —was not widely adopted until the 1960s, when the evidence from multiple fields was so overwhelming that it could no longer be dismissed.[7]

Now we know that Pangea actually existed. Three hundred million years ago, our planet consisted merely of one supercontinent and one super-ocean. As Pangea broke up, however, it created additional oceans and seas. The Atlantic emerged after the Americas split from Europe and Africa. Crucially, even as the lands surrounding the Atlantic Ocean drifted apart, their contours continued to fit like pieces of the same jigsaw puzzle. In other words, opposite coasts of the Atlantic have always remained *relatively close* to one another, with an *S* of ocean snaking between Europe and Africa on one side and the Americas on the other.[8]

Meanwhile, the ancestral Panthalassa evolved into the Pacific Ocean

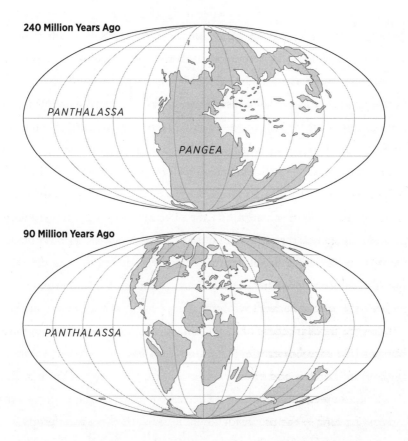

240 Million Years Ago

PANTHALASSA

PANGEA

90 Million Years Ago

PANTHALASSA

that we know today. It is smaller than its super-ocean predecessor and continues to shrink every day, as the American continent drifts westward in the direction of Asia. Yet even in this diminished incarnation, the Pacific remains the mother of all oceans, colossal compared to all other bodies of water and possessing the forbidding shape of an oval or a flattened circle with its east-west axis being the longest — precisely the direction that mattered most to the navigators whose story appears in this book, men who wished to go from the Americas to Asia and back. Not surprisingly, the Pacific has acted as the greatest obstacle to the movement not only of latter-day humans but also of all living creatures for tens of millions of years.

. . .

As long as the supercontinent lasted, plants and animals were able to move across the land more or less unencumbered. Most famously, dinosaurs were found on every continent, including Antarctica. About sixty-six million years ago, however, when North America had largely decoupled from Eurasia and South America had become completely detached from other landmasses, a meteorite smashed into Earth, bringing the dinosaur era to an end and causing a major redistribution of life on our planet.[9]

The most accepted scenario runs something like this: All was stable until a meteor fell on the coast of Yucatán. The object in question was about six miles in diameter, sizable but not big enough to inflict serious physical damage on Earth. For living creatures, however, the impact was devastating. The meteor moved so fast that it pierced the atmosphere in about one second. The first indication that something was amiss must have come as a blinding flash of light followed by a sonic boom far louder than anything humans have ever heard. More alarming must have been the rumbling of the ground as the meteor burrowed itself into the crust of Yucatán to a depth of about twenty-five miles. The worst came an instant later. As the asteroid became vaporized inside the hole, a brutal shockwave erupted as flaming rock and "ejecta," hurtling in all directions and reaching the atmosphere's highest layers. The narrow shaft carved by the asteroid on impact widened into a massive crater one hundred miles across, and a fireball resembling a mushroom cloud from an atomic bomb but incomparably larger emerged from it. Much of what is now Mexico, the United States, and Canada burst into flames as incandescent debris rained down all over the region, igniting fires and scalding animals roaming in the open or flying around. This great pulse of heat eventually died down. The ejecta, however, lingered in the atmosphere for months, causing an "impact winter." An environment that previously had been too bright and hot now overshot in the opposite direction. "The land became so dark that you could not have seen your hand in front of your face," wrote geologist

Walter Alvarez, one of the chief proponents of the killer asteroid theory. All green plants withered, producing a shutdown of photosynthesis and a collapse of the food chains based on them. Temperatures all across the world dropped precipitously. The mega-death that occurred sixty-six million years ago ranks as one of the five deadliest mass extinctions in all of life's history.[10]

The dinosaurs are the most widely recognized victims, suffering losses of one hundred percent. But the devastation went well beyond dinosaurs. Perhaps eighty-three percent of all lizards and snakes also vanished, even though they were smaller and therefore could find shelter more easily and required less food to survive. Birds went nearly extinct as well. Even mammals, the ultimate "winners" of that mass extinction, initially experienced reductions of seventy-five and up to ninety percent in some parts of North America.[11]

Life staged a comeback in time, but in a world far more geographically fragmented than before. A few hardy species remained viable all over the globe. Ferns, for instance, were among the first to recolonize the charred, acidic, and devastated lands. They were so successful that pollen specialists have detected a "fern spike" right after the asteroid's impact. Other species endured in different regions but quickly diverged from one another. Mammals are the most notable case. For tens of millions of years, they had lived in the dinosaurs' shadow. Once the great reptiles were gone, however, they experienced what some scholars have termed an "explosive" adaptive radiation. Different types of mammals—including us—emerged in some places but not in others. The same was true for many new species of plants and animals. Cacti, for example, arose exclusively in the Americas. Today about two thousand species can be found all over the continent, living in environments ranging from very dry deserts like the Atacama in northern Chile and the Baja California Desert in Mexico, to lush rain forests in southeastern Brazil and Central America, to grasslands in the United States and Canada. Yet up until five hundred years ago, when humans began dispersing them in sailing vessels, cacti did not exist anywhere outside the Americas.[12]

Precisely because many organisms were originally confined to one continent even though there were favorable conditions for their subsistence on other landmasses, some managed to cross the open ocean over tens of millions of years. Exactly how these "oceanic dispersals" occurred remains a matter of conjecture, but it is easy to imagine rafts of floating vegetation and animals as a mechanism. Storms cause rivers to swell and carry logs, branches, and vegetation. Sometimes a pile of debris collects behind a natural obstruction like a large rock or a tree until the storms become too strong, finally dislodging it and causing it to rush downriver and hurtle out into the ocean. British navy officers interviewed by nineteenth-century naturalist Alfred Russel Wallace reported seeing many such rafts of vegetation floating hundreds of miles from shore. They could be sizable. A British admiral recalled seeing them around the Philippines, "with trees growing on them, so that they were at first mistaken for islands." Animals were frequently trapped on them. Witnesses mentioned monkeys, squirrels, and even large felines traveling in spinning piles of wood along the Amazon River.[13]

Oceanic dispersals are extremely instructive because they reveal what is biologically possible, showing what oceans could be crossed and in what direction and which ones constituted insurmountable barriers. The Atlantic, for instance, has been breached several times. One hundred million years ago, South America became something of an island unto itself, having broken off from Africa and decoupled from North America (until about three and a half million years ago, when the Isthmus of Panama finally connected the two halves of the hemisphere). South America therefore existed in "splendid isolation" for tens of millions of years, as one scholar has put it. Yet several dispersals from Africa occurred during this time. South America was originally rodent-free, but a type of rodent called caviomorphs—related to guinea pigs, chinchillas, and capybaras but different from mice and rats—irrupted into it between fifty-five and forty-one million years ago. The closest relatives to the South American caviomorph rodents live in Africa, clearly indicating the source population. Primates followed suit. Again, South America possessed no primates at first. Yet a monkey that scientists call *Chilecebus carrascoensis* somehow got across the Atlantic Ocean thirty-five to twenty million years ago. To succeed, any primate had to be small and extremely resilient. To judge by the extant fossils, *Chilecebus carrascoensis* weighed less than two pounds and had a skull barely two inches long. This intrepid voyager would give rise to all New World monkeys, including spider monkeys, capuchins, and marmosets.[14]

As far as we know, about a dozen species have made it across the Atlantic Ocean, including rodents, primates, bats, tortoises, a blind snake, and even a weak-flying bird called the hoatzin. Of all these creatures, geckos and skinks were particularly capable of surviving long oceanic passages, as they hid underneath branches and laid eggs resistant to desiccation and even short-term immersion in seawater. Yet, irrespective of individual capabilities, two main factors explain these successful crossings. First, the closest two points across the Atlantic (Kabrousse, Senegal, and Touros, Brazil) now lie about 1,740 miles apart and, thirty or forty million years ago, perhaps half that distance. Nine hundred miles is far but not overwhelmingly so. Second, the rivers of western Africa constitute excellent launching pads to catch western-moving Atlantic currents leading to the Americas. Although crossing the Atlantic has never been easy, the biological record shows that it has occurred from time to time, and what is true for geckos and rodents applies no less to humans. When Christopher Columbus set out to cross the Ocean Sea in 1492, he and his crew were embarking on a voyage that other species had already made successfully.[15]

Other oceanic paths have been less common. The reverse Atlantic passage from South America to Africa, for instance, has played a much smaller role in the dispersal of species. Negative evidence cannot settle the matter definitively. South American organisms may well have crossed but been attacked on arrival, or perhaps they survived in Africa but without leaving much of a trace. Still, it is striking that no terrestrial vertebrates are known to have made the eastward passage across the Atlantic.[16]

Dispersals across the Pacific are more daunting still. Some species do exist on both sides of the Pacific Ocean, as we have seen. Marsupials live in the Americas (opossums and shrews) and in Australasia (kangaroos, koalas, Tasmanian devils, etc.). Intriguingly, a tiny arboreal marsupial from South America known as the *monito del monte* is more closely related to Australian marsupials than to its American cousins. Could this be the first terrestrial mammal to cross the Pacific? Recent research shows that marsupials originated in South America and migrated to Australia tens of millions of years ago, when there was a land connection via Antarctica or at least great proximity among these three landmasses. The same holds true for other lineages distributed on both sides of the Pacific, including birds, frogs, and turtles.[17]

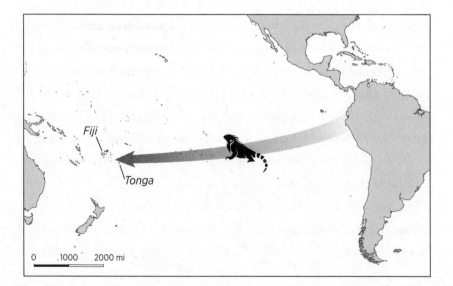

The only terrestrial vertebrate that seems to have survived a transpacific passage of six thousand miles is an iguana. The vast majority of iguanas are indigenous to the New World. Yet one genus called *Brachylophus* lives in the South Pacific islands of Fiji and Tonga. How did it get there? A passage from Central or South America would have taken a minimum of six months and more likely a year or more. Like geckos, iguanas are well suited for oceanic dispersals. They are able to obtain water from the plants they eat and possess nasal salt glands and thick skins that protect them from dehydration. Their presence not only on the American continent but also on many surrounding islands demonstrates their ability to travel across stretches of ocean. The Galápagos Islands, for instance, lie about six hundred miles away from the coast of Ecuador and are home to no fewer than three species of land iguanas as well as one marine iguana that lives on land but dives into the ocean to procure food, foraging on seaweed and reaching exposed rocks completely surrounded by water.[18]

Still, it is one thing to drift on logs for a couple of weeks and quite another to endure a six-thousand-mile passage. After several months adrift and no food left, any voyaging iguana would have perished. Nonetheless, some biologists have proposed a possible solution. The stowaways may have spent much of this journey as eggs. *Brachylophus* has an unusually long incubation period of seven, eight, or even nine months, one of the longest of any iguana. It is possible then that thirty or forty million years ago an unsuspecting group of iguanas, some in the form of eggs, may have dispersed by means of an epic rafting passage in which everything went right. Yet even if *Brachylophus* was somehow able to cross much of the Pacific, few other terrestrial vertebrates ever did until humans began making inroads in far more recent times.[19]

Except for the Arctic and the Antarctic, the islands scattered across the Pacific constituted the last frontier of human exploration and colonization on our planet. It was only about five thousand years ago — the blink of an

eye in terms of the human experience—when an island-hopping chain began forming. Over time, it would cross the great ocean. The chain started
in southern China, and the first links were quite straightforward. Early
seafarers from the Asian mainland explored and colonized large nearby
islands such as Taiwan and the Philippines. Their descendants, however,
faced a most extravagant labyrinth of islands, atolls, and stepping-stones
of diminishing size and availability of food resources as they ventured
deeper into the Pacific. Around 1500 BCE, these oceangoing pioneers took
a major first leap, a breathtaking passage of nearly fifteen hundred miles,
reaching the Mariana Islands, the archipelago containing Guam due east
from the Philippines. We will never know whether this event was deliberate or accidental; it may well have involved conditions of extreme hunger
and survival. Nevertheless, the fact that it happened at all, along with the
existence of ancient words for nautical terms like sails, points to a culture
with great navigational expertise.[20]

The next push required significant adaptations. Seafarers in a broad area
comprising Taiwan, the Philippines, the Bismarck Archipelago, and per-

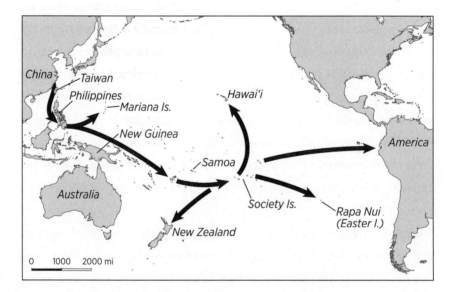

haps the colonizers of the Marianas themselves came to rely less on rice and more on tropical plants such as coconuts, bananas, and breadfruit as well as pigs, chickens, and dogs. Thus transformed, they ranged deeper into the great ocean, covering altogether about twenty-five hundred miles. Their perilous movements are clear from their distinctive pottery style known as Lapita, the languages they spoke, and the foods they carried. By 900 BCE, they had reached Tonga and Samoa, roughly a third of the way toward South America.[21]

A hiatus of more than fifteen hundred years followed that promising start, however. A second wave of colonization did not get under way until around 900–1000 of our era. What explains this prolonged pause? And why did seafarers suddenly start exploring again? Scholars still argue whether it was innovations like the double-hull canoe, sea-level fluctuations that revealed new lands and thus smaller sea gaps, novel forms of social organization, fortuitous changes in wind patterns due to El Niño events, or sheer luck. Whatever the reason, the voyages of this second wave rank among the most extraordinary feats of maritime exploration in all of history. Polynesian seafarers first had to negotiate the fifteen-hundred-mile gap separating Samoa from the Society Islands in what is now French Polynesia. After establishing a foothold there, these intrepid colonizers seem to have solved all remaining navigational and provisioning problems and, in one extraordinary pulse around the 1100s–1200s, explored and settled all remaining islands of East Polynesia, as far east as Rapa Nui (Easter Island), as far north as Hawai'i, and as far south as New Zealand.

These explorers also may have reached the Americas, thus completing the great human chain across the Pacific. If they had gotten four-fifths of the way across the Pacific and were capable of finding minuscule islands in the middle of the ocean, why would they have stopped short or missed an entire continent? As of this writing, DNA evidence indicating contact between Polynesians and pre-Columbian Native Americans had just become available. Polynesian populations in Palliser, the Marquesas,

Mangareva, and other islands in what is now French Polynesia bear traces of Native American ancestry dating back to the twelfth and thirteenth centuries. This new genetic information jibes well with the overall timing of Polynesian colonization of the Pacific and explains the presence of food items like coconuts and sweet potatoes across Polynesia and the American continent prior to Columbus.[22]

Pacific Islanders picked their way across this extravagant labyrinth with traditional methods. Captain James Cook in 1769, Don José de Andía y Varela in 1774–75, and other Western explorers down through the nineteenth century heard much about these techniques. In recent decades, too, anthropologists and sailing enthusiasts have learned from Polynesians and Micronesians who still practice these way-finding procedures. In an era of satellites and global positioning systems, it is hard to grasp the raw skill involved in such methods of ocean navigation that dispense with all instrumentation and rely solely on the detailed knowledge of the stars' movements, awareness of the winds and currents, and the uncanny ability to read a thousand clues from the skies and the water. As they could not see islands beyond ten or twelve miles distant, early Pacific navigators had to deduce their proximity by observing birds returning to their nests, paying close attention to the cloud formations, interpreting minute disruptions in the ocean swells, and catching sight of seemingly unimportant floating debris. Caroline Islanders employed a method of navigation known as the *etak* system. To keep track of their progress while going from one island to another, navigators visualized a third island off to one side of their canoes as a reference point. As they moved forward, the reference island changed its alignment with respect to the background stars, as the map illustrates. The passage thus became divided into stages, or *etak*, defined by successive alignments as Native voyagers completed one segment after another until reaching their destination.[23]

These navigation systems required extraordinary powers of observation and a lifetime of practice. Yet they worked well, enabling Polynesians

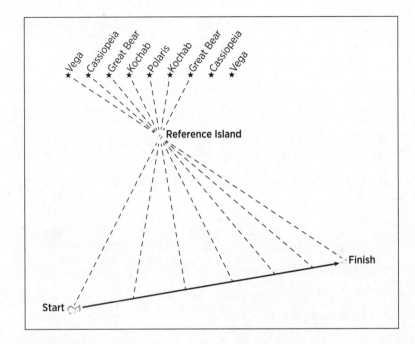

and Micronesians to move reliably across the islands, rendering what may seem to us like dangerous passages into routine voyages. Pacific Islanders were able to make themselves at home in this perilous world. Peoples from nearby continents still visited from time to time, and so life went.

In a few tumultuous decades in the fifteenth and sixteenth centuries, however, a small community of seamen from the continents devised new technologies of navigation that came to revolutionize the world. These newfangled techniques enabled peoples from the continents not just to hop to the nearby islands but to cross entire oceans at a time, finally overcoming vast physical obstacles that had been in place for tens of millions of years.[24]

A stretch of Mexico's Pacific coast in 1550. The "Puerto de Navidad" is on the bottom right, connected to a lagoon containing two small islands. North of Navidad, one can see Guadalajara, a substantial Spanish city represented with four blocks in a grid pattern. Nomadic Indians armed with bows and arrows, waging war, taking captives, and torturing them, appear at the upper-left corner.

1

A Global Race

*N*avidad is a small tourist town on Mexico's Pacific coast. About a four-hour drive south from Puerto Vallarta, it is an ideal place to hide from the world. In the sixteenth century, however, it was positively remote. No proper road led into Navidad, only a dirt path that ended at a horseshoe bay. A mangrove-choked, mosquito-infested lagoon was connected to the bay; and where bay and lagoon came together, a cluster of tumbledown huts sprouted. Illness and famine visited the hamlet with frequency. Just a few years earlier, the Native peoples of the region had launched the so-called Mixtón War, a massive rebellion that had nearly dislodged the Spanish presence in all of western Mexico.[1]

Clearly this was no place for a major shipyard or construction project. Acapulco would have been much better. Only the need for secrecy had tipped the scales in favor of this dilapidated harbor far north of Acapulco; and thus in 1557 some of the best carpenters and blacksmiths in all of Mexico began arriving in town.

Money seemed to be no object to the Spanish crown spearheading the secret effort. Navidad offered no suitable building materials, so nearly everything had to be brought in from distant lands: nails of all sizes from Spain, rope and rigging from Nicaragua, large trees for the masts from Oaxaca, anchors and sails from Veracruz, water barrels from Acapulco. The logistical challenges were at times alarming. The artillery pieces, for instance, had to be shipped across the Atlantic, moved on barges through the Isthmus of Tehuantepec, hauled for sixty miles on a road so rough that hundreds of Indian laborers had to rebuild portions of it to allow the carts to pass, and finally reembarked on the Pacific coast to Navidad. The cost of all this was prohibitive. Altogether the building project at Navidad ran to more than half a million pesos, or *ten times* the amount that the Spanish crown had invested in Columbus's voyage of discovery seven decades earlier. Yet the money kept flowing, and the construction proceeded in spite of a work stoppage and an earthquake that brought down what few stone structures existed there.[2]

After three years of unremitting frustration and expenses, the ribcage of a vessel of more than five hundred tons burden and another one of more than four hundred tons became visible. In any major European port like London, Antwerp, Seville, or Lisbon, such wooden skeletons would have attracted residents' attention. At Navidad they were downright incomprehensible, like two dinosaur eggs in a chicken coup. They were quite possibly the largest ships ever built in the Americas up to that time. Christopher Columbus's flagship in the 1492–93 voyage of discovery, the *Santa María,* had weighed barely one hundred tons. Ferdinand Magellan's largest circumnavigation vessel in 1519–1522, the *San Antonio,* had been about 120 tons. The two galleons at Navidad were four or five times larger. Still without masts or rigging, these two large hulls were eased into the water in 1563. They floated! The event was so momentous that the town staged a celebration. A special delivery of liquor had been necessary to mark the occasion. The people at Navidad had myriad questions, but the shipbuilders said only that the vessels would be used for coastal trade between Mexico and Peru, an explanation that fell somewhere on the spectrum between the extremely dubious and the absurd.[3]

The fleet being assembled at Navidad, which would ultimately entail four vessels, was unusual in one final respect. Expedition leaders generally enlisted their men right on the spot, even for long-distance voyages. Recruiters often set up tables by the docks, within sight of the ships, and signed up passersby. Not in this case. Although some locals may have been offered contracts, the majority of the crew members came from distant corners of the Spanish possessions and even from beyond. The pilots hailed from Europe: three Spaniards, a mysterious Frenchman, a man possibly from Venice, and a Portuguese pilot passing as a Spaniard. A greater power was evidently coordinating the recruiting effort. Indeed, from Spain and France (around six thousand miles away from the coast of Mexico), the Spanish king had been monitoring the progress at Navidad closely. Philip II, the monarch after whom the Philippines were named, had been dispatching letters and requesting the participation of specific individuals. He was bent on assembling the best possible crew, a dream team of sorts equal to the enormity of the task at hand.

One of these handpicked individuals was an Afro-Portuguese man named Lope Martín. He hailed from Portugal's southern coast, the Algarve, the preeminent maritime region of the world at that time, where Black people performed the most menial and grueling jobs aboard Portuguese and Spanish ships of exploration. Lope Martín was a free mulatto and an immensely talented navigator who always seemed to know just what to do aboard a sailing vessel. Over the years, he had risen through the ranks until becoming a licensed pilot, the highest occupation to which someone like Lope Martín could ever aspire. After accepting a very high salary, he signed on to the secret mission at Navidad, one meant to give Spain ascendancy in a global competition with Portugal to establish regular contact with Asia. This all-out race had dragged on for seven decades, and during this time Portugal had built a seemingly insurmountable lead by rounding Africa and India to trade with the fabled "Orient." Meanwhile, Spain had been held back by the immensity of the Pacific Ocean. The extraordinary navigator Martín and others met at Navidad to reverse Spain's fate.[4]

Like many other things in the history of the world, this global race had started with Columbus. After his 1492–93 voyage, the Spanish crown had wasted no time in claiming the Caribbean islands that the Admiral had visited. Just as quickly, however, the Portuguese objected to such claims. By then Portugal had been combing assiduously through the Atlantic for decades and naturally regarded Columbus's venture as an intrusion. The two Iberian powers had been at war before, and Columbus's discoveries opened a dangerous new rift. Spanish diplomats asked Pope Alexander VI (a Spaniard by birth) to intervene, and the pontiff's breathtaking solution was to divvy up the Atlantic Ocean and its surrounding lands between the two rival monarchies. A line running from the Arctic to the Antarctic and passing 370 leagues west of the Cape Verde Islands would separate their respective spheres of influence, according to a treaty signed by Portugal and Spain in the small town of Tordesillas in 1494. Portugal would be free to discover and claim any island or mainland "*to the right of the line,* going east from it, or north or south, as long as the ships belonging to the King of Portugal do not cross the line itself." Meanwhile, Spain would be able to explore "*to the left of the line,* going north or south from it, and all those lands will belong to the King and Queen of Castile and Aragon and their successors forever." All other nations and empires would have opposed such an unfair division of the world between only two powers, but alas, they had not been parties to the treaty. For Portugal and Spain, the Treaty of Tordesillas seemed a proverbial win-win arrangement.[5]

This division worked well enough in the Atlantic Ocean. It gave Portugal a free hand in all of Africa plus a slice of Brazil, while Spain gained

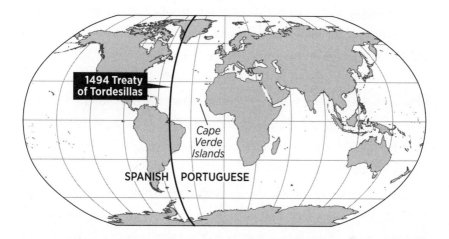

rights of exploration over the rest of the Americas. Beyond the Atlantic, however, this line of demarcation set the stage for an all-out race for the Far East and its immense riches in silk, ceramics, spices, and other wondrous products. The two upstart Iberian empires would eventually sail around the world in opposite directions. Always keeping "to the right of the line," Portugal rounded Africa, then India, and eventually burst into Southeast Asia. Meanwhile, Spain kept "to the left of the line," exploring the American continent, finding an opening between the oceans, and crossing the Pacific into Asia. This decades-long competition pitted against each other two neighboring nations that spoke mutually intelligible languages and were frequently ruled by monarchs related by blood or through marriage. Yet this familiarity did not make their rivalry any less ruthless. They poached each other's pilots and mathematicians, did their best to keep their charts and geographic discoveries secret, and waged bloody war in remote parts of the world to deny each other bases of operation.[6]

What made this contest all the more startling was the stark differences between the two competitors. To put it bluntly, it was a race between a dolphin and an elephant. With a population of barely one million by 1500, Portugal was just too small to take over the world. Lisbon was a very modest capital and base of exploration of around forty thousand people. As it expanded through western Africa, Brazil, India, Malaysia, Indonesia, Japan, and China—even if only to establish trading forts or *feitorias*—the Lusitanian nation became overstretched. Everyone at home was scrambling to keep things running or consumed by one of these ventures halfway around the world. Still, what Portugal lacked in population it more than made up for in experience, cutting-edge nautical technology, and clarity of purpose.[7]

In contrast, the kingdoms that coalesced into Spain contained some five to seven million inhabitants, easily dwarfing Portugal in human and material resources. Yet this aggregation of kingdoms was difficult to manage. Some of them possessed significant maritime experience: elephants do swim. Yet the core of this composite monarchy, the Crown of Castile, was more terrestrial than Portugal. This land orientation is evident in the cities where the Spanish court tended to reside: Valladolid, Toledo, and finally Madrid, right in the middle of the Iberian Peninsula, as far as possible from any coast or sea.[8]

There is no better way to get a sense of these two contenders and understand the nature of the race than by following in Columbus's footsteps. He lived in Portugal for a decade before moving to Spain and setting the contest in motion by proposing to his new hosts "to reach the east by way of the west." Columbus's initial arrival in the Iberian kingdoms had been entirely unplanned. Pirates had attacked the ship on which he was traveling and a great fire had broken out, forcing everyone to jump into the water, "and Columbus, who was a strong swimmer," a near-contemporary chronicler informs us, "swam for two leagues [seven miles] to the closest land, holding onto an oar to get some rest along the way." The twenty-five-year-old Columbus washed up on Portugal's southwestern tip in 1476. It was probably the farthest he had ever been from his native Genoa. Up to that time, Columbus had been trading wools and textiles on behalf of his family, mostly within the Mediterranean.[9]

The São Jorge Castle looms at the top of Lisbon's highest hill. Farther down lies Lisbon Cathedral, a Romanesque structure dating back to the twelfth century. On the water-front, one can see a broad beach area with many vessels being prepared before casting off.

Once in Portugal, the future "Admiral of the Ocean Sea" remade his life. After drying off his clothes and resting his weary limbs, he made his way to Lisbon where he found a community of Italian financiers, merchants, and nautical experts deeply involved in Portugal's ventures of exploration. This group included Columbus's own brother, Bartholomew Columbus, who had moved out of the family household years earlier and relocated to Portugal. The two brothers formed a partnership and made a living by drawing nautical charts and selling books. A contemporary who met Columbus in those years described him as "a dealer in print books of great intelligence although little book learning, and very skilled in the art of cosmography."[10]

Lisbon, surrounded by massive walls except along the waterfront, was a town on the move at the time of Columbus's arrival. Sitting on the highest hill was the Castle of São Jorge, a structure that looked ancient even in the fifteenth century. It had a commanding view of the Tagus River and the Atlantic Ocean. In the 1470s through 1490s, when Columbus lived in Lisbon, the castle remained the nerve center of Portugal's exploration activities. A huge map of the world mounted on gold-plated wood in a cavernous room signaled Portugal's grand design. Officials bustled around the premises, keeping accounts, levying taxes, and organizing sales of exotic goods coming from Africa as well as from Asia and America later on. Some of these items were on display, including two lions kept in a pen to impress visitors.[11]

Venturing outside the castle, Columbus would have entered a grid of narrow streets, diminutive plazas, houses, churches, and synagogues — some of which can still be seen in Lisbon's Alfama district. After wending his way down the hill for about ten minutes, past the cathedral and the shops farther down, he would have arrived at the Ribeira das Naus, or literally the "Riverbank of the Ships," a jumbled collection of shipyards and warehouses. If the castle was where the monarch and his officials resided, the shipyards attracted hundreds of carpenters, caulkers, pilots, sailmakers, sailors, instrument providers, food suppliers, artillery experts, and many other artisans connected to the building and provisioning of the fleets. Space was scarce on the riverbank, as ships in various stages of completion crowded one another while workers swarmed about them to get them ready to depart at very specific dates to take advantage of the best sailing season depending on where they were going.[12]

Columbus's chart-making business gave him direct access to this vibrant maritime community, and so did his private life. He made a habit of hearing Mass at Todos-os-Santos (now the French embassy in Lisbon), a convent just north of the riverbank where daughters and widows of the knights of the Order of Santiago lived. Unlike regular nuns, these *comendadeiras,* as these privileged women were called, had a special dispensation to marry if they so wished. Always relying on his Italian connections,

Columbus struck up a conversation with a woman named Dona Felipa Moniz Perestrelo. Felipa's grandfather had been an Italian nobleman who had moved to Portugal early in the fifteenth century; and Felipa's father had been an explorer on behalf of the Portuguese crown in the middle decades. A casual conversation blossomed into friendship and culminated at the altar. After the wedding, Columbus went to live with Felipa and her widowed mother. It did not take long for the older woman to recognize that her son-in-law "was inclined toward matters of the sea and cosmography" and told him at length about her late husband's exploits on the islands of the Atlantic. "And seeing that her stories of these voyages gave the Admiral much pleasure," Columbus's son and first biographer would later explain, "she gave him the writings and sea-charts left by her husband. These things excited the Admiral still more."[13]

Columbus spent a decade in Portugal, developing his nautical knowledge and conceiving his audacious plan. His training proceeded along multiple avenues. On a practical level, he traveled in the company of Portuguese seamen and learned from them about voyaging in deep-blue water. In 1478, less than two years after his accidental arrival in Portugal, Columbus cast off into the open Atlantic to purchase sugar on the island of Madeira. In 1482, he boarded a ship that ranged even farther, following the African coast until reaching the coast of Ghana, close to the equator. The future Admiral drew many lessons from these Portuguese voyages: "Africa is twice as long as Europe," he scribbled in the margins of Pierre d'Ailly's *Ymago mundi* (1410), one of his favorite geography treatises, adding later that "the torrid zone of the world is habitable because the Portuguese sail in that region and it is thickly populated."[14]

Yet his most important nautical insight had to do with the gigantic wheel of winds and currents that circles the North Atlantic Ocean with regularity, now called the North Atlantic Gyre. Portuguese navigators had stumbled on this vast circular flow earlier in the century when they began exploring western Africa. At first they had merely followed the coast in

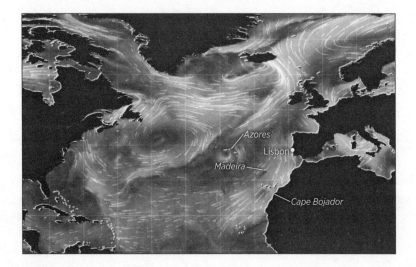

a southerly direction along Western Sahara. But when they reached the bulge of Africa at Cape Bojador, they ran into a major problem: strong winds blew consistently from the continent toward the middle of the Atlantic Ocean, and the currents ran in the same direction, reinforcing the effect of the wind. This made Cape Bojador a veritable point of no return. As one contemporary put it, "The currents are so terrible that no ship, having once passed the Cape, will ever be able to return." For twelve years, the Portuguese persisted in this daunting passage but failed every time.[15]

To go beyond Cape Bojador, fifteenth-century Portuguese navigators had to take a leap of faith, letting themselves go into the Atlantic Ocean very far from shore in search of more favorable conditions. Through trial and error, they perfected a maneuver that they called *la volta do mar largo* (the loop around the great sea), or *la volta* for short in Portuguese and *la vuelta* in Spanish. It consisted of sailing away from the African coast for hundreds of miles in a northwesterly direction before turning around in mid-ocean back to Portugal. Their growing awareness of this gigantic ring of currents and winds in the North Atlantic was both exhilarating and full of possibilities. In 1492–93, Columbus used the southern half of the North

Atlantic Gyre to propel his fleet toward the Americas and the northern portion of it to return to Europe.[16]

Apart from learning from working seamen, Columbus met a group of experts in the employ of King João, extraordinary mathematicians and cosmographers convened from time to time to advise the Portuguese monarchy on oceangoing ventures and to solve any problems related to them. During Columbus's stay in Portugal, these experts devised a novel method of determining latitude (north-south distance) based on the altitude of the sun. Latitude was less difficult to establish than longitude (east-west distance), as is generally known. But it was hardly trivial or "child's play," as author Dava Sobel writes in her well-known book about the British clockmaker who solved the longitude problem by inventing a marine chronometer. In fact, measuring latitude reliably in the middle of the ocean was difficult and constituted a necessary step to venture successfully first into the Atlantic and then into the enormous Pacific.[17]

To appreciate the breakthrough achieved by King João's experts in the early 1480s, we need to begin with what existed before. Pilots of the thirteenth, fourteenth, and fifteenth centuries—right up to Columbus and well after him—navigated by a system generally known as dead reckoning. Starting from a known location or "fix" marked on a map, all early pilots needed to do was point their compasses toward their intended destination. By keeping track of only two variables—direction and distance—they were able to plot their progress on a chart and arrive safely most of the time. Small errors were tolerable in passages confined to comparatively small bodies of water such as the Mediterranean, the Baltic, or the coastal regions of the North Atlantic. As one of the foremost Portuguese cosmographers of the sixteenth century explained, "No great errors arose [in the Mediterranean] since most days navigators had sight of land and knew where they were, and they did not need to carry astrolabes or other instruments to measure altitudes because they followed their sailing directions and thus kept track of their progress forward."[18]

Things were very different in the Ocean Sea. As the Portuguese ventured deeper into the Atlantic, they were forced to confront the limitations of dead reckoning navigation. After spending weeks far from coasts, islands, or any other identifiable geographic features, they had no way of confirming their position independently. We can only imagine the frustration of Portuguese pilots in the middle of the Atlantic attempting the *volta* and having to rely on a series of uncertain estimations originating in a very distant port. In theory, they could track their progress on a chart, but such plots could be utterly misleading, as small inaccuracies in direction and distance eventually built into significant and even colossal errors that could lead to complete disorientation and death.

The only independent point of reference was the stars. At least since the 1460s, Portuguese navigators began noticing how the height of the North Star in the night sky provided a clear indication of how far north or south they were. To illustrate with the most extreme examples: a sailor near the Arctic Circle would see the North Star almost directly overhead, while a second navigator near the equator would find the same star barely above the horizon. Naturally, while sailing along western Africa, Portuguese pilots came to associate specific stretches of that coast with certain altitudes of the North Star. At first they used rough approximations such as "the height of a lance" or "the height of a man," but eventually they resorted to cross-staffs and astrolabes to increase the accuracy of their north-south estimations.[19]

This system worked well enough until Portuguese navigators ranged too far south. In 1471 they crossed the equator and observed anxiously how the North Star dipped below the horizon and disappeared entirely from view. Deprived of their guiding star, pilots and cosmographers began scanning the southern sky for a suitable replacement and eventually found the Southern Cross. Yet this transition took decades. In the meantime, King João II summoned his experts, who set out to devise a far more elegant and sweeping solution to the problem of establishing latitude.[20]

Like any other star, the Sun could serve as a reference to determine north-south distance. But the great luminary posed two challenges. First, while the North Star remains almost perfectly stationary (because Earth's rotation axis is closely aligned with the North Star), the Sun describes an enormous arc across the sky over the course of the day. Its altitude must therefore be measured exactly at noon. Fifteenth-century navigators did not possess accurate clocks, so they had to start measuring a half hour or so before noon, taking the altitude continuously until the Sun had passed its zenith and was clearly on the way down. Of all the observations, navigators then selected the highest one, evidently corresponding to noon. This altitude was very high but almost never exactly ninety degrees because most places on Earth are either to the south or to the north of the spot where the noontime Sun is directly overhead and forms a perfect right angle with respect to the horizon. The residual shadow, however small, could therefore be used to determine north-south distance or latitude.[21]

All of this was possible in theory if not for the second complication. The Sun's path across the sky changes during the year. As we know, in the summertime, the Sun's path across the sky is higher and longer and thus the days are equally longer, while in winter, the Sun's trajectory is lower and shorter and consequently the days are shorter. This happens because Earth orbits around the Sun at an angle of 23.5 degrees. This slight axial tilt makes the wonders of the seasons possible, but it also causes the spot on Earth where the Sun is directly overhead at noon to wobble north and south — from the Tropic of Cancer to the Tropic of Capricorn and back again in the course of the year. This constant north-south displacement of the point on Earth that is directly underneath the Sun is called solar declination. In practice, it constrained the applicability of the method of establishing north-south distance to a two-day window. "If you want to know the ship's reckoning by the altitude of the Sun, take the Sun at noon when you leave port," instructed one of the navigational manuals of that era, "and after one or two days at sea, take the altitude of the Sun again and you will note the difference between one and the other." Beyond this two-day window, however, the solar declination would render any estimations dangerously off. It was a major limitation. Nevertheless, one could still envision a stunning mathematical solution. Astronomers could calculate, *in advance of the voyage,* the Sun's declination for every day of the year and compile a so-called declination table that pilots could then use to determine latitude accurately, on any day included in the table, anywhere in the world.[22]

Land-based astronomers aided by spherical models of Earth surrounded by movable rings representing the trajectories of various celestial bodies had been able to determine latitude by the noontime altitude of the Sun and perform all the necessary calculations to take into account the solar declination for centuries. Yet such involved procedures had been beyond the capabilities of working pilots, few of whom had any formal training in astronomy or mathematics. Some were actually illiterate. Therefore, devising a simple, workable declination table was the last obstacle before unleashing the full power of solar navigation; and King João's experts were closing in on a new system. Like many other innovations achieved collectively, this one has given rise to a great controversy about who deserves the credit, especially given the varied national backgrounds of the king's experts. One of them was a merchant from Nuremberg, Germany, named Martin Behaim, who had arrived in Lisbon a few years earlier and taken part in various voyages of exploration. Behaim was very well versed in mathematics and astronomy and "boasted about being a disciple of Johannes Regiomontanus, a famed astronomer among the professors of this science," according to the preeminent Portuguese chronicler of that era. On the strength of this contemporary endorsement, later scholars have considered Behaim the chief innovator — an open-and-shut case of German knowledge diffusing to a peripheral nation.[23]

Yet a close examination of the declination tables reveals that the source was neither Behaim nor Regiomontanus but two Jewish mathematicians from the Iberian Peninsula. The older and more established of the two was a Spanish astrologer from the university town of Salamanca named Abraham Zacuto, who devoted several years of his life to calculating sixty-five astronomical tables that tracked the positions of various celestial bodies. By all accounts, Zacuto was a phenomenal mathematician and astronomer (in addition to being a rabbi, lexicographer, and historian), and his tables were nothing short of a tour de force. He lived in Spain in the early 1480s and therefore was not among King João's circle of experts — although, after the expulsion of the Jews from Spain in 1492, Zacuto would relocate to Lisbon and accept the position of "astronomer to the king." Even though he was not physically present, his calculations had been well known in Jewish astrological circles throughout Iberia at least since 1478, when a Hebrew version of his text and tables began circulating. Yet Zacuto's contribution could have gone unnoticed had it not been for the second key figure, a Portuguese Jew named José Vizinho. He happened to be among the king's experts and may well have been a disciple of Zacuto or at least well acquainted with his work. Vizinho instantly recognized the utility of Zacuto's numbers. The first five tables provided the Sun's declination for the years between 1473 and 1476. These results could not be readily applied after 1476 because his calculations were thrown off by the intervening leap year. Nevertheless, it was possible to update Zacuto's declination table. On his own or with Zacuto's assistance, Vizinho compiled a new table, starting in March 1483 and ending in February 1484.[24]

Thus began a new method of navigation by the altitude of the Sun. It was better than anything the Portuguese — or anyone else around the world for that matter — had ever used before, as it allowed pilots to work in broad daylight anywhere in the world and resort to very simple rules and straightforward tables to determine latitude. Even today, short of using a global positioning system, sailors who want to be protected against electronic failure carry published declination tables (*The Nautical Almanac*) and sextants to determine their latitude at sea. The tables and sextants (which superseded the astrolabes) may be more accurate these days, but the method has remained the same for more than half a millennium.[25]

This innovation was great news in the community of navigators in Lisbon—Columbus among them. He followed closely as Behaim, Vizinho, and the other experts arrived at a straightforward system of finding latitude that all pilots could use. In 1485, King João dispatched Vizinho to Guinea (Sierra Leone) to measure the height of the Sun and conduct an astronomical survey of that coast. Columbus witnessed the session when the mathematician submitted his findings after his return. As the future Admiral of the Ocean Sea reported, "Master José [Vizinho] gave an account of everything to His Most Serene Highness, the King of Portugal . . . and the king sent navigators to Guinea and other places and it was always found that the observations were in agreement with Master José's measurements." The method of navigating by the altitude of the Sun would prove essential to Columbus during his New World voyages and to those who would later venture into the Pacific, as we shall see.[26]

Columbus was thoroughly transformed in Portugal, not only by the nautical knowledge he gained but also by his growing obsession with the idea to "reach the east by way of the west." In 1483 or 1484, the future Admiral mustered enough courage to explain his project before the Portuguese king and to make a formal proposal. King João II heard him out but ultimately turned the matter over to his expert mathematicians and astronomers. They were not impressed. According to the leading chronicler of that era, "They all considered the words of Cristovão Colom as vain and founded on imagination and things like the Isle of Cipango [Japan] of Marco Polo." It did not help that Columbus grossly underestimated Earth's size. As far as the king's experts were concerned, this Genoese petitioner was bound to perish in the middle of the Ocean Sea well before reaching Asia—as would have undoubtedly happened had he not stumbled first on America. Finally, Columbus's plan was out of sync with Portugal's fundamental strategy of going down and around the African coast to beat a path toward India and then to the Far East. Compared to this systematic approach, Columbus's wild dash across the Atlantic seemed like a distraction at best and likely a foolish waste of lives and money.[27]

With the double blow of no hope of royal sponsorship and Felipa's sudden death in 1484, Columbus decided to leave Portugal and try his luck in Spain. He submitted his proposal to the Catholic sovereigns, Ferdinand and Isabella, in 1486–87 and again in 1491. They had it examined by a junta of experts much as had happened in Portugal. The Spanish elephant was nothing if not lucky. The experts at Valladolid and Santa Fe raised objections—some reasonable and others less so—but in the end left the door open for royal support of this harebrained scheme. The rest of the story is well known. Perhaps the Spanish monarchs sensed that this Genoese man, steeped in the latest Portuguese navigational methods and with real sailing experience in the Atlantic, would be as good a bet as any. Fresh from their victory over the last Muslim enclave on the Iberian Peninsula, Ferdinand and Isabella signed off on the project in the spring of 1492.[28]

Columbus's exploits loom so large in our understanding of the past that other great discoveries recede into the background. In truth, any reasonable observer at the turn of the sixteenth century would have conceded that, even after Columbus's famous voyages, Portugal's lead in the global race had widened until becoming almost unassailable. Portuguese navigators reached the tip of Africa in 1488 and found the route to India a decade later. King Manuel I of Portugal took pleasure in writing lengthy letters to the Spanish monarchs, his in-laws and rivals, informing them, "Our Lord has miraculously wished India to be found" and telling them about the spices, precious stones, elephants, exotic peoples, and the immensely profitable trade carried on there. "We are still awaiting news from the twenty-five ships that we sent the previous year [1502]," Manuel gloated to Ferdinand and Isabella in one of his letters, "and after they come back in September there will be time to send some more."[29]

In the meantime, Spain could point to only a few Caribbean islands and inklings of an unknown continent, but no precious spices, porcelain, or silk. The new lands did offer some gold, but they never replaced the original quest of finding a western approach to the incalculable riches of the Far East. Spaniards explored the continent blocking their way, looking for a passage that would connect the Atlantic with the Pacific. They came up empty-handed until Fernão de Magalhães—a Portuguese defector like the Afro-Portuguese pilot Lope Martín a generation later—put Spain back in the race. Ferdinand Magellan had come of age during Portugal's torrid expansion into Asia in the 1500s. Yet he had a falling-out with the Portuguese crown and went knocking on neighboring doors. It is difficult to overstate the significance of Magellan's move to Spain.

Magellan caught up with the roving Spanish court at the town of Vall-adolid. For someone accustomed to the sound of waves and the proximity of sailboats, it must have been strange to have to journey to the middle of Iberia to propose a maritime venture in a town surrounded by agricultural fields and interminable plains. He did not arrive alone but was accom-panied by two brothers, Rui and Francisco Faleiro, both cosmographers whose reputations exceeded Magellan's. The trio complemented one an-other well. Magellan came across as a man of action who had fought in India, Malaysia, and North Africa, while the Faleiros were armchair aca-demics. As they waited for an audience with the Spanish king in February and March of 1518, the Portuguese visitors grew unsettled by what they heard. The new monarch, Charles I, was an awkward eighteen-year-old who had come from Belgium just a few months before and had great diffi-culty communicating in Spanish let alone Portuguese. Worse, the trio had to tread carefully in a court riven by a power struggle between Charles's advisers recently arrived from Belgium and the old Spanish officials from the previous monarch.[30]

Interestingly, during the early negotiations Rui Faleiro rather than Ma-gellan emerged as the leading voice. The older of the two Faleiro brothers,

Rui was deferentially referred to as a *bachiller* (or *bacharel* in Portuguese), the highest university degree one could get at the time. Before leaving Portugal he may have been considered for a new chair in astronomy established at the oldest university in the kingdom (what is now the University of Coimbra) by the Portuguese king himself. It was the highest position in the field. One of the reasons that perhaps impelled Rui Faleiro to join Magellan in Spain was being passed over for this prestigious appointment; academic rivalries and pettiness were already alive and well in the sixteenth century! In spite of this setback, and notwithstanding a rumor that "he was possessed by a familial demon and in fact knew nothing about astrology," Rui Faleiro remained a top European cosmographer. Sixteenth-century Spanish chronicler Gonzalo Fernández de Oviedo described Rui Faleiro as "a great man in matters of cosmography, astrology, and other sciences and humanities." There is little doubt that he was extremely accomplished if mercurial and mentally unstable. Rui's younger brother Francisco Faleiro was just as talented and would go on to find long-term employment in Spain as a leading nautical expert. Together the two Faleiros and Magellan were very credible petitioners.[31]

On the day of the audience, Magellan and Rui Faleiro arrived not with charts as would have been expected but with "a globe that was very well painted and showed the entire world, and on it Magellan traced the route that he would follow." The two petitioners explained that they intended to cross from one ocean to the other "through a certain strait that *they already knew about.*" Even though the globe was detailed, the portion of South America where the strait was supposed to be had been left intentionally blank. Magellan and Faleiro had evidently taken some precautions in case anyone present at the audience should wish to steal their project.[32]

Their knowledge of a passage between the oceans—the alpha and omega of many New World explorations—would have been more than enough for the royal sponsorship. But Magellan and Faleiro went further. As one witness at the audience recounted, "They offered to *demonstrate* that the Moluccas [Spice Islands] from where the Portuguese take spices to their country are on the side of the world that belongs to Spain, as agreed by the Catholic Monarchs and King Juan of Portugal." The 1494 Treaty of Tordesillas had established a line of demarcation running from pole to pole through the Atlantic but did not contemplate extending the line to the other side of the world. As Portugal and Spain, however, had continued to sail in opposite directions, such an antimeridian had become necessary. Measuring longitude or east-west distance was still extraordinarily difficult in the early sixteenth century, so no one knew quite where to draw this line in the distant Pacific. All the same, in the early 1510s the Portuguese had planted trading forts in Malaysia and the Spice Islands while Spain had stood by helplessly. Yet in the winter of 1518, Magellan and Faleiro had become persuaded that the Spice Islands were actually on the Spanish side, a conclusion all the more startling in Spain because it was coming from these top *Portuguese* navigators and cosmographers.[33]

Magellan had become convinced that the Spice Islands were on the Spanish side after carefully studying the Portuguese sailing charts (mostly unavailable to Spanish navigators). By adding up the east-west distances of the passages from Portugal to the tip of Africa, on to India, and all the way to Southeast Asia, he had persuaded himself that the Spice Islands were simply too far away and so beyond the Portuguese hemisphere. This in itself was intriguing. But during the audience with the Spanish king, the two petitioners also promised to confirm this potentially explosive geopolitical idea by means of a more technical method. For this part of the proposal, Magellan turned to his partner, the extraordinary Rui Faleiro.[34]

Measuring east-west distance and finding the antimeridian was possible in theory. One obvious method would have been to take the time along the Tordesillas line, travel to the other side of the world, and locate a line exactly twelve hours apart. Unfortunately, this solution required a timepiece unaffected by the pitching and rolling of a ship, a mechanical feat that would not be achieved until the eighteenth century. Navigators also tried to find the antimeridian by means of astronomical events like eclipses visible simultaneously in different parts of the world. Yet pilots could never depend on such rare events for their daily work.[35]

Instead of looking at the sky, the two Faleiro brothers focused on an earthly phenomenon. On long voyages, Portuguese navigators began observing how the compass needle did not align exactly with "true north" as shown by the North Star. Instead, it often pointed slightly to the left or the right of it. Not everyone agreed that such misalignments between magnetic and true north were even real. In those days, compass needles had to be detached from time to time from the boxes where they were suspended and re-magnetized by striking them against a lodestone. Therefore the variation was often chalked up to de-magnetized or faulty needles or otherwise explained away by the idiosyncrasies of Genoese or French compasses or some other maritime lore.[36]

As they roamed east and west across the world, however, Portuguese pilots came to the realization that the misalignment increased and decreased regularly and affected not one or two but *all* compasses. Navigators developed a specialized language to refer to this curious behavior. They said that the needles would *nordestear* (northeast), meaning that they would point to the east from true north in some parts of the world or that they would *noroestear* (northwest) in others. Today, the difference between magnetic and true north is called magnetic declination, and Portuguese charts of the early 1500s reveal an astounding awareness of it. The famous Cantino Planisphere, a colorful chart smuggled out of Portugal and taken to Italy in 1502, shows the African coast in striking detail; no contemporary map even comes close to depicting the cone of Africa so accurately. Interestingly, the southernmost tip is identified as the "Cabo das Agulhas," or "Cape of the Needles," so named because at that precise place the compass and the North Star became perfectly aligned and the magnetic declination was zero. Portuguese mariners evidently recognized the "Cape of the Needles" as a place of great nautical significance.[37]

Magnetic declination was immensely exciting because it could help establish the all too elusive east-west distance or longitude. The Faleiros were among the chief proponents of this method; Rui became convinced that a correlation existed between magnetic declination and east-west distance. He was not mistaken. Anyone with a basic compass in the continental United States today can approximate longitude. In San Francisco, for instance, the needle points to about thirteen degrees east of true north. Farther east, in Denver, that difference dwindles to about eight degrees. Along the Mississippi River, the magnetic declination approaches zero. By the time one gets to Chicago, magnetic north is nearly four degrees *west* of true north. In New York City, that difference has increased to twelve degrees. In other words, magnetic declination increases or decreases depending on one's east-west location within the continental United States.[38]

During the Age of Exploration, this magnetic declination method would have been a very practical way to approximate longitude, requiring no additional instrumentation, tables, or calculations. But this system had two drawbacks. First, because of the turmoil in our planet's core, magnetic declinations change. Recent reports about the north magnetic pole wandering away from Canada and toward Siberia have made us aware of this instability. Any method based on Earth's fickle magnetic field would therefore have required some updating. This was a minor inconvenience, however, compared to the second one: the system simply did not work in many, if not most, places on Earth. A magnetic declination map of the world—that is, a map displaying lines with the same magnetic declination—reveals their wavy and capricious arrangement. Magnetic declination would have indeed served to approximate east-west distance in the North Atlantic, but it would have been utterly confusing along some of the equatorial regions—where the compass needle would not have budged over vast distances—or in areas of the Pacific and Indian Oceans where the lines run in perplexing directions.[39]

Faleiro did not possess a magnetic map of the world and therefore could

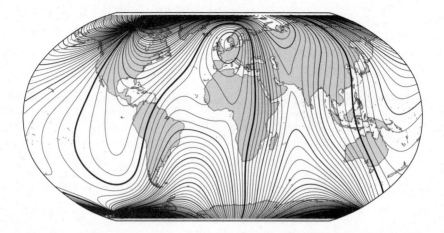

not have anticipated that his system, although viable in the North Atlantic, would be fatally misleading in a passage around South America and across the Pacific Ocean such as the one he and Magellan were proposing. Yet none of this mattered at the time. During the early negotiations, Faleiro was convinced of the soundness of his method, while the Spanish monarchy was bent on reaching "the east by way of the west" to catch up with Portugal. Spain thus backed up Faleiro and Magellan, placing a second and colossal bet.[40]

Against all odds, Magellan's voyage succeeded. The Portuguese captain employed by the Spanish crown not only found the strait at the southern tip of South America that still bears his name but also crossed the Pacific Ocean in one swoop for the first time in recorded history. The suffering was extreme. Of the five ships that had started out from Spain in 1519, only one damaged hull with tattered sails returned in 1522 with eighteen survivors, after having crossed the Pacific, negotiated the Indian Ocean, and ascended through the Atlantic back to Europe. Magellan himself perished in the attempt. Yet his voyage demonstrated that, although vastly larger than anyone imagined, the Pacific was crossable and could well become a new gateway to the extraordinary riches of Asia.[41]

The race was suddenly back on. In the wake of Magellan, Spain dispatched at least one overland and *seven* maritime expeditions in the 1520s, 1530s, and 1540s to open this new route. All ended in disaster. Some ships ran aground in the treacherous waterways of the Strait of Magellan, others sank in storms or were defeated by the vast distances of the Pacific, and yet others became stranded on the opposite side of the world and succumbed to attacks by Pacific Islanders, Southeast Asians, or the Portuguese.[42]

Expedition planners learned three crucial lessons from these failures. First, sending fleets all the way from Spain via the Strait of Magellan and across the Pacific was not practical. Instead, the best strategy consisted of establishing a port on the western coast of the Americas to serve as a launching point for the transpacific voyages. Second, although long, it was feasible to sail from the Americas to Asia aided by two belts of favorable currents and winds that existed above and below the equator.

The third and most painful lesson, however, was that, once in Asia, there was no return to the Americas. Magellan's men had been the first to experience this predicament. After reaching the Spice Islands, one of the ships, the *Trinidad,* attempted the first return across the Pacific Ocean in 1522. Wisely, the pilot first sailed to a northern latitude of forty-two degrees (around Japan's northernmost island and opposite the coast of Oregon) to get out of the contrary currents and winds and catch the other side of the North Pacific Gyre. Only then did the *Trinidad* point its bow toward the coast of North America, thus starting an agonizing passage that would claim the lives of thirty—out of fifty—crew members through exposure and lack of provisions before the last survivors finally gave up and turned back to Asia. Magellan's famous voyage is often referred to as a *circumnavigation,* the first spin around the world, as if he had set out to prove that the world was round. In reality, Magellan's armada ended up circumnavigating the globe only because it could not sail back the same way it had come. Another Spanish fleet reached the Spice Islands in 1527 and attempted the *vuelta* unsuccessfully not once but twice in 1528 and 1529. A third Spanish fleet made it across the Pacific and tried the return voyage once again in 1543 and 1545. Every time the ocean refused to yield a passage home. A Spanish missionary in Asia (and future saint) named Francisco Xavier drew a clear lesson from all of these failures: "It is necessary to tell the Emperor not to send any more fleets via New Spain [Mexico] to discover these islands because so many of them have been lost. The storms are so great and in such a manner that the vessels have no way to save themselves."[43]

2

Dream Team

The empire paused for fifteen years before dispatching another expedition, this time the secret endeavor originating in Navidad, across the great ocean. When the order finally came down in 1557, it was given not by Charles—the Belgium-born Spanish monarch who had approved Magellan's voyage and the disastrous expeditions that followed—but by his son Felipe. Like his Hapsburg relatives across Europe, Philip was born and bred to rule. But unlike most of them, he was extremely dedicated and well adapted to the life of the court—with a fondness for hunting, jousting, and spending time with jesters. When Philip was sixteen, Charles went abroad for fourteen years to attend to various European entanglements, leaving his son as regent. By necessity, Philip grew up as Spain's day-to-day ruler.[1]

By the time Charles finally abdicated, the prince was ready to assume his duties. Philip II became the hardest working of monarchs, "never losing an hour, for he is all day among his papers." As he himself admitted, "I am so starved of sleep because I need to spend most nights reading the papers that other business prevents me from seeing during the day." This punishing routine was self-inflicted, as he insisted on making decisions on everything, from the placement of toilets at the Escorial palace to the details of a plot to "kill or capture" Queen Elizabeth of England. In recognition of his administrative dedication, and because the Spanish Empire attained its greatest size and power during his long reign, Philip II is known to posterity as the "prudent king." Yet he was far from prudent. As his most insightful biographer makes clear, we can better understand Philip as a man overwhelmed by his enormous realms, obsessive to a fault regarding every decision, and dangerously convinced that he was doing God's work. As a result of these qualities, he issued several ruinous orders. (Dispatching an "invincible armada" against the British Isles is his best-known blunder.) Yet he was equally capable of getting behind risky projects, persisting beyond reason, and occasionally succeeding.[2]

It is impossible to pinpoint when Philip first became interested in the quest to open the Pacific route. We know that in 1543, the year he began acting as regent of Spain, a fleet reached Asia for the third time after Magellan. Vague rumors about the fate of these men circulated at the court, but after a five-year absence, a few hardy survivors finally returned. The Spanish expeditionaries had departed from the coast of Mexico and crossed the Pacific in a surprisingly uneventful passage. Yet as soon as the voyagers tried to establish a foothold in the Philippines, they were forced to battle elusive islanders armed with poisonous daggers and lances. As their main objective was to discover the return trip, they mended their ships and made two valiant attempts to get back to America in 1543 and 1545. Both failed. The Spaniards were stranded halfway around the world. Worse still, as they moved from island to island in search of friendlier hosts, they depleted their provisions. "We had to eat many creatures and plants of which we had no knowledge," recalled one of the friars accompanying the expedition, "especially the large lizards that are brown and shiny [monitor lizards], and not many of those who ate them remain alive today." Even the levelheaded expedition leader, a tall and aristocratic man named Ruy López de Villalobos, changed his opinion about the wisdom of establishing a beachhead in the Philippines. "Do not waste any more resources or time except to come to our rescue," he wrote to his superiors in 1545, "as there is nothing of value in these lands." In the end, Villalobos and his men surrendered to the Portuguese stationed in the Spice Islands just south of the Philippines. The Lusitanians regarded this band of ragtag survivalists as trespassers but agreed to throw them in the hold of their ships and transport them via the long way home, first to India and then to the Iberian Peninsula.[3]

At the time of the survivors' arrival in Spain in 1548, Philip could do little, as he was still in the process of consolidating his power. Five years into his regency, the prince was able to act with surprising independence within Spain. Yet his father the emperor retained control over sensitive international affairs—and the Villalobos expedition had turned decidedly controversial. Since learning of the arrival of a Spanish fleet in the Philippines, the Portuguese had accused their neighbors of encroaching on their side of the world. Philip's father had thus refrained from sending additional ships or even mounting a rescue mission to avoid further antagonizing the Portuguese monarch, who also happened to be his brother-in-law.[4]

Nonetheless, the Villalobos expedition produced at least one tangible result. The Philippines, a dazzling archipelago of more than seven thousand islands, had gone by different names in Iberia and remained only hazily known. Magellan had called it "el archipiélago de San Lázaro" because his ships had arrived there on Saint Lazarus Day (and probably, like Saint Lazarus himself, Magellan on landfall felt as if he had risen from the dead). Much of the contemporary documentation refers vaguely to "las Islas del Poniente," or the Islands of the West (or better yet the Islands of the Sunset), because from Spain it was necessary to sail toward the setting sun to reach them. The survivors of the Villalobos expedition added striking new details. They called the enormous island in the southern sector of the archipelago (Mindanao) Caesarea Karoli in honor of Emperor Charles V.

As a nod to the Spanish prince, they also gave the name "la Isla Filipina" to the sizable island in the eastern sector (Samar). As Philip cemented his power during the 1550s, this name gained traction in letters, reports, and maps, and eventually was extended to the entire archipelago.[5]

The emperor abdicated at last in 1556. Most expected the retiring ruler to maintain a presence around the court for continuity. Instead, he went into seclusion at the Monastery of Yuste in western Spain, where he was able to escape his earthly duties. Suddenly, Philip found himself alone and free to make decisions about the entire empire guided only by his judgment and conscience. In his prime at twenty-nine, the new monarch went into a frenzy of activity over the next few months. Philip devoted most of his waking hours to micromanaging a war with France. But he also set aside time for other matters, including dispatching a peremptory order to his personal representative in Mexico, Viceroy Don Luis de Velasco, "to explore the Islands of the West, and colonize them, and put them in good order." This implied finding the return voyage through the Pacific Ocean.[6]

Philip's instructions were striking for several reasons but particularly because they gave Viceroy Velasco "all the power and authority to make those discoveries." In the past, the Spanish monarchy had generally partnered with entrepreneurial individuals in ventures of discovery. Magellan, for instance, had approached the crown with the idea of finding an alternative route to the Far East and had secured some financing for such a venture. Later on, wealthy conquistadors in the Americas like Hernán Cortés and Pedro de Alvarado took the lead, getting loans, building shipyards, and raising armadas before seeking the royal blessing for their transpacific ventures. In this case, the crown itself would seize the initiative, relying on its vast human and material resources to procure everything needed. All this activity would be coordinated by Velasco, "a trustworthy man who enjoys our full confidence," according to Philip. From his perch in Mexico City, Don Luis would plan the venture from the ground up, build a fleet, hire the best crew available, and bring the project to fruition—a difficult task for a man with no nautical experience who may never have seen the Pacific Ocean. Yet the viceroy relished the challenge.[7]

Don Luis was a peculiar man who in some respects resembled Philip—noble birth, administrative experience since the age of fourteen, a deep sense of duty to crown and God, and obsessiveness in every decision. But Don Luis differed from the Spanish king in that he was perennially short of money. As viceroy of Mexico, Don Luis earned an enormous salary, and as the king's personal representative and living image in Mexico, he was expected to maintain a certain level of luxury. Yet in this Don Luis went well beyond the call of duty. He was a gregarious man who surrounded himself with relatives, friends, supporters, and hangers-on. "Every day his table was set for thirty or forty people, and indeed for anyone who wished to dine with him, of the proper class, of course," one contemporary remembered, "and they were all treated to great meals of ten or twelve courses and this lasted all the time that he was here in Mexico." Don Luis also loved horses. An accomplished rider, he kept a stable "worthy of a king," with dozens of beautiful animals trained by an expensive horse master. He was equally passionate about bullfighting. Every Saturday, at the head of a hundred cavalrymen and their servants, Don Luis rode to the nearby woods of Chapultepec, where he had built a bullring, and they spent the day with a half-dozen wild bulls imported from the Chichimec frontier. The viceroy offered food to all the cavalrymen and their servants, "and it was always a banquet so that they were always talking about celebrations and feasts." The viceroy's lifestyle far exceeded what he could afford. "My salary is not enough for the expenditures that I am forced to make," Don Luis complained to the king as early as 1553, as he would continue to do over the years, "and given my outstanding loans, I do not wish to repay everything in the afterlife. I implore Your Majesty to grant me an adequate salary." The viceroy's complete disregard for his financial circumstances is at times baffling. He was married to Doña Ana de Castilla y Mendoza, a descendant of a fourteenth-century Castilian king. Worried about the transatlantic passage and the uncertain accommodations in Mexico City, Don Luis initially traveled to Mexico alone. But with the passing of the years, the viceroy began preparing to bring Doña Ana to his side. He lived in a palace that had belonged to Moctezuma, the last Aztec emperor. Don Luis was not satisfied with the building, however, so he embarked on a major renovation, adding several rooms and making costly modifications. The viceroy racked up an enormous debt that he indeed would take all the way to his grave.[8]

Apart from his spendthrift ways, the viceroy was a hands-on administrator. When he received the king's order at the end of 1557 to send an armada to the "Islands of the West" along with what amounted to a royal blank check for "all the power and authority to make those discoveries," Don Luis set to work immediately. As he knew practically nothing about matters of the sea, he began by surrounding himself with explorers, shipbuilders, mapmakers, and anyone who could offer advice. Through his vast network, the viceroy quickly identified numerous experts, with whom he held discussions. These consultations became so extensive that the king felt the need to reprimand Don Luis for "communicating this business with so many people," and thus alerting the Portuguese to Spain's latest bid to conquer the Pacific. The viceroy replied with an old Spanish saying that shows his determination: "When one is doing work on the house with axes and hammers, the neighbors usually know about it." In other words, the Portuguese would inevitably find out about the mission, but what really mattered was its success.[9]

Don Luis's primary adviser was a larger-than-life adventurer named Juan Pablo de Carrión, a figure well known in Spain today because of a recent comic, *Espadas del fin del mundo,* based on one of his many exploits. At the ripe old age of sixty-nine, Captain Carrión led an attack on a band of Japanese pirates and samurai operating in the northern Philippines, a rare showdown between European swords and Japanese katanas. In the comic, Carrión comes across as a swashbuckling adventurer getting too long in the tooth, a sort of Don Quixote or Diego Alatriste in a Pérez-Reverte novel.[10]

This was merely one late incident in a lifetime of adventure. Four decades earlier, Carrión had enlisted in the disastrous Villalobos expedition

Juan Pablo de Carrión, circa 1582.

across the Pacific and had been one of the few to make it back alive to Spain in 1548. In spite of returning penniless and physically diminished, he promptly entered the service of the archbishop of Toledo as treasurer. At that time he also met a young woman named Isabel Medina and "knew her carnally," as the Holy Office of the Inquisition would later put it. When Captain Carrión moved to the port of Seville in 1549 to participate in the shipping business there, he took Isabel with him. Those were heady years for them. Yet a few bad deals led to Carrión's imprisonment for debts amounting to a fortune of more than 100,000 ducats. Isabel remained in Seville and faithfully visited the captain in jail. So life went until 1553, when, in a turn of events reminiscent of *The Count of Monte Cristo,* Carrión bribed his prison guards, escaped, and went to hide in Isabel's house while he waited to board a ship bound for the Americas. All along, Carrión and Isabel had lived together but without being married. This was very troubling to Isabel, who apparently changed her name to Doña María de Sotomayor at that time to protect her true identity. Now that the captain was a fugitive from the law and at her mercy, however, Doña María saw her opportunity. As Carrión would declare to the inquisitors, "She tried to persuade me to marry her before taking passage, and after much pleading and many arguments threatened to denounce me to the authorities if I refused." If we are to believe the captain's version, he had no choice. One early morning, Doña María took a cloaked Carrión to the chapel of San Lázaro just outside the city walls, where a witness was already waiting. The bride had arranged for a discreet ceremony. As Captain Carrión continued to insist that their marriage was not valid, relations ended badly when he finally left for the port of Sanlúcar de Barrameda to take ship for the Americas.[11]

Carrión's destination was Mexico, where, always resourceful, he found his way to Don Luis's sumptuous table. His arrival in Mexico City was like a godsend. Here was a man with a commanding presence and real experience crossing the Pacific, capable of overcoming the most trying circumstances, and comfortable in ports and fleets around the world. The viceroy and the captain got along famously from the start. Both were nearly the same age — forty-seven and forty-five, respectively. They may have known each other since childhood, as they both hailed from the town of Carrión de los Condes (thus the name Juan Pablo de Carrión) or at least from the same general region in north-central Spain. It is unclear how much Don Luis knew about the captain's legal troubles in Seville. Regardless, Carrión became Don Luis's right-hand man.[12]

Before construction of the vessels could commence at Navidad, Don Luis, Carrión, and other nautical experts had to decide on the optimal number of ships. Prior transpacific fleets had ranged between two and ten.

A single vessel was the most economical, but it would have been intolerably risky, as any leaks, collisions, or groundings would have been fatal. Two or more ships would lessen the risk, allowing those aboard a sinking vessel to transfer to another. Yet too many vessels made coordination difficult and added considerably to the cost. The expedition planners initially settled on a minimal fleet of two ships, probably with the intention of maximizing the size of each. When it came to crossing the Pacific, the larger the vessel the better, as it would cut through the waves and weather storms more easily, like a floating fortress designed to last for months without sight of land and withstand attacks from other ships or from land.[13]

After agreement was reached on the optimal configuration, construction began in the distant port of Navidad. In the meantime, the viceroy dispatched Carrión to Spain to report in person to the king and to request artillery and merchandise for trade in Asia. The captain's first port of call was none other than Seville, where he may have gambled on an amicable resolution to his status as a fugitive of the law. After all, he was returning as the leader of the most important venture of exploration in the whole empire. It is more likely, however, that Carrión and Don Luis had arranged things in advance and perhaps even secured a pardon. All we know is that the captain had no trouble carrying out his mission in Spain. At the time of the captain's arrival, Philip II was abroad waging war on France, so Carrión transacted his business in Seville with the Council of the Indies, the powerful committee in charge of all New World affairs. The monarch's absence could well have resulted in delays, but the never-sleeping Philip sent immediate instructions to his councilors, "and within thirty days, they sent me back to Mexico with all the munitions and artillery pieces that we had requested," the captain recalled. Carrión also used his stay in Seville to rekindle his relationship with Doña María. The couple took up residence in a house where, according to one witness, "the two ate at the same table, slept in the same bed, and had the type of conversations that a husband and a wife would have." They even discussed traveling together to the Americas, but, according to the captain, Doña María could not overcome her fear of crossing the Atlantic.[14]

On his return to Mexico, Carrión learned that the construction effort at Navidad had stalled. This was especially troubling because the viceroy, Don Luis, decided at the same time to expand the fleet to three ships and eventually to four. Such a gargantuan building project would go nowhere without a high-ranking official residing permanently at Navidad, with sufficient authority to hire and fire workers and mobilize large sums of money. Don Luis thus commissioned the ever adaptable captain "to put pressure and haste and diligence into the construction effort" and commanded "all officials, caulkers, carpenters, and everyone else at that port of Navidad to obey and execute all the orders given by Juan Pablo de Carrión." This important commission, however, condemned the captain to the epidemic-prone and mosquito-infested port of Navidad for nearly five years. It could have been an especially trying period in the captain's life. Yet he found ways to make it bearable. During his travels to and from Navidad, he met Leonor Suárez, a wealthy widow who owned a cacao hacienda in Zapotlán, strategically located midway between Navidad and Guadalajara. Carrión would later swear to the inquisitors that he had been "uncertain and confused" about the validity of his marriage in Spain. He also declared that several persons from Spain had told him that Doña María de Sotomayor had died. Caught in this maelstrom of misinformation and contradictory emotions, Captain Carrión wedded Leonor and had children with her. Yet word about the captain's earlier marriage began to circulate. Some of the mariners at Navidad had known Carrión in Spain and had met Doña María. One of them had actually stayed in their house in Seville and observed them living as a couple. Carrión's own brother, Andrés Cauchela, boasted to a group of mariners spending the night in a road hostel — and perhaps after a few drinks — that the captain "had been married in Spain and had a woman in Seville." Bigamy was common among conquistadors and explorers. But in this particularly high-profile case, the murmurs spread through Mexico and across the Atlantic, where Doña María, still living in Seville, eventually found out about her husband's second marriage to a wealthy widow in Mexico.[15]

All along, Captain Carrión believed that he was, as he put it, "la lumbre del negocio," literally "the fire of the venture." His experience and knowledge seemed unmatched. He had crossed the Pacific, beheld with his own eyes the Islands of the West, and—as a result of his commissions in Spain and Navidad—knew the most about the logistics and politics surrounding the fleet. It is hard to fault the captain for assuming that during the passage he would serve in a leading capacity. Yet Carrión's prolonged absence from the decision-making center of Mexico City resulted in a confrontation with a second nautical expert named Andrés de Urdaneta.[16]

Urdaneta had been sailing the Pacific even longer than Carrión and possessed a storied pedigree. As a teenager, nearly forty years earlier, Urdaneta had befriended some of the survivors of Magellan's expedition, especially Juan Sebastián Elcano, the Spanish captain who had taken over from Magellan and completed the historic first voyage of circumnavigation. Urdaneta and Elcano hailed from nearby towns in the Basque Country in northern Spain. The young Urdaneta had entered Elcano's service and become his protégé and apprentice. Thus began Urdaneta's life as an explorer. In 1525, the Spanish crown recruited Elcano for a follow-up expedition to Asia, and the old seaman decided to take along his pupil. They departed from the port of La Coruña, passed through the Strait of Magellan, crossed the Pacific Ocean, and circumnavigated the world for the second time in history. Elcano had died along the way, and Urdaneta had spent eight years marooned in Southeast Asia, becoming proficient in Malay, the lingua franca of navigation, and learning much about the winds and currents in that part of the world. He had even started a family there and had brought back to Iberia a daughter named Gracia de Urdaneta.[17]

• • •

After that adventure of a lifetime, Urdaneta decided to take up residence in Mexico and for a few years continued to probe the Pacific Ocean, combining occasional maritime forays with land-based service to support himself. Yet his life ultimately evolved. In 1552, at the age of forty-four, he traded his cape for a robe and his boots for hemp sandals and entered an Augustinian monastery in Mexico City. Urdaneta spent a year as a novice. The veteran explorer must have cut a peculiar figure, as his cohort in the monastery consisted of adolescents between thirteen and fifteen. Nonetheless, Urdaneta had gained permanent admission and set a new course: "I promise to live in renunciation of all personal possessions, in chastity, and in accordance with the Rule of our glorious Father Saint Augustine, until death," his oath reads. He went on to study for the priesthood and became ordained around 1558. As a priest-friar, Urdaneta joined the monastery's hierarchy. "It is as if he had devoted all his life to religious affairs," a fellow Augustinian marveled, "and as if he had forgotten all the things he had seen in the world and had never lived in it." His good standing is evident in his appointment as master of the novices, instructing aspiring Augustinians during the start of their spiritual lives.[18]

Urdaneta's second career was evidently in full bloom when the viceroy of Mexico attempted to recruit the friar-mariner, presumably for a position in the fleet that Don Luis was assembling at Navidad. Yet nothing came of these conversations. Urdaneta's reluctance is understandable. At the Augustinian monastery, he lived a basic but predictable life with guaranteed meals and membership in a close-knit community, something particularly comforting to an aging man without a wife. "I am over fifty-two years old," Friar Urdaneta stated later, "and the illnesses and hardships that I have suffered since my youth make me want to live out the rest of my life in quiet and peace." Urdaneta's dogged refusal eventually forced the viceroy into a circuitous way of obtaining the friar's services. Both men lived in Mexico City within a short distance of each other. Yet Don Luis had to send a missive across the Atlantic asking the king of Spain to write back to Urdaneta (and to his superior in the monastery) to prevail over Urdaneta's objections. Philip obliged. "I have heard that before your religious state, you went aboard the [1525] fleet of Loaysa and crossed the Magellan Strait," the letter began, "and because of your great knowledge of those lands, your understanding of the art of navigation, and because you are a good cosmographer, it would be of great effect if you went aboard the ships." Urdaneta could scarcely refuse a direct order from his monarch.[19]

To his credit, after acquiescing, the friar-mariner immersed himself in the project. "Even though it is a very wide sea," Urdaneta had said of the Pacific, "there is no reason to think that a path exists only from here to the Spice Islands but there is no way to return." He seemed to have strong opinions about everything. With respect to the port of Navidad, for instance, he believed that it had been foolish to set up the shipyard in a remote port that offered no easy access to building materials and that was prone to illness. "The carpenters and other artisans who are supposed to work on the ships refuse to go there even when offered good salaries," Urdaneta noted, "because they become sick there and the foods that they require for their sustenance, like wine, oil, and other things that come from Spain, are extremely expensive." He wrote to the Spanish king and asked that the shipyard be moved from Navidad to Acapulco (a solution that at least in the short term would have been even more disruptive and expensive). Urdaneta also advocated developing an independent naval infrastructure on the west coast of Mexico. If the expedition across the Pacific succeeded in planting a Spanish colony in Asia, more ships would be needed in the future to resupply such a colony. Therefore, instead of importing finished products like artillery all the way from Spain and at great expense, it would be much better to import skilled ironworkers to jump-start such an industry in Mexico. "In this land there is good copper in quantity," the friar pointed out, "and although the artillery made from these materials usually cracks very quickly, it is believed that with better purification methods one can make excellent weapons." Urdaneta's plan of development was extensive. It called for importing hemp seeds (*Cannabis sativa*) from Spain in order to use the plants to make cordage and cables in Mexico, and contemplated setting aside plots of land to grow hardwood trees for the ships' hulls and masts. Knowledge transfer was at the core of his plan. Coopers, carpenters, sawyers, ironsmiths, cordage makers, and other artisans would come from Spain to teach local workers, particularly mestizos and mulattos, "who would be compelled to learn, although paying them just salaries."[20]

At every turn, the friar-mariner and the captain seemed to be on opposite sides. Whereas Urdaneta could not understand the choice of Navidad, Carrión had initially supported it. Whereas Urdaneta emphasized an independent New World naval industry, Carrión had traveled to Spain to bring back navigational equipment and artillery. They could still compromise in matters of construction and provisioning. But no middle ground was possible with regard to the fleet's route and destination, and Carrión's prolonged absence from Mexico City left him out of the decision-making process. Urdaneta's influence over Don Luis became decisive. The friar was well spoken and persuasive, and his vast knowledge not only of the technical aspects of the art of navigation but also of Southeast Asia made him a formidable adviser. "Andrés de Urdaneta has the greatest familiarity with those islands and is the best cosmographer in all of New Spain," wrote the viceroy, explaining his reasoning to Philip in 1560, "and he and I alone drew up the plans of the expedition."[21]

For all his knowledge and experience, Urdaneta's proposed route bordered on insanity. He intended to go to New Guinea. To get there, the friar planned to descend from Navidad until reaching the Southern Hemisphere all the way to twenty-five or even thirty degrees of southern latitude—much too far south—where the fleet would start looking for New Guinea. Urdaneta admitted that negotiating the equatorial region might be challenging because of "the great calms that must be avoided," but he

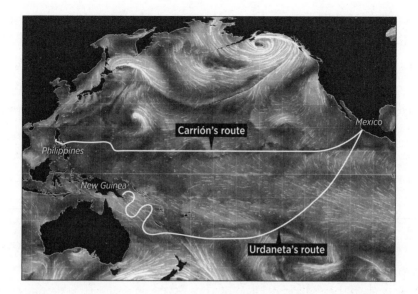

was confident that the pilots would find enough wind if they started from Mexico between November and January.[22]

Understandably, Carrión opposed Urdaneta's proposal from the start. Why attempt an unknown passage instead of the proven, straight, and elegant trajectories of the two previous transpacific voyages in 1527–1534 and 1542–1548? Captain Carrión was especially adamant about establishing a Spanish base in the Philippines and nowhere else. "Those are the islands where we have friends," he said, "and where eight Spaniards from our own fleet have remained." Indeed, Spanish fleets had been visiting the archipelago since Magellan, "and some of our people know the language, the main ports, and even the names of the principal lords of those islands." The Philippines were also densely populated in some places and possessed abundant foodstuffs to sustain a Spanish colony; they even had cinnamon, one of the spices so valued by Europeans. Yet the archipelago's greatest attraction was strategic. It was an impossible-to-miss bull's-eye of "eight large islands and many small ones interspersed among them, all within sight of one another," and in the same latitude as Mexico. The Philippines were quite simply the most convenient gateway to Asia and, once there, the possibilities were endless. "To the north is China at about two hundred leagues [seven hundred miles] of distance," enthused Carrión, "and to the south are the Moluccas [the Spice Islands], and the way toward them [from the Philippines] is well understood." Last and most important for the mission at hand, the Philippines afforded Spanish navigators the most propitious base from which to attempt the elusive return to the New World.[23]

Two vastly different life experiences had given rise to the two competing routes. Captain Carrión had seen with his own eyes the highway of winds and currents connecting Navidad (at nineteen degrees of northern latitude) with the Philippines (between five and nineteen degrees). "When we went in the [Villalobos] fleet of 1542," Carrión recalled, "we found excellent winds and good seas, departing from the port of Navidad and navigating west and southwest, where we know some of the islands and ports to get fresh water, and the route is known and proven." In contrast, Father Urdaneta's knowledge harked back to an earlier era when the fleets still departed from Spain, crossed the Magellan Strait, and ascended through the southern Pacific Ocean, venturing into the fickle equatorial regions until reaching the Spice Islands. Urdaneta had never gone directly from Mexico to the Philippines and thus had no experience with the winds and currents that had impressed Carrión so much.[24]

Although Carrión's arguments were more convincing, Urdaneta insisted on going to New Guinea. The friar made much of the fact that the Philippines were "on the side of the world that belonged to Portugal," not Spain. He was so adamantly opposed to going to the Philippines — except to top off provisions or rescue stranded Spaniards — that he threatened to quit the expedition if the archipelago was selected as the target. Urdaneta's uncompromising stance was once again rooted in his personal story. At the time of his first visit to the Spice Islands in 1526, Urdaneta had nearly perished at the hands of the Portuguese. He had found that the

Lusitanians were already deeply entrenched in the region, having forged alliances with various local lords and built a fort on the tiny island of Ternate, one of the very few sources of cloves in the world. (According to a contemporary report, there were only five islands with clove trees at the time.) The Portuguese reaped extraordinary benefits from their yearly shipments of cloves, nutmeg, and mace and were not willing to give up their monopoly easily. When a Spanish fleet carrying Urdaneta had pulled into the neighboring island of Tidore (also featuring stands of clove trees), the Portuguese had initially exhibited some restraint. But as the Spanish began building a fort of their own, hostilities broke out. Not yet twenty years of age and already in command of thirty men, Urdaneta experienced the conflict between the two nations in the flesh. In March 1527, he was traveling on a ship along with his men when a barrel of gunpowder exploded, causing Urdaneta severe burns to his face. To relieve his pain, he jumped into the ocean. The Portuguese and their local allies, observing both the explosion and Urdaneta's dive into the water, immediately went in hot pursuit, shooting at him. "I remained alive only because I am a good swimmer," Urdaneta recalled, "and I was so burnt that I was confined to a house for twenty days." The young navigator, who bore the scars for the rest of his life, had no desire to relive similar hostilities in the Philippines in his old age.[25]

From a legal perspective, Urdaneta was correct. The Philippines *were* on the Portuguese side of the world. As a practical matter, however, New Guinea would have been an inferior choice, as it was in the Southern Hemisphere and therefore ships departing from Mexico would have been forced to sail through the Intertropical Convergence Zone along the equator. In this region, the winds of the Southern and Northern Hemispheres come together and the prevailing weather is fickle and treacherous, ranging from violent thunderstorms and unpredictable squalls to calms that can last for weeks. The additional risk of getting there seemed hardly worth it, as New Guinea itself possessed few attractions other than its relative proximity to the Spice Islands. Carrión had been there in 1544 and commented that all he saw were "a few naked blacks, and even though we communicated and bartered with them, only obtained miserly foodstuffs and very little rice."[26]

Remarkably, the viceroy of Mexico not only backed Urdaneta but also went on to build the entire venture around the friar. When it came time to appoint an expedition commander, Don Luis passed over Carrión — who had arguably done the most to push the project forward and whose plan made the most sense from a nautical perspective — and instead made a puzzling choice. Miguel López de Legazpi had served for decades as a scribe and accounting official at the Casa de Moneda, or Minting House, in landlocked Mexico City, a post that scarcely prepared him for a major transpacific voyage. "We could not have chosen a more convenient person and more to the liking of Friar Andrés de Urdaneta, who is the person who will in fact direct and guide the voyage," Don Luis confided in Philip, "because both come from the same land and are friends and will get along." Captain Carrión was less charitable. "Miguel López de Legazpi is from Urdaneta's home region and both are intimate friends," the captain commented; "he has no experience in exploration and doesn't know the first thing about navigation and will defer to the friar in everything." Today, Legazpi streets and monuments exist in Navidad, Guadalajara, Acapulco, Mexico City, Madrid, Manila, and elsewhere; and the historic voyage that is the subject of this book is generally known as "the Legazpi expedition." But in truth, Legazpi started out as an incidental commander whose chief attribute was his ability to get along with the Augustinian friar.[27]

If Viceroy Don Luis de Velasco had lived longer, Urdaneta would have gotten his way, and today we would live in an alternate universe in which Spanish was spoken in New Guinea, Australia, and New Zealand. But as fate would have it, Don Luis became very ill in 1564 and died on July 31, four months before the fleet's scheduled departure. His funeral was the

most elaborate ever conducted in Mexico, "and this magnificence was en-
hanced by the soldiers and General [Legazpi] who were about to leave,"
recalled one witness, "and they all carried their weapons and black flags
and other signs of mourning, and it was something to behold." Don Luis
would have approved. Yet his unexpected death left no time to consult
the king on the life-or-death matter of destination for an expedition that
had been in the making for nearly seven years and was finally ready to
cast off.[28]

Five venerable men had been ruling Mexico jointly with Don Luis. All
six had been members of the so-called Audiencia of Mexico, a committee
with broad executive, legislative, and judicial powers. Predating the doc-
trine of separation of powers, the Audiencia was like a cabinet, Congress,
and Supreme Court rolled into one. After Don Luis's death, the five remaining officials naturally stepped up to fill the vacuum. Their ability to
rule, however, was severely compromised. One of them was already in
his eighties and perhaps bordering on senility. Another one was almost
completely deaf — an ironic circumstance, as the Audiencia members were
called *oidores,* or "those who hear" — and in fact had asked to be relieved
from his post. One final drawback applied to all five. One year before Don
Luis's death (down to the day), a high-ranking official appointed by Philip
II had arrived in Mexico to carry out an investigation into Don Luis's performance as viceroy. Over the summer of 1563, Jerónimo Valderrama had
crossed the Atlantic and survived a shipwreck in the Caribbean for the
sole purpose of conducting what was then known as a *visita,* or a royal
inspection routinely performed on important officials nearing the end of
their term. As *visitador,* Valderrama wielded enormous power and thus invited anyone with complaints against Don Luis to come forward. In the
course of his investigation, the *visitador* Valderrama had learned about the
viceroy's scandalous granting of power and riches to his allies, friends,
and family. Don Luis had married his daughter to the richest silver baron

o (Diego de Ibarra), granted the *encomienda* of Xilotepec to his
's family, given the *encomienda* of Tecamachalco to his nephew,
the list went on. This wholesale trafficking in influence (notorious
en in an era when nepotism and conflicts of interest were tolerated) also
extended to the members of the Audiencia, who came under suspicion
during the royal inspection.[29]

In an atmosphere of great uncertainty, the *visitador* Valderrama turned
his attention to the Navidad project. At the outset, the *visitador* was shocked
by the cost. "I pray for the success of this venture to China," Valderrama
wrote to Philip, "yet they have spent three hundred thousand pesos, without counting the expenditures for artillery and other things in Seville, and
I will be pleased if they request only one hundred thousand more before
the ships depart." For a deceased viceroy characterized by his spendthrift
ways, the fleet at Navidad had been by far his most extravagant undertaking, surely exceeding half a million pesos. The *visitador* also objected to the
selection of Legazpi, the Mexico City accounting official, as commander.
"He is a very good man and a fearful Christian," Valderrama commented,
"but he is completely unprepared in matters of war . . . and lacks experience for an undertaking of this magnitude." The *visitador* was even more
alarmed by the appointment of Mateo del Sauz, a veteran of the wars in
Peru, as the highest-ranking military officer of the expedition. In Valderrama's own words, Sauz was "a great traitor" who could well become "another Lope de Aguirre," a reference to the deranged soldier who two years
earlier had hijacked an expedition up the Amazon River, murdered his
ranking officers, and defied the king of Spain by declaring the absolute independence of the kingdom of Peru. Valderrama was partly correct. There
were Lope de Aguirre–like figures in the transpacific expedition. But the
military commander was not one of them.[30]

The *visitador* and the Audiencia members made one final decision intended to correct the late viceroy's excesses. Even though Commander Le-

gazpi had already received instructions to go to New Guinea, the royal officials, with merely a few weeks before the fleet's departure, quietly solicited
additional opinions. They consulted many experts, probably including
Captain Carrión, who happened to be in Mexico City at the time. It did
not take long for the officials to conclude that the plan in place was sheer
madness. Going to New Guinea "would be venturing into a completely
unknown path and require an enormous detour to reach the Islands of the
West," the Audiencia explained to Philip, "whereas the other route [to the
Philippines] would be very straight, well known, and established."[31]

At last, the *visitador* and the Audiencia had come around to Captain Carrión's point of view. Yet changing the fleet's destination at the eleventh
hour would have been extremely disruptive. It would have caused the immediate withdrawal of Friar Urdaneta and, along with him, Commander
Legazpi, several subsidiary captains, many soldiers, and all the Augustinian friars who were to Christianize the peoples of Southeast Asia. Caught
in the dilemma of sending the fleet on a suicidal mission or disrupting it
severely, the Audiencia opted for a decidedly unorthodox solution. Pub-
licly, New Guinea remained the fleet's destination, thus ensuring Friar
Urdaneta's participation. Moreover, Captain Carrión, who still harbored
hopes of going along with the fleet, was ordered to stay behind. The *visitador* Valderrama became convinced that the captain had maliciously delayed
the outfitting of the expedition for his own benefit "and had done other
wrong things," a vague condemnation that hinted at mismanagement of
royal funds or perhaps at the captain's bigamy. To the outside world, all of
this would appear as a clear endorsement of the late viceroy's plan and a
complete triumph of Urdaneta's faction.[32]

Secretly, however, the Audiencia drafted another set of instructions and
then summoned Legazpi on September 1, 1564. With all five Audiencia
members in attendance, the *visitador* Valderrama informed a startled fleet
commander that he would not be going to New Guinea after all but to

the Philippines, and administered a most solemn oath. With his right hand on a Bible, Legazpi pledged to carry out this new mission and, on pain of "disloyalty to the king of Spain," promised not to reveal the new destination to anyone. The instructions would remain in a sealed envelope until the ships were one hundred leagues (about 350 miles) into the Pacific. It would amount to a dangerous gambit that would play out in the middle of the ocean.[33]

3

Navidad

*I*n the span of a few weeks, between September and November 1564, 380 expeditionaries — and as many as a thousand people or more if we count family and friends accompanying them — rode or were carted into the port of Navidad. Their impressions on arrival may have been positive. At the end of the rainy season, the Pacific coastal plain in western Mexico would have been an interminable carpet of green interrupted only by chocolate-colored rivers and streams. The view toward a secluded horseshoe bay surrounded by verdant hills, reaching almost to the water, would have been equally alluring. The town itself, however, was underwhelming. It consisted of a few makeshift huts and a couple of stone houses on a lip of sand between the bay and the entrance to a lagoon. The place was so insignificant that absorbing a sudden influx of hundreds of outsiders must have required a great deal of improvisation. Except for the highest-ranking officials, who may have enjoyed special accommodations in a house or perhaps aboard one of the nearly completed ships, almost everyone had to camp by the beach or around the town.[1]

Very rapidly, the expeditionaries must have grasped the conditions they would endure until leaving. In theory, the heat should have been bearable. Temperatures in September through November hover around eighty-five degrees Fahrenheit at Navidad—and in the sixteenth century, during the Little Ice Age, perhaps somewhat lower. Yet with the heat stuck day and night in a narrow range and the humidity approaching one hundred percent, the overall effect was oppressive, sapping the energy of the newly arrived and clouding their minds. The marshy environment contributed greatly to their discomfort. It supported an array of insects and arachnids, particularly of the biting kind: dense clouds of mosquitos, of course, but also midges (*jejenes*), horseflies (*tábanos*), bedbugs (*chinches*), blister beetles (*cuereres*), scorpions (*alacranes*), and spiders of all sizes and shapes. Beginning at dusk, this tenacious army of biters attacked and tortured all humans residing at the port and made every night a true ordeal. Before regular fumigation was introduced some decades ago, locals still resorted to procedures like rubbing mud on their bodies or keeping smoky fires in their houses through the night. If the dark hours were difficult, the days were exasperatingly long, and the expeditionaries were confined mostly to the town. Venturing into the mangroves and forests would not have been prudent: a snakebite or an encounter with a predator like a river crocodile (*Crocodylus acutus*), a jaguar (*Panthera onca*), or a venomous Mexican beaded lizard (*Heloderma horridum*) was always a risk. A dip in the lagoon would have been the simplest way to escape the heat and the bugs and get some relief from the exuberant environment, but swimming in the bay was dangerous because of the strong riptide that could carry away even good swimmers.[2]

From the time they first set foot in Navidad, the visitors had to adapt to an unvarying new diet that consisted primarily of turtles (eggs, meat, and blood) as well as some corn, beans, and occasionally fish. As the nesting season was unfolding during September–November, marine turtles were plentiful both along the bay and inside the lagoon. Such food, however, proved challenging to Europeans, who regarded bread, wine, olive oil, and land animal meat as the essential building blocks of any true meal. Infuriatingly, there was in fact plenty of wine, vinegar, bacon, cheese, fava beans, and garbanzos in Navidad. Yet all these foods had been set aside to provision the ships and were therefore inordinately expensive or unavailable, and the entire province of Michoacán had sent all its wheat to make *bizcocho,* or hardtack, a type of unleavened bread eaten on sea voyages.[3]

Navidad was a notorious deathtrap, especially at the end of the rainy season, when the abundance of water was thought to cause "fevers and swelling of the stomach." The first and most important task of the expeditionaries therefore consisted of not falling ill. As they had come from temperate regions in central Mexico or farther afield in Europe, Africa, and Asia, they had to grapple with a new set of pathogens from the semitropical coastal plain. Sources mention the alarming tendency of newcomers to develop fever, diarrhea, and vomiting. From then on, there were only two prognoses: an extremely slow and unnerving recovery or a gradual worsening of the condition that ended in dehydration and death. Unfortunately, there was no escaping this rite of passage while waiting for the final provisioning of the ships. Many expeditionaries developed the dreaded symptoms, among them Friar Lorenzo Jiménez, one of the six Augustinian friars, who was never able to turn the corner. There was some medical attention. One of the viceroy's earliest appointments at Navidad had been a barber-surgeon from the Basque Country named Damián de Rivas. Besides cutting hair and trimming beards, Rivas was handy with the scalpel to make incisions or sever veins, letting blood out of his feverish patients to restore their humoral balance according to the dominant medical theory of the time. Better trained (although probably no more effective) was a "physician and surgeon" called Gabriel Sánchez Hernández. He was to be the expedition's chief doctor but had been dispatched to Navidad several weeks before departure because his services were so badly needed. The last resort was Father Melchor González, a tireless priest who dispensed spiritual comfort to the dying.[4]

Those who remained reasonably healthy and curious would have been immediately struck by Navidad's sheer diversity. As the port's population swelled from a few dozen to several hundred, it turned into something of a Babel of races, nationalities, classes, and occupations. Native Americans were ubiquitous. Coming from nearby towns such as Tuxpan and Xilotlán, they had been compelled to abandon their families, homes, and fields and go to Navidad to work for token compensation according to a system of corvée labor known as *repartimiento*. For these Indigenous peoples, service at the port was yet another labor sinkhole that they had to endure, like the silver mines or the road construction projects. Also common were African slaves, purchased by the viceroy and dispatched to Navidad to aid in the building effort. Some had been Christianized and spoke Spanish, but many others, the so-called *negros bozales,* had been imported directly from Africa. Particularly visible was a team of Black slaves constantly moving cargo from various towns into Navidad and managing a train of twenty-seven mules and two horses.[5]

Spaniards constituted the largest share of the expeditionaries, as one would expect. The catchall appellation *español,* however, masked yet more diversity. Friar Urdaneta and Commander Legazpi were both from the Basque Country, so a disproportionate number of voyagers hailed from that region. As Basque is a non-Indo-European language, they enjoyed a private means of communication completely impenetrable to all other Spaniards — far more so than, say, English, German, or Russian. Galicia in the north of Spain, Castile in the middle, and Andalusia in the south were also well represented at Navidad. Although these historic kingdoms were linguistically and culturally closer to one another, the differences between them were greater in the sixteenth century than today and inevitably led to cliques and divisions within the crew and the two companies of soldiers.[6]

A fixture of all early voyages of exploration was the high proportion of non-Spaniards. They could account for as many as a third (according to some regulations) and up to half (as in the case of Magellan's expedition) of all crew members. The Navidad fleet was no different. The documentation mentions a Belgian barrel maker, a German artilleryman, an English carpenter, Venetian crew members, a French pilot, two Filipino translators, and so forth. Portuguese mariners made up the largest and most conspicuous foreign group: at least sixteen could be counted at Navidad. Spaniards regarded them as rivals but also valued their nautical skills. The Afro-Portuguese pilot Lope Martín, our protagonist, was among them.[7]

Lope Martín was from Lagos, an old port near Portugal's southwestern tip that had historically served as a stepping-stone from Europe to Africa. In the summer of 1415, a powerful fleet had gathered there before crossing the Mediterranean to capture Ceuta. In later years, Lagos had turned into Prince Henry the Navigator's base of operations. Famous local pilots included Alvaro Esteves (who charted the "gold coast" of Africa) and Vicente Rodrigues (one of the foremost pilots to India). As Portuguese fleets had traced the contours of western Africa, Black slaves had flowed back into Lagos, giving rise to a sizable slave and free population of African ancestry. This contingent did much of the work around the city, in the harbor, and aboard the ships of exploration. Many of the apprentices and sailors in Lagos were Black slaves whose salaries were pocketed by their masters or free Blacks engaged in the harsh life of the sea.[8]

Lope Martín was, as we have seen, a free mulatto, that is, a person of mixed Afro-Portuguese descent. Although little is known about his early years, he must have cut his teeth aboard Portuguese and Spanish ships of exploration, carrying sacks of flour and climbing ratlines to the top of the mast. The fleets outfitted all along the southwestern coast of Iberia, on both the Portuguese and Spanish sides, constantly required fresh recruits like him. Towns like Huelva, Moguer, and Palos de la Frontera had supplied Columbus with a crew willing to risk their lives across the great ocean in 1492. Less than one hundred miles in length, this stretch of Portuguese-Spanish coast was at the time the preeminent maritime region in the world. Somewhere in this exploited and often brutal milieu, where knife fights could erupt over insignificant incidents, Lope Martín went from page (children of eight to ten) to apprentice (older and more experienced) to mariner (twenty and older and in possession of a certificate), all the while voyaging to Africa, the Americas, and perhaps as far as Asia. Lope Martín's passages likely ended in different Portuguese and Spanish ports. These comings and goings must have taken him away from his native Lagos, well inside Portugal, toward the Spanish border, and finally to Seville, the only Spanish port open to trade with the New World.[9]

Through the years, this remarkable Afro-Portuguese man was able to climb to the pinnacle of his career by becoming a licensed pilot. This was rare in an era when the vast majority of naval officers, shipmasters, and pilots were white Europeans. Lope Martín was not the only mulatto pilot working in the Spanish fleets; there were a handful, but still rare enough to stand out. His trajectory was also unlikely because, to ascend from ordinary sailor to pilot, he had to acquire a great deal of knowledge and pick up many new skills. Sailors were "mostly ignorant and unlettered people," as one sixteenth-century naval writer put it, while the pilot's craft had become notoriously technical by the middle of the sixteenth century. Among other things, it required measuring the altitude of the Sun at noon with an astrolabe, using declination tables, and performing a series of mathematical calculations. Lope Martín must have mastered the material, taken the required courses, and passed the examinations at the House of Trade in Seville, a powerful agency that not only regulated all Spanish commerce with the Americas but also trained and licensed pilots. A *piloto mayor,* or chief pilot, oversaw these activities, a post that had been occupied by the likes of Amerigo Vespucci (of "America" fame) and Sebastian Cabot (explorer of the North American coast along with his father, John Cabot).[10]

Any person wishing to become a pilot had to be at least twenty-four years of age, "of sound upbringing," and possess a minimum of six years of sailing experience. In the examiners' eyes, Lope Martín's African ancestry was undoubtedly a shortcoming, but perhaps his extensive seagoing experience compensated for this. Additionally, according to the regulations, aspiring pilots needed to own their nautical charts and demonstrate proficiency in mathematics, astronomy, and cartography. Lope Martín must have passed all the tests. Yet there was one final contretemps. The House of Trade had to certify the nationality of all candidates. Being a Spaniard was preferable and often indispensable. When the chief pilot requested proof of Lope Martín's nationality, the pilot must have done what many of his Portuguese predecessors had: produced forged or irregular documents showing that he was from Ayamonte, a town on the Spanish-Portuguese border but on the Spanish side. This would explain why most of his contemporaries believed that Lope Martín was from Ayamonte while a few knew that Lagos was in fact his real place of origin. To make sure that his application went through, Lope Martín may have added a bribe, another standard practice. House of Trade officials were not inclined to look into such irregularities too closely. Spain was in dire need of competent pilots, and Lope Martín was extraordinary.[11]

The scarcity of pilots delivered benefits, too, to taking Lope Martín to the New World. While the Afro-Portuguese man was in the process of obtaining his license in Spain, on the other side of the Atlantic, the viceroy of Mexico had begun recruiting navigators for his secret project at Navidad. By 1561, four years into the project, Don Luis had been able to hire only three pilots, so he asked Philip II to dispatch two more, "trained in the navigation of the ocean sea." This was of the utmost importance. A poor choice could doom the fleet even before departure. Friar Urdaneta was expected to make all the important decisions about the overall route across the Pacific. Each of the four vessels, however, would still need a pilot for its daily operations. (Interestingly, Urdaneta had no formal appointment as a pilot but would be traveling as a passenger and nautical expert.) Indeed, the expedition planners contemplated not one but two pilots aboard each ship, "given that on such a long passage, one may be lacking"—a very terse way to refer to the expected high mortality. In spite of such ambitious plans, by the fall of 1564, when the vessels were ready to set sail, of the eight pilots needed, only six were on hand. All of them were extremely accomplished, the very best that a viceroy and a king working together could procure. Three were indisputably Spanish, one was a Frenchman, another one was possibly a Venetian, and completing the list was Lope Martín. Our protagonist was not selected as lead pilot. That honor went to Esteban Rodríguez, a Spaniard from Huelva who was offered the princely sum of one thousand ducats for the duration of the voyage. At seven hundred ducats, though, Lope Martín was not too far behind. Less than a month before departure, he made his way to Navidad to inspect the ships and meet the crew.[12]

The shipyard was at the core of the activities of the diverse workforce at Navidad. Today no one knows where the original construction site may have been located. In 1587, three decades after the secret construction we are tracking in this story, Thomas Cavendish and his men took Navidad by surprise and "set fire on the houses," the English pirate wrote, "and burnt two new ships of 200 tons the piece which were in building there on the stocks, and came aboard our ships again." It is likely that the shipyard would not have been on the ocean side of Navidad, exposed to the waves and occasional storms sweeping through. Hurricanes are always a threat on that coast. In 1971, Hurricane Lily (Category 1) knocked out the electricity for days. A Christ with his arms nearly ripped off still on display at the local church is a reminder of the power of the elements. More recently, Hurricanes Jova (Category 2 in 2011), Patricia (Category 5 in 2015), and Willa (Category 5 in 2018) have made close passes. Given the risks, it is probable that the shipyard was somewhere inside the lagoon in a more sheltered environment with calmer waters.[13]

Somewhere around Navidad, four ships lay at anchor in a state of near completion: two huge galleons and two much smaller vessels. Safety and living conditions onboard would vary dramatically depending on the ship. The most privileged would travel aboard the flagship, called the *San Pedro,* a hulking structure of about 550 tons burden. Accustomed as we are to the sight of cruise ships carrying six thousand passengers and oil tankers approaching four football fields in length, the *San Pedro* would appear small to us, especially for a transpacific adventure. It must have been about sixty feet in length and nineteen feet across, about the size of a large private sailboat these days. At that time, however, the *San Pedro* was probably the largest ship ever built in the Americas. Size mattered. In rough seas, smaller craft were tossed around, testing their physical integrity and exhausting their crews, while heavier ships were more stable and forgiving. The *San Pedro* would also enjoy the protection afforded by the smaller vessels in the fleet, scouting ahead for shoals and making sure that there was deep enough water for the flagship to pass. On the day of departure, those boarding the *San Pedro* could count themselves extremely lucky.[14]

At the other end of the spectrum, those piling into the smallest of the four vessels, the *San Lucas,* could expect a very different experience. At a mere forty tons, it was essentially a souped-up boat of about twenty-nine feet in length and eight feet across. The *San Lucas* was what sixteenth-century mariners referred to as a "patache," or tender, a small, shallow boat intended for coastal navigation rather than deep-blue sailing. It would carry a minimal crew of twenty in cramped conditions, working day and night, trimming sails, throwing lead lines, signaling to the other vessels, and keeping lookouts for hidden and not-so-hidden dangers ahead. If caught in a mid-ocean storm, these twenty men would face the full impact of the large waves and strong winds and would have to struggle mightily to steady the course. Even without a storm, they would run a great risk by crossing the world's largest ocean with only eight casks of water and modest food stores.[15]

. . .

Fleet Commander Miguel López de Legazpi had ample powers to distribute the voyagers as he saw fit. Sometime in September 1564, he made the
two-week journey from Mexico City to Navidad, took formal possession
of the four ships in a scripted ceremony, and got down to business. His
orders were to carry between 300 and 350 men because "all the provisions
have been calculated for that number and, although plentiful, if more people go, they would become scarce sooner." Erring on the side of caution
would have been wise. Yet Legazpi ended up admitting 380 voyagers, an
excessive number probably forced on him by prominent passengers who
insisted on taking their servants. The commander also had been instructed
to prohibit all Native Americans, Africans, and women, whether married
or single, from joining the fleet, except for "a dozen black men and black
women of service." Women must have taken part in this risky adventure
under conditions that we can only imagine, and the same is true for Black
slaves and Native Americans. In a letter to the king, the expedition commander summed up this human microcosm in a single sentence: "It consists of 150 people of the sea, 200 soldiers, 6 friars of the order of Saint
Augustine led by Friar Andrés de Urdaneta, and some people of service
for a total of 380."[16]

Legazpi needed to strike a delicate balance in the distribution. On the
one hand, it made sense to assign the most capable navigators, the best
troops, the most loyal supporters, and the expedition leadership to the
most seaworthy ship, the *San Pedro,* to maximize the chances of reaching
Asia. This was all the more sensible because, once on the other side of
the ocean, Commander Legazpi would have to dispatch a vessel back to
America to attempt the elusive *vuelta.* On the other hand, Legazpi needed
to appoint officers, pilots, and mariners loyal to him in all four ships, and
distribute the resources equitably to make sure that the fleet remained together and more or less contented under his command. If we are to judge
by the final distribution of passengers, he neglected this second objective.[17]

The fleet commander ended up assigning the entire expedition leadership to the flagship *San Pedro,* which would carry Legazpi along with all his relatives and friends, sixteen in total, the royal officials, and three of the five surviving Augustinian friars, including Urdaneta, all "in proper accommodations." The concentration of navigational resources in the flagship was notable. It had two assigned pilots—Esteban Rodríguez, the lead pilot of the entire fleet, as well as a somewhat mysterious Frenchman whom Spaniards called Pierres Plín (or sometimes Plún)—in addition to Friar Urdaneta. But that was not all. One of the other friars aboard the *San Pedro,* Martín de Rada, was also a reputed cosmographer and "a great arithmetician," according to one source, and "one of the greatest arithmeticians, geometricians, and astrologers in the whole world," according to another. Therefore, no fewer than four world experts would be traveling aboard the *San Pedro,* discussing their estimates and comparing their plots across the ocean. Their collective experience and knowledge (and probably the charts and instruments available to them) easily surpassed that of all the others.[18]

The second vessel in the fleet, the *San Pablo,* was only slightly smaller than the flagship at four hundred tons. It would carry the military commander, Mateo del Sauz, along with his one-hundred-strong company of soldiers. Sauz was a veteran of the wars in Peru. He had risen against the Spanish crown and been pardoned by a later viceroy provided he left Peru within two months and never came back. "This pardon had spared him from being hanged, drawn, and quartered," as the *visitador* Valderrama had quipped, "but it hardly qualified him for additional service on behalf of His Majesty." Nonetheless, Legazpi must have been satisfied by the formerly treasonous Sauz's loyalty. He not only supported Sauz's appointment as military commander but also gave him the second-largest vessel in the fleet along with two excellent pilots.[19]

At eighty tons, the third ship, the *San Juan,* was a big step down from the first two and something of a self-contained operation. The captain and pilot were brothers, Juan and Rodrigo de la Isla (or sometimes Rodrigo de Espinoza). During the outfitting of the fleet, Juan de la Isla had demonstrated his vast administrative and maritime acumen. He traveled to Veracruz to procure nautical equipment and oversee the transportation of artillery pieces across the Isthmus of Tehuantepec, and went to Oaxaca to select and cut down large trees to manufacture the masts of all the vessels in the fleet. His brother Rodrigo was no less experienced and capable. He was an excellent pilot who had impressed the viceroy and his advisers greatly. Although Juan and Rodrigo would be risking their lives in a smallish vessel capable of carrying only about forty people, these two siblings and their dependents constituted a compact and able group.[20]

The last vessel, the tender *San Lucas,* with capacity for only twenty, was a gamble from the start. For unknown reasons, the appointed captain failed to appear in Navidad. "Because I have been informed that he is still in Mexico City and has no intention of coming," Legazpi wrote on November 19, a mere two days before departure, "I name Don Alonso de Arellano as captain on behalf of His Majesty. He is a gentleman and willing to serve, as is assumed and trusted of him." Don Alonso was the most socially prominent individual in the entire expedition. Indeed, the Arellanos were among the noblest and best-connected families not just in Mexico but throughout the Spanish Empire. Hernán Cortés, the conqueror of Mexico, had married Doña Juana Ramírez de Arellano de Zúñiga, daughter of the second Count of Aguilar. He had gone on to strengthen this dynastic connection by marrying both of his children to members of the Arellano clan. Don Alonso, the man present at Navidad, appears to have been on the main line of the Arellanos but conceived out of wedlock and therefore illegitimate. Nonetheless, Don Alonso counted several highly placed relatives in both Mexico and Spain. The wording of Arellano's appointment is revealing. The honorific "Don" (reserved for people of noble descent in the sixteenth century, unlike its wider usage today) precedes his name, and the document specifies that he was "a gentleman." The appointment also makes clear that Legazpi knew Don Alonso by reputation only, as his willingness to serve was "assumed and trusted of him" ("como de él se presume y confía"). In all likelihood, Commander Legazpi was acquainted with Don Alonso only superficially and, with less than forty-eight hours to go, chose him as captain on the basis of his social prominence.[21]

Acting as sole pilot of the *San Lucas* would be none other than Lope Martín.

Before departing, the expeditionaries went over basic procedures derived from decades of hard-earned experience of Pacific exploration. Some were obvious: "You will prohibit any dealings between your men and native women because, in addition to offending God, such relations produce great harm," or "If any native were to bring you cooked food, wine, or water, make sure to have them eat and drink first." Others stemmed from specific incidents that had occurred in the past: "Whenever the ships are moored in populated lands, you will keep guard on the ropes, especially at night, because the natives try to cut them or pull the ships ashore to run them aground." Yet other admonitions seemed excessive. For instance, Commander Legazpi's galleon would constitute his fortress and castle during the entire voyage, and under no circumstance was he to go on land. If an Indigenous leader requested a parley, Legazpi would ask that person to come aboard instead. If that was not possible, the fleet commander could always dispatch one of his officers, but only after the leader had left one of his own kin aboard the fleet, who would not be released until after the safe return of the Spanish envoy. Only in extreme circumstances was Legazpi authorized to get into a rowboat and approach the land, and in these rare cases he would be surrounded by many soldiers and well within range of their powerful artillery.[22]

Preserving Legazpi's life was a top priority. Yet, as the instructions went on to observe, "all of us are at the mercy of death." An ironclad procedure was therefore in place for such an eventuality. No second-in-command had been named. Bitter experience had shown that designating a successor could incite rivalries, mutinies, and murder. Instead, Legazpi's replacement was to remain unknown until the time of his death, when the survivors would be permitted to look in the commander's cabin for a steel coffer "of about one palm in length and one hand and two fingers in width." This hidden box, "nailed shut and wrapped in cloth with three royal seals," contained a piece of paper with the name of the substitute commander. Should this person die too, a second steel coffer, slightly smaller than the first but similarly closed, wrapped, and with three royal seals, bore the name of the third person in the line of command. The identities of the two replacements were wholly unknown to the expeditionaries—including Legazpi and the two chosen successors themselves. Now we know that the first (and surprising) replacement was the once treasonous military commander Mateo del Sauz, and the second was the expedition's royal treasurer, Guido de Lavezaris, a man of Genoese ancestry who had been involved in earlier attempts to find a practicable route to Asia. Clearly, Pacific exploration was dangerous as much for the forces of nature as for the human element, an insight that we shall have ample occasion to confirm.[23]

The days before casting off were frantic. Indigenous workers and Black slaves must have been under tremendous pressure to load the bacon, hardtack, chickpeas, wine, and other victuals. The perishables had to be carried into the ships at the last minute to avoid spoilage, although in reality the tropical fauna had already started ravaging them. Even busier than the port workers were the expeditionaries themselves. They needed to acquire many items like weapons, goods for trade in Asia, additional food for the voyage; or, conversely, they had to dispose of their property. After all, they were about to embark on the journey of a lifetime and might not be back in the Americas for years, or perhaps forever. Preparations also needed to be made for the worst possible outcome. Each of the four ships had a person "of good conscience and reputation" appointed as a "holder of goods" (*tenedor de bienes*). All voyagers were required to register with this person, providing their names, showing proof of the salaries assigned on signing up, and naming their beneficiaries in case of death. Inevitably these transactions and arrangements took more time than expected. Religion played a primary role in sixteenth-century voyages of exploration, and Commander Legazpi did not take such matters lightly. Prior to embarking, all expeditionaries had to confess, take communion, and hear a Mass of the Holy Spirit.[24]

Three days before leaving Navidad, Commander Legazpi wrote a brief letter to the Spanish king underscoring the "enormity and importance of this venture" and currying royal favor: "I have taken over this enterprise and spent a great deal of my patrimony to supply and equip myself and thus deserve your consideration." Just hours before leaving and already aboard the flagship *San Pedro,* Urdaneta also put pen to paper to commend "Andrés de Mirandaola," his nephew, "who is also going in this armada as a royal administrator, and I implore Your Majesty to grant him this appointment in perpetuity." The friar-mariner also used the opportunity to write on behalf of the five surviving Augustinians, "for we are the first to participate in this great enterprise, and we have worked hard and this should count for something in your judgment and favor."[25]

4

A Disappearance

On Monday, November 20, 1564, all voyagers boarded their respective ships, ready to depart. At 2:00 or 3:00 a.m. on Tuesday, in the darkest hour, the flagship finally fired a salvo. A crier said something along these lines: "Ease the rope of the foresail, in the name of the Holy Trinity — Father, Son, and Holy Spirit, three persons in one single true God — that they may be with us and give us a good and safe voyage, and carry us and return us safely to our homes!" Crew members proceeded to untie the mooring ropes or lift the anchors while others raised the sails. Slowly, the *San Pedro* turned toward the immensity of the Pacific Ocean. Moments later, the other vessels went through the same motions. The fleet must have cleared the bay by sunrise and continued to catch glimpses of the Mexican coast for several hours.[1]

Life aboard the ships followed new rhythms and obvious improvements over Navidad. The mosquitos and other insects vanished almost instantly (though not the fleas and lice), and the ocean breeze provided effective relief from the heat. The expeditionaries also gained immediate access to foods that had been denied to them before. Each soldier received a daily ration of one pound of hardtack and either a pound of meat or half a pound of dried fish along with fava beans or chickpeas. Doled out in three square meals a day, this was more than enough. Every Sunday afternoon, some cheese was added to the ration for variety. The liquids on offer were also generous: three pints of water per day along with wine, enough not only to keep hydrated but also to soak and soften the hardtack. Commander Legazpi had said nothing to the four ship captains about the distribution of spirits, but we know that the crew members would never have consented to crossing the Pacific without this indispensable tonic for the body and mind. Indeed, alcohol was an important tool, deployed especially during storms to steel the mariners' resolve and "warm their stomachs."[2]

These rations were tangible improvements. Yet the negatives far outweighed the positives, beginning with the cramped conditions. To understand the sailors' circumstances in a way that makes sense to us, we must imagine a good-sized urban apartment occupied by about one hundred strangers. A single toilet — but no shower or sink — would have to do for everyone, along with a very rudimentary kitchen and no furniture other than sea chests (wooden boxes) scattered all over the deck and below and serving as chairs and tables as needed. Two or three times a day, pages brought out platters of food into which everyone stuck their fingers liberally to get the best pieces of meat or servings of chickpeas. At night, everyone but the most privileged had to find a reasonably level surface to sleep on — always too close to others — and try to get some rest in spite of the noises, odors, and constant movement. Spending merely a week in these conditions would have been taxing, yet the expeditionaries had to endure this for months.[3]

Aboard the ships, there was strict regimentation. Everybody "without skipping anyone if not for illness" was assigned daily to a four-hour shift. This could occur at any time of the day or night, with the worst shifts having evocative names like "drowsiness," or *modorra* (from midnight to four), "dawn," or *alva* (from four to eight), and so on. The time was measured carefully with multiple hourglasses, or *ampolletas,* that had to be turned without fail every thirty minutes, and the assigned tasks ranged from moving barrels and serving as lookouts to pumping out the awful-smelling water that always collected at the bottom of the ship. Those on shift could also be ordered to perform navigational duties like hoisting and trimming sails, not only because the crew was spread too thin but also "to get everybody trained and accustomed to such work in case of necessity." The remaining twenty hours of the day were far more leisurely. With so much time to kill, the expeditionaries were tempted to play cards or engage in other games of chance, betting their daily rations, clothes, and weapons. Of course, all of this was strictly prohibited, as was invoking the name of God in vain or using profanity, a constant occurrence among seamen. Any of these infractions could lead to punishments ranging from public shaming and withholding of one's daily ration to imprisonment and torture for repeat offenders.[4]

The first four days of the journey were uneventful. But on Saturday, November 25, Commander Legazpi requested all captains, pilots, and high-ranking officers to come aboard the flagship, *San Pedro,* for a mid-ocean meeting. Just conveying this order accurately to the other three vessels—some of which may have been sailing miles away—and then transferring two or three individuals from each of these ships into rowboats and then onto the towering *San Pedro* must have been difficult and time-consuming. All six pilots, including Lope Martín; all four captains, including Don Alonso de Arellano of the tender *San Lucas;* all five Augustinian friars, including Urdaneta; all royal officials; military commander Mateo del Sauz; and a few others—around twenty-five men in total—were in attendance at this unexpected gathering hundreds of miles from the continent. The fleet commander must have dreaded the moment when he would have to disclose the existence of a second set of instructions from the Audiencia of Mexico which he had kept secret from everyone else. The notary aboard the fleet broke the royal seals and read aloud until reaching the key paragraph: "You will steer toward the Islands of the West without entering the Moluccas [Spice Islands] because that would be contrary to our arrangement with his Most Serene Highness, the King of Portugal, and instead you will go to the Philippines, which are not on the Portuguese side but within His Majesty's demarcation."[5]

We will never know the full range of emotions that flared up at that mid-ocean meeting, but Urdaneta received the news as a personal affront. The Philippines *were* on the Portuguese side, as he had made abundantly clear to Philip II four years earlier. "The Philippines and the Spice Islands are on the same meridian," Urdaneta had written to the monarch without a shred of doubt, "and both are well within the Portuguese demarcation." This is why the friar had advocated going to New Guinea all along. The new orders ignored this exchange between the friar and the king, reverted to a mistaken geography, and risked a serious military engagement with the Portuguese in Southeast Asia. Friar Urdaneta also must have spared a thought or two for his old nemesis Captain Juan Pablo de Carrión, who had always proposed going to the Philippines and had evidently gotten the last word. Carrión had been forced to stay behind, but his brother, Andrés Cauchela, had joined the expedition as a royal accountant and was present at that meeting. Above all, the unveiling of the new orders strained relations between the two most important men of the expedition: the fleet commander, who had withheld vital information from the other, the man who was supposed to guide it. Legazpi had to admit that the sudden change of plans "affected the friars greatly," adding that "they would not have come on the voyage had they known [the true destination]." The opinionated Urdaneta did not hide his anger, but he could hardly quit or retaliate in any meaningful way in the middle of the ocean.[6]

After the pilots and captains returned to their vessels, the fleet immediately changed course to "west-southwest and heading straight to the
Philippines." There was one additional adjustment. Since departing from
Navidad, the flagship had sailed at the head of the squadron. After the
mid-ocean meeting, Commander Legazpi ordered the tender *San Lucas*
to move to the front, perhaps in recognition of Lope Martín's extraordinary seamanship or merely as a precaution. Martín and his crew would be
scouting ahead for rocks, islands, atolls, and other dangers. The *San Lucas*
would remain in constant communication with the other ships, using flags
during the day and lanterns at night. If the wind picked up and it became
necessary to lower some of the sails to reduce speed, all four ships agreed
on a signal so all would slow down at the same time and remain together.[7]

After taking the lead, however, the *San Lucas* began pulling ahead.
Lope Martín's instructions had been to stay within half a league (about
two miles) of the flagship, yet he steered as far as two leagues (seven miles)
ahead. In fair weather, this would still have been acceptable. Yet on December 1, 1564, several clouds gathered during the day and developed into
an evening storm. The flagship lowered the mainsail and made the signal
to slow down, but the *San Lucas* forged ahead into the impenetrable darkness until it disappeared.[8]

Hours later Lope Martín sounded the alarm and informed Captain Don
Alonso de Arellano that the other ships were nowhere to be seen. The pilot
explained that the *San Lucas* was "low on the waist" and therefore could
not slow down too much because the cross-sea would dump water over
the deck and swamp the vessel. Don Alonso immediately ordered lanterns
to be placed at the stern and on top of the mainmast, but the separation
continued during the next morning and over the next few days. Indeed,
it became permanent. The weather had something to do with it. With the
passing of the days, however, Legazpi, Urdaneta, and others aboard the
flagship suspected that the mulatto pilot, perhaps in collusion with Don

Alonso, had abandoned the fleet deliberately. Whatever the real reason, a mere ten days after leaving Navidad, the expedition became something of a race. The three largest vessels with the lion's share of the resources remained together, while the smallest craft, commanded by a cipher of a nobleman and steered by a remarkable pilot, struck out on its own.[9]

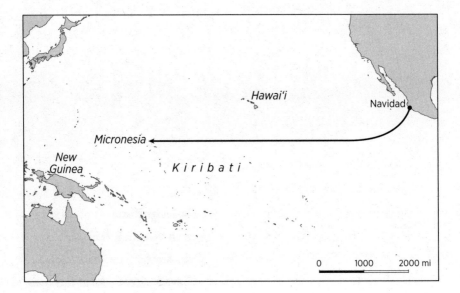

5

Mar Abierto

*T*he voyagers' first hurdle was to cross the longest stretch of open water in the world. After leaving the port of Navidad, they would not
see land for six thousand miles, or about three-fifths of the way across the
Pacific Ocean. The Hawaiian Islands would have been ideal for a stopover,
but Europeans would not know of their existence until 1778, when Captain Cook chanced on Kaua'i. Instead, Legazpi, Urdaneta, Don Alonso,
Lope Martín, and the others followed what they believed to be the best
trajectory to the Philippines, a very straight path across the ocean that
passed hundreds of miles south of Hawai'i and hundreds of miles north
of Kiribati for a disquieting month-and-a-half passage through a trackless,
seemingly never-ending expanse of water. The utter loneliness of that sector of the great ocean is hard to imagine.[1]

An ordinary person standing on the deck of one of the four ships in the
fleet would have seen nothing but water. Yet the pilots possessed a mental
map of the Pacific that included currents, winds, areas of calm, islands,
and subtle clues floating around or in the skies that were critical to orient-
ing them. This mental map had evolved over the decades, as oceangoing

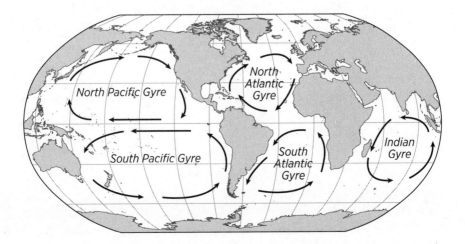

expeditionaries came to understand the general circulation of winds and currents around the world, applied novel technologies to establish their position on the high seas, and culled all relevant geographic and biological information from preceding voyages. It was a collective enterprise spanning six generations of pilots, cosmographers, seamen, mathematicians, astronomers, mapmakers, and instrument makers.

By far the most crucial insight was that gigantic wheels of winds and currents, now called gyres, circle the oceans with regularity. Five main such circular flows exist in the world: two in the Atlantic, two in the Pacific, and one in the Indian Ocean. Gyres change constantly and are affected by atmospheric phenomena like El Niño, which causes the winds to slacken around the equatorial Pacific. Yet the gyres of today are quite comparable to their predecessors five hundred years ago because they arise from the same slow-changing factors: Earth's rotation on its axis and the overall shape of continents and oceans. The spinning of our planet causes the air to be deflected to the right in the Northern Hemisphere and to the left in the Southern Hemisphere. In turn, the circling winds transfer some of their energy to the ocean as air molecules collide with the surface and set the water in motion. Known as the Coriolis effect, this peculiar air and water circulation is neither intuitive nor easy to explain. But from the vantage point of humans wishing to cross oceans, what matters is that gyres amount to veritable highways, because alongside them both winds and currents flow in the same general direction, like conveyor belts. In an era before motorized vessels, being pushed along by the currents and having the wind at one's back made all the difference between the possible and the utterly impossible. Among other things, the Atlantic gyres enabled Columbus to go from Spain to the Caribbean and back, and permitted the long-distance interactions that followed—including the forcible transportation of 12.5 million Africans across the Atlantic. The Pacific gyres allowed Magellan to cross the Pacific and made possible Spain's subsequent explorations of Southeast Asia down to the Navidad venture.[2]

Humans have brushed against portions of the five principal gyres of the world from time immemorial. Yet understanding their overall shape and using them purposefully for long-distance navigation is a development of the last few centuries. Except for the Indian Ocean—a case apart on account of the seasonal winds of the South Asian monsoon—it was not until the early 1400s when navigators began a systematic process of discovery of the gyres, beginning with the two in the Atlantic Ocean. This work began quite by accident while the Portuguese were exploring the western coast of Africa. Sailing from Portugal to the bulge of Africa was trivial thanks to the favorable winds and currents pushing the ships. But returning the same way proved more difficult the farther south the fleets went, until Cape Bojador in southern Morocco emerged as something of a point of no return. To go beyond Cape Bojador, Portuguese navigators had to let themselves go with the dominant winds and currents deep into the Atlantic for hundreds of miles westward until arriving at a region of variable winds, where they could finally try to double back toward Portugal. The *volta do mar largo* (the loop around the great sea) was a maneuver not suited for the faint of heart.[3]

The discoverers of this daring trajectory are unknown, not only be-

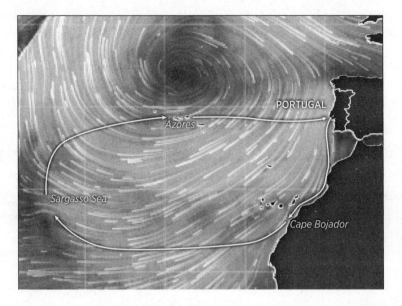

cause the Great Lisbon Earthquake of 1755 destroyed much of the extant historical documentation but also because of Portugal's deliberate secrecy to prevent competitors from learning about this revolutionary method of ocean navigation. Nonetheless, by 1446 the *volta do mar largo* had become so commonplace that even ordinary passengers knew about it. That year, eighty Black men aboard thirteen canoes, armed with bows and arrows dipped in poison, ambushed Nuno Tristão's fleet off the coast of Senegal. Only five young men in one caravel survived the attack. Their sole hope of returning to Portugal was by means of the *volta*. A cabin boy, the only survivor with some sailing experience, refused to pilot the caravel because of his "limited knowledge of the art of navigation." Fortunately, one of the passengers, aptly named Aires Tinoco (*aires* meaning "winds"), rose to the challenge and volunteered to steer, following the contours of the North Atlantic Gyre, a maneuver that he must have seen performed before. They spent two agonizing months until emerging, almost as if by a miracle, close to the port of Lagos in the Algarve.[4]

As they gained in experience, Portuguese seamen came to understand the North Atlantic not as a featureless expanse of water but as a space with peculiarities and clear signs. After sailing down the African coast and veering into the Atlantic for hundreds of miles, experienced pilots knew to look for the "Sargaço," a floating mass of seaweed that exists to the west of the Cape Verde Islands between twenty and twenty-five degrees of northern latitude. *Sargassum* gathers in the becalmed areas close to the center of the North Atlantic Gyre, but contrary to myth, it is never thick enough to impede the movement of vessels. This "Mar de Sargaço," as it became known, is quite simply a circular pool of warmer water held in place by the colder waters of the circling gyre. Its whereabouts offered a major clue to Atlantic voyagers. Having reached the Sargasso Sea, pilots sailed toward its northern limits to make sure that they had traveled sufficiently west and north to begin turning back toward Europe. From this increasingly familiar region in the middle of the Atlantic, the next target was the Azores, an archipelago of nine islands with deep-green valleys and volcanoes, which were still about nine hundred miles away from the Portuguese coast. As it was hard to make landfall precisely on one of these islands, sailors scanned the skies for another biological clue: "a seagull with red legs and other small birds." It is no coincidence that the Portuguese explored and colonized the Azores in the 1430s and 1440s, the very years of experimentation with the *volta do mar largo* (or *volta do Sargaço,* as it was also known). From the Azores, the final stretch home was due east with favorable winds and currents.[5]

The North Atlantic Gyre was a major find, but it turned out to be only half of the story. In the 1470s, the Portuguese crossed the equator and stumbled on a second gyre in the South Atlantic. Once again, it was necessity that prompted the discovery of this second great wheel of winds and currents. As the Portuguese sailors could not make any further progress in their Atlantic explorations by staying close to the African coast, on account of the contrary elements, they were forced again into the open Atlantic, this time venturing in a counterclockwise direction, away from the continent until practically crossing the entire ocean and nearing the coast of Brazil. This detour enabled Portuguese vessels finally to catch the southward-moving Brazil current and eventually to double back east toward the tip of Africa. This *volta* around the South Atlantic—a maneuver similar to the one in the North Atlantic but longer—could take up to three months of sailing without sight of land.[6]

As early as 1500, Vasco da Gama, the great discoverer of the sea route from Portugal to India, penned a concise but unmistakable characterization of this second *volta* in the instructions that he left to his successor: "You should always go around the sea until reaching the Cape of Good Hope." The recipient of such sound advice was Pedro Álvares Cabral, who followed da Gama's words so closely that he drifted to the coast of Brazil, where he spent a few days before continuing eastward to India. Over the years, Portuguese seamen became familiar with the contours of the South Atlantic Gyre, as is evident in the so-called *roteiros* (*derroteros* in Spanish, *rutters* in English, *routiers* in French, and so on), or sailing instructions, occasionally penned by pilots to facilitate the task of future navigators. The South Atlantic *roteiros* alerted pilots to approach the coast of Brazil well to the south of Cabo de Santo Agostinho; otherwise they risked being knocked off course by the currents and pushed into the Caribbean, a disastrous turn of events that could delay the voyage by several months. Farther south along the Brazilian coast, pilots were warned to steer clear of the Abrolhos, a group of islands and reefs off the present-day state of Bahia. ("Abrolhos" comes from *abre olhos,* or "open your eyes" in Portuguese.) Once the fleets doubled back toward the tip of Africa, the only intervening land was Tristan da Cunha, a group of remote islands in the South Atlantic, first sighted in 1506, precisely during the early exploration of the South Atlantic Gyre.[7]

Sixteenth-century navigators probably did not understand that Earth's rotation is what causes the ocean gyres. It would not be until the early nineteenth century when Gaspard-Gustave de Coriolis worked out the

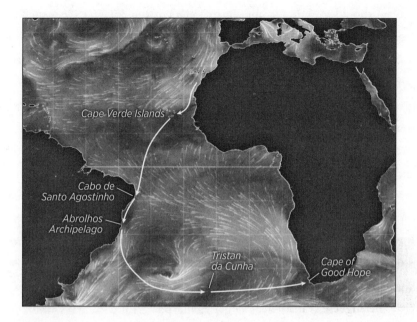

mathematics of the forces in a rotating system. Yet five hundred years ago, Portuguese pilots clearly referred to the *ventos gerais* (general winds) to distinguish them from more localized and variable winds. They also knew that these *ventos gerais* formed two rotating systems on either side of the equator. "When you have passed the equator and reached the general winds, you need to go with them for as long as possible," a pilot named Bernardo Fernandes counseled in 1550, "because with them you will reach the Cape of Good Hope latitude." Evidently seamen like Fernandes had a clear mental image of the gyres.[8]

If the Atlantic possessed two symmetrical wheels of currents and winds, it was reasonable to assume that the same was true in the Pacific. Magellan was likely the first to transfer this scheme from one ocean to the other. During his early years in Lisbon, he had the opportunity to learn about the Atlantic gyres. As a page and employee at the royal palace in the 1490s and early 1500s, Magellan received formal instruction in ocean navigation and rubbed shoulders with leading practitioners of the Atlantic *voltas* such as Vasco da Gama. In 1505, at the age of twenty-five, Magellan joined a fleet bound for India and thus had his first direct experience with the Atlantic gyres. He would go on to spend seven formative years in Asia, where his growing knowledge of the cutting-edge navigational technologies of his time proved decisive.[9]

Magellan's 1518–19 proposal to the Spanish crown to cross the Atlantic and the Pacific assumed that both oceans had general winds. He downplayed the difficulties of navigating on the high seas and instead focused on finding a passage between the Atlantic and the Pacific. Remarkably, he succeeded at locating it, but getting through it turned out to be far more difficult than anyone expected. The famous strait at the southern tip of South America is narrow (barely a mile wide in some places), leaving crews very little room to maneuver while facing powerful contrary winds and enormous tidal changes. Magellan and his men thus had to wrestle with the elements for thirty-eight harrowing days, tacking back and forth until finally they emerged into a comparatively calm ocean that Magellan misleadingly named "el Mar Pacífico." Thus began a new phase in this journey of discovery.[10]

Magellan's trajectory across the Pacific seems preternatural when we consider the gyres: he sailed parallel to the Chilean coast while being pushed by favorable currents and winds and then veered west at around thirty degrees of southern latitude (close to the center of the South Pacific Gyre), thus catching the westward-moving band of winds and currents to get across the ocean. Today, *World Cruising Routes* recommends *exactly* such a course to cross the Pacific. Nonetheless, weeks after that first and very accurate turn, Magellan and his pilots decided to continue on a northwesterly path, eventually crossing the equator and overshooting their intended target, the Spice Islands, which lay in the Southern Hemisphere, as they knew well. In other words, Magellan's fleet deliberately abandoned the South Pacific Gyre, entered the fickle Intertropical Convergence Zone

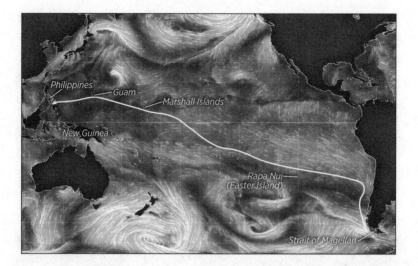

along the equator, and ventured into another gyre that, as far as anyone knew at the time, might or might not have existed. Whatever the reasons for this perplexing northward drift, Magellan and his companions crossed the great ocean in one swoop for the first time in recorded history. In a single voyage, they gained knowledge about the general circulation of winds and currents in the Pacific which had required decades of painstaking work by the earlier navigators of the Atlantic.[11]

It is ironic that Magellan is known to posterity as the first circumnavigator of the world, as if he had somehow intended to show that the world was round or to pioneer a new commercial route. In reality, the Spanish Empire retraced Magellan's tortuous trajectory only once more, in 1525–26. A youthful Urdaneta participated in that expedition and his opinion was clear. "The route from Spain to the strait found by Magellan is too long," he wrote in his report, "and the strait itself is long, unpopulated, with a brief summer and a long winter, tempestuous, and very dangerous." From then on, all transpacific voyages departed from the western coast of North America and came to depend on the vagaries of the North Pacific Gyre.[12]

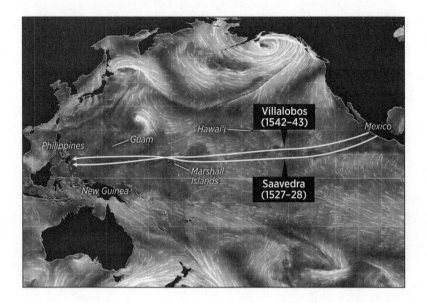

In this multigenerational effort to chart these global gyres, the next stage came in the form of two straight and elegant crossings of the Pacific. None other than Hernán Cortés spearheaded the first one. Barely nine months after he toppled the Aztec Empire, Cortés's scouts reached Mexico's west coast and established an outpost. "I have started building ships and brigantines to explore all the secrets of that coast," this irrepressible conqueror of Mexico wrote to the Spanish monarch in 1522, "and this will undoubtedly reveal marvelous things." Cortés considered leading an expedition from Mexico to the Spice Islands himself, but in the end named his cousin Álvaro de Saavedra Cerón as captain. The Saavedra expedition of 1527–28 proved calamitous. A storm in the middle of the Pacific dispersed the three ships in the fleet—two of which were never heard from again, as if swallowed by the ocean. The flagship *La Florida* struggled from the start because water kept pouring in through the keel close to a pin. The crew was forced to operate a pump day and night just to keep afloat. Remarkably, the *Florida* survived this initial challenge, withstood the mid-ocean storm, and overcame a second leak, eventually crossing by means of a direct path. The *Florida* benefited from favorable winds and currents all the way from Mexico to the Philippines and was able to cover impressive daily distances of between 90 and 140 miles, and as much as 250 miles if we are to believe one of the surviving logbooks.[13]

The second arrow shot across the Pacific, the Villalobos expedition of 1542–43, essentially retraced the previous track and confirmed that the best way to sail from the Americas to Asia was indeed via a straight path across the ocean just north of the equator. Wind maps of the North Pacific show a broad westward-moving band of winds (and currents) between five and twenty-five degrees of northern latitude, connecting Mexico and the Philippines. Wide, continuous or nearly so, and quite regular all year round, this portion of the North Pacific Gyre amounts to a veritable highway across the ocean, far easier to locate and navigate than the northern portion for the return trip, as we shall see.[14]

Just as earlier Atlantic navigators had used the Sargasso Sea to orient themselves, the Saavedra and Villalobos expeditions began identifying some of the Micronesian — that is, tiny — islands on the way to the Philippines. To get a sense of the difficulty, we need to consider that all the Micronesian islands add up to 271 square miles, or a quarter of Rhode Island, the smallest state in the United States, but are scattered over a patch of the Pacific that is roughly the size of all the contiguous states in the Union. Still, the Saavedra expedition was able to sight a group of low-lying atolls they grandly called "las Islas de los Reyes," or "the Islands of the Kings" (probably the present-day Faraulep Atoll at 8.6 degrees of northern latitude). More promisingly, the Villalobos expedition spotted a small island with many coconut palms and thickly inhabited (likely the present-day island of Fais at 9.7 degrees of northern latitude). The captain called it Matalotes because, as they passed, some of the islanders paddled toward the vessels and called out in cheerful Spanish, "Buenos días, matalotes," or "Good morning, sailors." Somehow they had interacted with Spaniards before.[15]

• • •

The Legazpi expedition pursued the same direct trajectory across the Pacific as the previous two voyages and benefited from the knowledge acquired up to then. The four vessels in Legazpi's squadron remained safely inside the band of favorable winds and currents of the North Pacific Gyre, covering the six thousand miles between Mexico and the first Micronesian islands in record time. At every stage of the journey, the pilots—the very best in all the Spanish Empire—knew their precise location relative to the North Pacific Gyre because they estimated their latitude (north-south distance) every day. They had begun this painstaking work right at the departing port of Navidad, where, independently from one another, they measured the angle of the sun with respect to the horizon at noontime with their astrolabes and then used a declination table to correct for the sun's altitude on the date of the measurement. The four surviving latitude readings at Navidad (19.5, 19.3, 19.25, and 19.5) are all within a third of a degree of the true latitude of 19.2 degrees. Considering the instruments and declination tables available in the sixteenth century, this was a negligible error and an extraordinary achievement. A third of one degree of latitude represents only twenty-three miles. Navigators would not have been able to spot a low island at a distance of more than ten or twelve miles, but at twenty-three miles, they would have been close enough to begin seeing floating vegetation, birds returning to their nests, and cloud formations indicating the proximity of land. In Columbus's time, navigating by the altitude of the sun had been an esoteric technique that produced very mixed results. Fifty years later, navigating by the altitude of the sun had become, if not routine, at least more common and infinitely more reliable. Legazpi's expert pilots were capable of great precision not only on land but also while standing on a heaving deck in the middle of the ocean. Here is a typical logbook entry: "Wednesday, December 6, 1564, we made 28 leagues following the same course," wrote pilot Esteban Rodríguez two weeks after departure, "and I took the sun at thirteen degrees and three quarters."[16]

Before the separation of the *San Lucas* from the rest of the fleet, the plan had been to go to the Philippines by way of the so-called "Islands of the Kings" (at nine degrees), "Matalotes" (at ten degrees), and a few others identified on earlier voyages. The distance between the coast of Mexico and these islands, however, was so vast that even extremely skilled pilots would have had a hard time estimating on what date, or even in what week, they had sailed far enough to be near them. The pilots were likely not to make landfall during an estimated window of time, and once that passed, they would not be able to tell if the islands they were seeking lay farther still, or behind them, or in some other direction.[17]

Anticipating such problems, the expeditionaries had agreed on a plan. "All will steer immediately to nine degrees of northern latitude, and then continue due west toward the Islands of the Kings and the Islands of the Corals, said to be at nine degrees," Legazpi had explained, "and then go to ten degrees toward the Islands of Reefs and Matalotes." Today this is called "parallel sailing" and consists of positioning the ships exactly in the latitude of the intended target well in advance and maintaining that latitude — correcting every day as needed — until reaching the destination. If they could just keep to a perfectly straight east-west line leading directly to the island that they were seeking, they would run into it *sooner or later*. But as the weeks went by, the pilots grew restless. Christmas came and went, New Year's Day passed, and no island came in sight. They kept measuring the altitude of the sun, a daily ritual that at least yielded consistent results, even though "the pilots could not agree completely, because some took the sun at nine degrees and others at nine degrees and one-quarter . . . and each pilot tried to justify his results and explain why the others were wrong."[18]

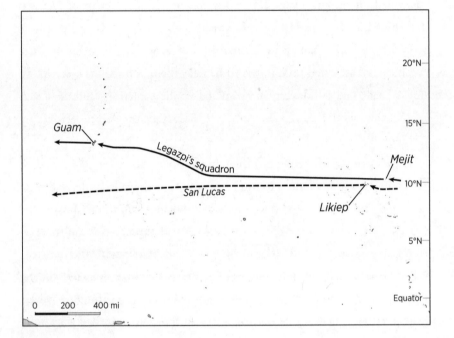

20°N—

15°N—

Guam

Legazpi's squadron

Mejit

10°N—

San Lucas

Likiep

5°N—

0   200   400 mi

Equator—

6

The Tiny Islands

*A*fter a month and a half, Legazpi and his men at last began encountering palm-fringed islands that seemed to rise out of nowhere. These jewels in the middle of the ocean were irresistible but extraordinarily treacherous. Some broke through the waterline, but others lurked just below the surface like deadly traps for passing ships. Enormous rings of sharp coral (atolls) formed placid azure lagoons teeming with fish, like visions from paradise. Yet attempting to stop there could easily turn disastrous.

Now known as the Marshall Islands, these volcanic columns rise straight up from the ocean floor. In the Cretaceous Period (145–65 million years ago), tectonic plates rubbed against one another, creating volcanoes that eventually broke through the surface. Yet since that time, the geologic activity had declined and the volcanoes receded. Thus, unlike the Hawaiian and other Pacific islands that lie in active volcanic zones, the Marshalls are constantly eroding and submerging, leaving ideal platforms for the coral to grow and form massive banks, perennially reaching for the surface as the islands themselves are slowly sinking. A mile-deep layer of dead coral, sand, and rock makes up the top portion of these columns. Close to the surface, the living coral often forms irregular rings enclosing shallow lagoons connected to the ocean through natural channels. Significantly, the coral tends to be steeper and more formidable in the direction that the currents—and thus the nutrients—come from. In other words, these coral islands are much harder to breach precisely in the direction from which the Spanish were approaching.[1]

A lookout on the flagship *San Pedro* spotted an island on January 9, 1565. A cannon shot signaled to the others to follow. After some hours, an elongated island came clearly into view. It was only about seven miles in length, "but the vegetation was lush and there were many coconut palms." Legazpi's three remaining vessels had been navigating at nine degrees in search of the Islands of the Kings, but the ships had accidentally drifted to ten degrees and serendipitously found this previously uncharted island (probably Mejit). After fifty days of continuous sailing, the expeditionaries were running low on water, and their urge to stop was overpowering. The three ships came very close to the island, "but it was completely surrounded by reefs, and we could not find a bottom." Commander Legazpi and his companions persisted, going from one end of the island to the other, probing different places to find a mooring. In the course of this exploration, they sighted "a little village with houses and palm trees and islanders walking by the beach and others going around in canoes." Throwing caution to the wind, the *San Pedro* approached the shore directly in front of the village, coming so close to it that the bowsprit (the pole at the front of the ship) touched land, and at that moment dropped anchor, "but could not find a bottom even though they had tied two ropes together." The smallest of the three vessels, the *San Juan,* also approached the island until nearly touching it, and lowered an anchor. Miraculously, it held on to something, at a depth of 150 fathoms, or nearly nine hundred feet.[2]

The larger two vessels, the *San Pedro* and the *San Pablo,* could never find a suitable anchorage in spite of their persistent searching. It was as if this

The lead pilot aboard the flagship, Esteban Rodríguez, took the time to sketch the first island that the fleet encountered on its way to the Philippines—possibly Mejit—on Tuesday, January 9, 1565. "The Indians here have beards," the pilot added in his logbook, "and for this reason our general gave it the name of the Island of the Bearded Ones."

elongated island emerged straight up from the depths of the ocean. The two unmoored vessels had to keep sailing close by at great peril of running aground while some of the men got into rowboats to reach the island and join those who had already gone ashore from the anchored *San Juan*. Commander Legazpi's grandson Felipe de Salcedo and the friar-mariner Urdaneta were among the members of the landing party. They were to take possession of the island and seek contact with the locals. On seeing the large vessels lurking in front of their village, however, the Micronesians had prudently sought refuge in the interior. The only ones left at the village consisted of a very old couple and a young woman with a baby. Father Urdaneta tried to communicate, using the Malay that he had learned in his youth when living in Southeast Asia for eight years, but neither the friar nor the other translators were able to understand the islanders' tongue. Still, the old man "appeared well disposed and the women's gestures were welcoming." The Europeans gave beads and other trade goods to them and communicated well enough through signs and by pointing at things. The old man returned the favor by giving them a tour of the village, "show-ing them their houses and the fruits that they had to eat, and giving them some to taste, and pointing to the fish that they had in great quantity both in piles and already cooked." It was a pleasant first encounter. The elderly couple and the younger woman probably did not understand that their is-land had become a part of the far-flung Spanish Empire. But the Spaniards would not be back for decades.[3]

That strip of land was only the first of what Legazpi's company would soon discover to be a forest of low-lying islands. The next morning, the fleet ran into a very characteristic atoll with a lagoon in the middle, quite likely Ailuk. "The island is all broken up and low," wrote pilot Esteban Rodríguez, "and even though we could not find a bottom around it, the shallow water between one part of the island and another reaches only up to the knee." The fleet commander likened such lagoons to mid-ocean "corrals," undoubtedly drawing on his pastoral Iberian background. By sunset, the expeditionaries had found yet more islands but could not stop at any because the anchors did not hold.[4]

Pilot Rodríguez sketched an atoll that came into view on January 10, 1565, possibly Ailuk Atoll. The dots represent coral, fringing a shallow lagoon in the middle.

. . .

Sailing many miles ahead of Legazpi's squadron and slightly to the south, the *San Lucas* also had to negotiate the jungle of basaltic columns in the middle of the ocean. The first encounter proved nearly fatal. A strong breeze was pushing the *San Lucas* around midnight on January 5, 1565, four days ahead of Legazpi's arrival at the atolls, when some of the men on the deck suddenly heard the sound of crashing waves. A calm evening turned to pandemonium in an instant. As the small ship continued its rapid forward momentum, streaks of foam and rock glistened straight ahead. They were about to crash into an incongruously shallow spot in the middle of the largest ocean in the world—possibly Likiep Atoll. Over the roar of the surf and shouts of alarm, the pilot Lope Martín barked orders to lower the sails "just as the helmsman made a sharp turn to port [left], prompted by Our Lady of Guadalupe, and this was our salvation because the breeze was strong. Had he turned the other way, we would have been lost," reported the nobleman captain Don Alonso de Arellano. The men of the *San Lucas* had narrowly avoided a direct collision, but the danger was hardly over. They scraped against rock and coral and then entered a shallow area. In the pitch darkness of the ocean, it was nearly impossible to see how to get back out into deeper water. The pilot ran to the front of the deck to scout the way forward, "but at that instant the sea pushed him out of the vessel, and he was saved only because he held onto a loose rope with one hand, and he was swimming so close to the rocks that he thought that the ship was already stuck." Mercifully, that night ended only in a scare. The *San Lucas* remained in the vicinity of the breaking waves and the next morning attempted to make landfall. "But the island was entirely surrounded by reefs," Don Alonso noted, "and we could not find a place to stop even though we came so close that a man could practically jump onto the reef." After that first harrowing encounter, the crew worried constantly about hitting land lying "so low that one could barely see it even when passing right next to it." Over the next few days, they journeyed through many islets and atolls.[5]

On January 7, the voyagers of the *San Lucas* saw in the distance a small canoe with a triangular sail, crossing from one island to another. They decided to follow it. Two men and a boy were aboard, sailing fast. By the time the *San Lucas* pulled near enough, the canoe had entered a shallow area where the deeper-keeled Spaniards could not follow. The voyagers signaled to the canoers to come to the ship. "And so they turned around, grabbed a line that we threw them, and climbed aboard," Don Alonso remembered, "and we gave them beads and a knife and offered a shirt to the boy, and they gave us coconuts and fish and all the water they were carrying." After this exchange, the canoers agreed through signs to lead a party of Spaniards to their houses in another part of the island (perhaps Kwajalein Atoll). Don Alonso, Lope Martín, and eight sailors got into their rowboat and tried to keep up with the fast-moving canoe as it glided over reefs and coral banks until arriving at a stretch of shore where the two men had built their homes. Two women and a child were there. The two men explained "that they were fishermen who had come from larger islands farther west and had set up camp there only for some time." Lope Martín remarked that no armada had ever visited that island, so he gave it the name of "the Island of the Two Neighbors" because only two families lived there.[6]

These islanders were the ultimate ocean dwellers, never straying more than a few feet away from the water and sustaining themselves through the bounty of the sea. "They live a thousand leagues away from the mainland, and their small islands are occupied by coconuts," marveled Don Alonso. "Anyone seeing these lands would think that they are like floating carpets, they are so small and so low that they would sink under the water in a storm." He was entirely correct. Typhoons do occur in this region and indeed swamp the low-lying islands. In the worst of such instances, Pacific Islanders had no other recourse but to fill the hulls of their canoes

Sixteenth-century documents make clear that Spanish expeditionaries were impressed both by the *paraos,* the boats used by Pacific Islanders, and by the skill of their operators. This is a nineteenth-century drawing made by a French admiral while visiting the Caroline Islands.

with fresh water, venture into the open ocean, secure the rigging, and wait out the storm, displaying extraordinary aplomb and seamanship. Less apparent to the Europeans was the extent to which these sea people, over the course of two or three thousand years of occupation, had thoroughly transformed the tiny coral islands. Originally no coconut palms had existed there. Early settlers had propagated them purposely to build their houses, clothe their families, weave rugs, and obtain practically every item required for their vessels, from the hulls, sails, and rigging to the food and water conveniently packaged in natural round containers. By cutting open the coconuts, they could also fashion cups and use them to drink the fermented sap and juice of the plant itself. "It is astounding that out of a single tree," remarked a later Spanish visitor, "these natives can make so many different things and fill all of their needs." The first inhabitants of the Marshalls may have "seeded" the islands in advance, leaving coconut plants in their seasonal visits before settling down permanently. They also introduced chickens (domesticated originally in South Asia) as well as breadfruit and taro (from Southeast Asia) and thus transformed what had once been a very challenging island world into an eminently livable corner of our planet.[7]

Although biased and uninformed, the voyagers' observations constitute our earliest sources on the original inhabitants of what are now the Marshall Islands. The visitors immediately noted the long beards of the males, reaching to the chest and sometimes all the way to the waist. Commander Legazpi called the first island that they saw "la Isla de los Barbudos," or "the Island of the Bearded Ones." In addition to their beards, Marshallese men let their hair grow "like women," according to Don Alonso, "but they comb it and tie it in a knot at the top of the head." Man buns were apparently in fashion in the sixteenth century. Predictably, Europeans dwelled on the nakedness of both men and women, although the women covered their private parts with garments made of palm tree fiber "that are very thin and beautiful." The expeditionaries found the islanders "attractive and tall," especially the women, although their opinions of their character were far less flattering. Don Alonso judged them to be "covetous," "great traitors," and, in short, "a people of the devil." Excursions into the villages afforded Europeans glimpses of their simple and effective material world, which included fishhooks made of bone, fishing nets, and "very well-made canoes." The voyagers were especially curious about their hosts' military capabilities, and some Spaniards remarked that they could not find "any defensive or offensive weapons," while others identified clubs, sticks with sharp points of bone, and slings.[8]

The expeditionaries of the *San Lucas* sighted many more islands on their way to the Philippines. On January 8 the ship arrived at an island that was small but densely populated. The men pulled their vessel as close as possible, threw a line, and signaled to the islanders watching from the shore to grab it. Instantly, several of them jumped into the water and took the rope. They were expert swimmers, infinitely better than the Spanish seamen, many of whom did not know how to swim at all. "And they began pulling us toward the land," the *San Lucas* captain recounted, "but some of the Indians did not think that allowing us ashore was such a good idea, so they pulled sometimes and let go of the rope at other times, and they kept us like this." As this discussion unfolded among the people holding the rope, other islanders jumped into the water or boarded their canoes and reached the European vessel to offer coconuts and other goods. They were so many that they threatened to overwhelm the *San Lucas*. After what seemed like an eternity of uncertainty and confusion, the Europeans finally cut the rope and began sailing away, "but the Indians were so covetous for what we carried in our ship, that we could not kick them out even when we were one league [more than three miles] away from their island." Don Alonso called it "la Isla de los Nadadores," or "the Island of the Swimmers," as a testament to their prowess in the water.[9]

Amidst the many atolls and low-lying islands that make up eastern Micronesia, there was little hope that the *San Lucas* would ever become reunited with the other vessels. Before the separation, the plan had been to head to nine degrees of northern latitude to visit the "Islands of the Kings" and the "Islands of the Corals," then steer to ten degrees, toward the "Island of Reefs" and "Matalotes," and finally on to the Philippines. Anticipating the possibility that one of the vessels could become accidentally separated, the expeditionaries had agreed on a contingency plan. The stray vessel would proceed immediately toward the next stopover island and wait for eight or ten days for the rest of the fleet to catch up. "And if the vessel could not make landfall or, having waited for ten days, had not reunited with the others," the written instructions read, "it would continue but not before its crew had marked a tree with a cross and buried below it a bottle with a letter describing everything that had happened and the route that it would follow." The theory was clear but the practice less so. Legazpi's squadron accidentally drifted from nine to ten degrees, while the *San Lucas* navigated between nine and eight degrees. This seemingly small difference of one or two degrees was more than enough to preclude a rendezvous. More fundamentally, none of the ships could stop in the coral-ringed islands of Micronesia. "In spite of our instructions to wait for the others, we could not do so because there was nowhere to stop," Don Alonso remarked later, "and we were barely twenty people strong between men and boys, some of whom were ill already, and we lacked weapons, all of which had been kept in the other vessels."[10]

Commander Legazpi nevertheless came to believe that the *San Lucas* had abandoned the rest of the fleet deliberately. He surmised that the pilot Martín, possibly in collusion with the nobleman captain Don Alonso, was a traitor to the Spanish crown, perhaps pursuing an independent plan of enrichment. As we shall see, such an accusation is at least excessive and quite likely unfounded, especially considering the trajectory of the *San Lucas* parallel to that of the other vessels and the geology of the Micronesian islands. The *San Lucas* remained within one degree of the agreed plan and could not stop for the same reason that Legazpi's fleet could not make landfall. Indeed, the separation became permanent not because of the *San Lucas*'s trajectory but because of Commander Legazpi's sudden decision to change course on Wednesday, January 17, 1565. On that day, Legazpi convened a mid-ocean gathering with his remaining pilots and captains. They had been sailing for nearly two months, and the pilots were convinced (mistakenly) that they were nearing the Philippines. Striking the archipelago at ten degrees of latitude or less—corresponding to the southernmost Philippine island of Mindanao—entailed a very real risk. Twenty years earlier, the southerly winds and currents prevalent in that part of the Philippine archipelago had made it impossible for the Villalobos expedition to "turn the corner of that island [Mindanao] and head north from there." Urdaneta himself had experienced the same contrary elements in the southern Philippines nearly forty years earlier. To avoid a repeat of such a scenario, Legazpi's navigators and captains agreed to "go up to thirteen degrees and then continue due west." After that unplanned turn to the north, it was certain that the *San Lucas* would never be able to rejoin the others.[11]

In this drawing by one of Legazpi's pilots, we can see on the left the contours of Guam. The Spanish gloss "surgidero y agua," or "landfall site and water," at the lower left identifies the exact bay where the fleet landed in January of 1565. At the top one can read "Esto no se descubrió," or "This part was not discovered." On the right, the Spanish pilot sketched a *parao*, showing its sails made of palm leaves — "velas de palma" — and an outrigger or secondary hull to stabilize it.

7

"The Island of the Thieves"

Sometime during January 1565, Legazpi's expeditionaries crossed into a new geologic region of the Pacific. They were gliding over the deepest gash in the world, the Mariana Trench, and sailing through a subduction zone where the Pacific Plate meets the Philippine Sea Plate, a region of volcanism and earthquakes. The low-lying islands of the Central Pacific suddenly gave way to higher lands, among them a north-to-south chain called the Marianas. This line of volcanic islands right on the path between Mexico and the Philippines was the first viable way station since leaving the American continent, in particular Guam, the most southerly of the Marianas as well as the largest island in all of Micronesia. Guam possessed lush high hills and many inhabitants, and offered foods unfamiliar to most Europeans, like the "long figs," as they sometimes referred to bananas. Ever since Magellan had serendipitously run into Guam in 1521, Spaniards had been aware of its existence. That early encounter with the local Chamorros had not gone well, however. They were tall, imposing, and extraordinarily eager to trade. Well before making landfall, dozens of outrigger canoes had come to surround Magellan's ships. The islanders had overwhelmed the Europeans, calling out from their boats, offering fish or coconuts, while others climbed aboard, forcing themselves on the travelers, urging them to barter, and appropriating any objects that were loose on the deck. When crew members tried to repel them, localized violence had erupted. Yet many Chamorros remained unfazed and continued to peddle goods. Some even cut off a skiff towed by one of the Spanish ships and made away with it. Magellan retaliated the following day. To retrieve the skiff, he went ashore with forty men and looted two villages, burned fifty houses, and killed at least seven. He also gave Guam the dispiriting name of "la Isla de los Ladrones," or "the Island of the Thieves," because, as the chronicler in Magellan's expedition explained, "its inhabitants are poor, ingenious, and very thievish."[1]

Forty-four years after Magellan, the *San Lucas* passed too far south of Guam, but the rest of the fleet under Legazpi ascended to thirteen degrees and caught sight of the island on the morning of January 22, 1565. The land appeared so large and so high that "all the pilots thought we were in the Philippines," Legazpi noted, "and the closer we got, the more certain of this they became." The only holdout was Father Urdaneta, who thought that it was "the Island of the Thieves." A disagreement among extremely skilled navigators of this magnitude was rare. The distance between Guam and the Philippines is 1,500 miles! All along, the navigators in Legazpi's fleet had been very consistent in their calculations of latitude. As we have seen, the variation had been at most a third of one degree, or twenty-three miles. Yet their longitude estimates, the dimension that mattered most when it came to crossing the Pacific, were anything but consistent.[2]

Finding longitude was challenging because it required an arbitrary, human-given point of reference. North-south distance is measured with respect to the equator, a line wrapping around the middle of our planet equidistant from the poles that everyone can readily understand. Every place in the world is either north or south of the equator (or right on it). In contrast, no comparable line exists for longitude, and therefore no place on Earth is either east or west except with respect to some other handpicked location. Today we start counting from a meridian line running through the Royal Observatory in Greenwich, just south of the River Thames in London (although the Greenwich meridian no longer passes through the line marked on the ground, as it has moved in the intervening time). Before Britain's ascendancy, however, Iberian navigators began measuring variously from Lisbon, Seville, Toledo, the Cape of São Vicente (the southwestern tip of Iberia), or the line dividing the world between Spain and Portugal according to the 1494 Treaty of Tordesillas.

Having common standards is an underappreciated but vital aspect of scientific progress, and early navigators could not agree on where to start when it came to measuring longitude. The French pilot aboard the flagship, Pierres Plín, for example, calculated longitude at Navidad before casting off. "At that port," Plín noted, explaining his result, "I found myself at 1,250 leagues from the line of reference along the Canary Islands that is ten leagues to the west of the Island of Hierro." It turned out to be a reasonable estimate. The east-west distance between Hierro and Navidad is about 1,400 leagues. Yet if this result was to have any value, the other pilots also had to start measuring from a prime meridian passing ten leagues west of Hierro. This was not the case. Plín's good measurement notwithstanding, one of the five Augustinian friars, Martín de Rada, was involved in a parallel effort and thus "carried an instrument of medium size to ascertain the longitude between Toledo in Spain and wherever God wants us to settle down across the Pacific." It would still have been possible to make longitude measurements from Hierro and Toledo compatible with each other, but this would have required knowing the east-west distance between these two places halfway around the world.[3]

Starting in Europe to establish longitude in the Pacific was just too cumbersome. As a practical matter, Legazpi's pilots tried to solve the east-west riddle in two ways. First, they kept a running tally of the distance traveled since departing from Navidad. Typical logbook entries include statements such as these: "Today we traveled twenty-nine leagues" or "There was very light wind during the day, so we set the distance at fifteen leagues." Ships did not come equipped with odometers or speedometers in those days, so pilots had to gauge distance and speed by sensing the strength of the wind, observing the trim of the sails, and looking at the passing bubbles every hour of the day and night. The pilots may have been extremely skilled, yet even small hourly and daily inaccuracies added up. After a month at sea, Commander Legazpi asked them how far the fleet had traveled since departing from Navidad. "Some of the pilots showed the ships 200 leagues [734 miles] ahead of where others said they were," the commander reported, "I don't know if on account of the tides and currents that we experienced." When the expeditionaries first sighted Guam after two months of sailing, the discrepancies had grown to 1,500 miles. Eyeballing distance was evidently not a satisfactory method to estimate longitude.[4]

For this reason, the foremost pilots in the world resorted to a second method based on the small angle between true north as observed by the North Star and magnetic north as indicated by the compass. As we have seen, Portuguese navigators began noticing how the compass needles almost never pointed straight north but deviated slightly to the east or to the west, a phenomenon that they described as "northeasting" or "northwesting" of the compass and today we call magnetic declination. Explorers traveling vast distances across the globe such as Columbus, Amerigo Vespucci, and others witnessed how their compasses shifted slightly but in unison, as if pointing toward a specific spot in the world. (At least one sixteenth-century cosmographer called it the "attractive point," a very early formulation of the North Magnetic Pole.) Some cosmographers posited that this slight displacement of the needles held the key to approximating the elusive longitude, among them the brothers Rui and Francisco Faleiro, as we have seen. Rui Faleiro had offered to determine the exact longitude of the Spice Islands with this revolutionary system during the negotiations with the Spanish king leading to Magellan's historic circumnavigation voyage. In the end, Rui Faleiro did not accompany Magellan—some sources claim that he went mad—but the crown still compelled him to explain his system in writing and also hired the younger Francisco Faleiro, a brilliant cosmographer in his own right. Francisco went on to explain the method in a published navigational manual and even proposed a "shadow instrument"—today we would call it an azimuth compass—to measure the gap between true and magnetic north more precisely.[5]

Legazpi's excellent pilots—including Lope Martín—may well have been acquainted with Francisco Faleiro's method and even with the cosmographer himself, who remained active in Seville nautical circles in the 1560s. The two pilots of the San Pablo, for instance, started wrestling with the longitude problem at Navidad. "At that port, we marked the direction of the compass needles, as is customary among mariners, to know the variation and distance from the true pole," Jaymes Martínez Fortún and Diego Martín explained in their logbook with disarming clarity, "and the needles pointed to the northwest by half a quarter with respect to a straight north-south line." Today the magnetic declination at Navidad is 6.53 to the *east* of true north, but if we use the most accepted geomagnetic model for the sixteenth century (January 1, 1590, is the oldest date available), the declination would have been 4.55 degrees to the *west,* entirely consistent with the pilots' assertion about "northwesting." What is more, the pilots' misleading-sounding measurement of "half a quarter" turns out to be uncannily accurate. Compass roses of that era were divided into thirty-two points of 11.25 degrees each (32 x 11.25 = 360 degrees). "One-quarter" was like saying one click of the compass, and thus "half a quarter" amounted to 5.6 degrees, or a mere 1.07 degrees off from the predicted magnetic declination at Navidad for that era. The two pilots of the San Pablo were almost exactly on the mark, and their continued observations on the way to the Philippines jibe extremely well with our estimates. As we would expect, magnetic declination diminished as the fleet traveled across the Pacific. Three weeks into the voyage, on Wednesday, December 13, 1564, the two navigators reported "no variation whatsoever between the North Star and the compass needle." According to our geomagnetic model, this line of zero declination would have been located about 1,500 miles west of Navidad (at a longitude of 125 degrees west), a distance that makes perfect sense given the fleet's overall trajectory and speed. When the expedition began encountering the first islands of Micronesia on January 12, 1565, the two pilots measured the declination again and recorded that the compass needles were now "northeasting by a quarter," or 11.25 degrees. Their accuracy is again hard to believe. The declination would have been 10.9 degrees to the east of true north at Ailuk Atoll according to our estimates, only one-third of a degree off from what the pilots reported! Not all of their measurements match ours so precisely — after all, sixteenth-century

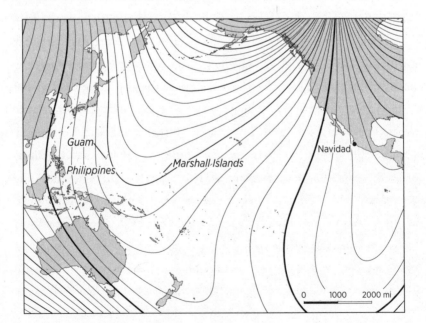

pilots expressed their measurements in imprecise clicks of the compass of 11.25 degrees. Yet all of their readings were consistent and painted the same basic magnetic picture of the Pacific.[6]

Magnetic declination confounded navigators and cosmographers from the fifteenth through the eighteenth centuries because, while it serves to derive east-west distance in some parts of the world, it is downright perplexing in others. In a passage such as the one pursued by Legazpi's fleet toward Asia, it was quite effective. Since Legazpi's pilots were measuring declinations across the Pacific for the first time, these values only satisfied their curiosity. Future navigators, however, could use them to gauge their east-west progress. They would expect their compass needles to "northwest" slightly at Navidad. For a couple of weeks after departure, the declination would diminish until reaching zero at a spot in the ocean that was easy to measure and indicated good westward progress. Future travelers would also know that from that point on, the compasses would "northeast" until getting to "one-quarter," at which point they were likely to run into the first Micronesian islands. The needles would continue to "northeast" and attain the highest declinations at a line between the first Micronesian islands and Guam (at a longitude of 162 degrees east), and then reverse course and begin their march back toward zero, something that would occur near the Borneo coast, west of the Philippines. All of this may seem like voodoo science to us, but to anyone risking his life across the largest ocean in the world, this longitude information was beyond precious. And yet, in some other parts of the North Pacific, this method could be fatally flawed, as is obvious from the wavy and capricious lines of a magnetic map of the region. The return trip across the mighty ocean, the awesome challenge facing the expeditionaries, would yield confusing magnetic declinations and thus a potentially fatal ending.[7]

Even today, catching the first glimpses of Guam from an airplane window after so many hours of ocean travel is exhilarating. We can only guess at the elation of Legazpi and his men at the sight of such a large and lush island on that Monday, January 22, 1565. The fleet was met far out at sea by no fewer than fifty canoes, similar to what Magellan's fleet had experienced, although this time the islanders refrained from attaching themselves to the Spanish vessels or climbing aboard. They stayed in their canoes or *paraos* "at a stone's throw distance." Violent encounters since Magellan's visit more than four decades earlier had taught both peoples to be circumspect. Nonetheless, the Chamorros "gave great voices to call our attention, and they pointed to different parts of the island where they lived, giving us to understand that they would give us much to eat." Wishing to make a good first impression, the Spanish commander ordered some knives, scissors, beads, and a mirror to be tied onto a piece of wood and cast adrift so the islanders could get it. The people on the *parao* that was closest to the Spanish flagship picked up the gift and pointed even more intently at a certain place on land.[8]

The fleet's final approach to the island was challenging with the swarm of *paraos* and distracting shouts coming from them. The greatest obstacle, however, was a shallow limestone platform surrounding Guam. This "shore bench," as geologists sometimes refer to it, fringes the island and extends up to half a mile out, preventing vessels with deep keels from getting near the land. The sea is too shallow inside the platform and too deep outside it, so it is not even possible to anchor. Visible from many beaches around Guam, this limestone platform has been a deterrent throughout history. In 1944, when American troops launched an amphibious assault to retake the island from the Japanese, the operation began with underwater demolition teams reconnoitering gaps in the platform and reefs and blasting boat lanes.[9]

Wisely, Legazpi's fleet bypassed Guam's treacherous southern tip where the limestone platform is widest and probed the island's western approach. It was sunset by then, however, so the ships had to pull away to a safe distance for the night. In the meantime, the islanders returned to their villages to light fires all along the western coast of Guam, still trying to lure the voyagers to their respective settlements. The next morning the three Spanish vessels resumed the search and found a promising bay (indicated as "surgidero y agua," or "landfall site and water," in the drawing at the beginning of this chapter). Legazpi probably knew about its existence in advance. Nearly forty years earlier (on September 4–10, 1526), Friar Urdaneta had stopped at Guam during the Loaísa expedition and perhaps still recalled where the best ports were. The three ships in the fleet almost certainly entered what is today Umatac Bay and anchored without difficulty.[10]

The Chamorro people wanted nothing more than to trade. Coastal villages throughout Guam had participated in a regional exchange with other islands as well as with the Asian mainland, a trade that included iron, an extraordinarily valuable material that did not exist on the island. Iron knives served as excellent weapons and tools, while iron nails were essential to build sturdy boats. "This is their gold," commented one contemporary Spaniard, "and they use it in all of their tasks and activities." Understandably, different Chamorro villages competed with one another fiercely to control and monopolize such a vital trade. This explains their venturing far out to sea to meet all passing vessels, their relentless peddling of goods, and their aggressive methods.[11]

"The Natives began coming from the entire coast in their *paraos*," the commander reported, "and we counted more than four hundred, the flagship alone being surrounded by more than one hundred." Each *parao* carried between four and six persons, so the islanders who gathered on Tuesday, January 23, 1565, could well have exceeded two thousand out of a total island population of perhaps thirty thousand. Yet not a single Chamorro dared to go aboard the galleons in spite of the commander's encouraging signals and occasional gifts. The canoes surrounded Legazpi's three ships from all sides as scores of Chamorros called out to the Spaniards insistently and held up "coconuts, sugarcanes, green bananas, and rice tamales, although each canoe brought very little: two or three coconuts, one or two sugarcanes, or two or three yams." When the peddlers learned that the visitors had iron, they did not want to trade for anything else, "and when we showed them our nails, they became so very addicted that they gave up everything for them." The friar-mariner must have had a facility for languages and an excellent memory. He came out on the deck and "said a few words in the Chamorro language from his previous visit, counting up to ten, and everyone was very excited." In return, one of the islanders shouted "Gonzalo," the name of a cabin boy who had deserted in the Marianas during Magellan's visit and who had lived there for years.[12]

That first day of trading, the Spanish got the better part of the bargain. Yet as the *paraos* continued to arrive in Umatac Bay to barter over subsequent days, some islanders came out ahead. Word spread that the Spanish wanted rice, so Chamorro merchants brought bundles of twenty-five to thirty pounds. "But because the Indians didn't want to come onto our ships and thus gave the rice to be hoisted with a rope," Legazpi recorded, "we found many loads full of sand with two fingers of rice at the top to hide their deception." The Spaniards also traded for coconut oil similarly hoisted in barrels that were later found to contain one or two fingers of oil at the top and the rest water, "and they played similar tricks, because, after we had thrown down the nails, they fled without any shame and went to another ship to do the same." Indeed, "these peoples are inclined to do harm," the fleet commander concluded, "and they seem delighted by their bad deeds, and whoever called it the Island of the Thieves had more than enough reason."[13]

Nonetheless, the trading at Umatac Bay would prove enduring. By the seventeenth century, this small bay would become the primary way station for Spanish fleets journeying across the Pacific. The water was deep enough for the galleons to anchor safely, and the surrounding hills protected them from the wind and storms. As the Umatac River flowed into the bay, fresh water was easy to obtain, as Legazpi's men found out after jumping ashore.

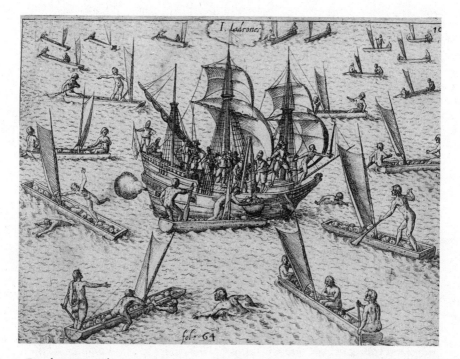

Dutch captain Olivier van Noort visited Guam in 1600. His experience with the local Chamorros was nearly identical to Magellan's and Legazpi's. Islanders aboard many canoes met van Noort far out at sea and competed with one another to trade. The Dutch captain reported that the Chamorros noisily shouted "hierro," or "iron," making clear what they wanted most.

The ships moved closer to the bottom of the bay to facilitate the uploading of water casks, "but the Indians suddenly started throwing rocks with their slings in such quantities that they hurt some of our people, and we had to use our harquebuses [a shoulder-supported matchlock gun] to drive them away." Remarkably, many *paraos* had continued to trade with the Spanish ships even while under attack. Over the next three days, the tenuous Spanish-Chamorro peace nearly came undone. On Thursday, the soldiers were still filling up water barrels at the Umatac River when some islanders offered help to carry them. "Everyone was together and in perfect peace and friendship," the commander recounted, "until one Indian wrested a harquebus from one of the soldiers and ran away; and the others fled too and turned to pelting those who were taking the water." Hours later they returned, saying that they wished to remain friends with the Spanish.[14]

On Friday, four days after having arrived, Commander Legazpi finally went ashore to take possession of Guam in the name of the Spanish crown. He walked around the beach, "cutting tree branches with his sword, pulling some grass, making stone monuments, and carving crosses into some of the coconut trees." The Augustinian friars said Mass. It is impossible to know what the islanders made of such strange proceedings, although more than eighty presented themselves to the Spanish commander, "and in return he gave them beads, and they were at times at peace and at times at war."[15]

For a brief moment, the expeditionaries considered forming a settlement in Guam. The largest island in Micronesia right on the ocean highway of winds and currents would have been ideal for moving across the Pacific, though less so for trade with Asia. Commander Legazpi gave up on the idea, however, partly because his instructions were very explicit about establishing the base in the Philippines, but also perhaps on account of the islanders' volatility. A final tragic incident made this clear. As the Spanish were filling up the last casks of water before their departure, a cabin boy named Ochoa de Arratia fell asleep on the island after the soldiers had returned to the ships for the night. No one noticed Arratia's absence until a great uproar erupted from the beach. A group of Chamorros had seized the cabin boy from the Basque Country, tied him spread-eagled, and used him as target practice, firing spears at him. By the time the Spanish soldiers came back, Ochoa de Arratia had sustained "more than thirty piercing wounds that had passed entirely through his body, and they also had stuck a sharp stick through his mouth that came out through the back of his head."[16]

8

The Far Side of the World

W hile Legazpi's ships spent a week in Guam, the *San Lucas* forged
ahead all the way to the Philippines. After what must have seemed
like an eternity of seventy days of navigation, on January 29, 1565, Captain
Don Alonso de Arellano, pilot Lope Martín, and the twenty-strong crew
of the smallest ship in the fleet were the first to lay eyes on the archipelago.
In the early afternoon, the men of the *San Lucas* began catching glimpses
of Mindanao, the southernmost of the Philippine islands. By the time they
had come close to the shore, the sun was barely above the horizon, and
a sudden shift in the wind started pushing the vessel relentlessly toward
the coast—what mariners call a lee shore. Almost in darkness, the crew
attempted to lower the rowboat to tow the *San Lucas* out toward deeper
waters. Yet the wind became so strong that during the maneuver the boat
smashed against the ship, breaking parts of both. In spite of their best efforts, the crew members could not prevent the *San Lucas* from running
aground. Completely exhausted, they gave up by 2:00 a.m. A carpenter
started nailing together a plank to transfer the food and other valuables
from the ship to the rowboat in order to move everything ashore. But the

wind shifted direction again, now blowing from land to sea, and according to Don Alonso, "the air had a sweet smell that greatly encouraged us." This breeze gained quickly in strength until it became powerful enough to free the *San Lucas*.[1]

The next day the vessel coasted for some time until it came to rest in a protected cove. It had covered about nine thousand miles since leaving the coast of Mexico. In all likelihood, the voyagers had reached the Davao Gulf. From the deck of the *San Lucas,* all that was visible was dense foliage, an impenetrable curtain of greenery. The forest floor appeared dark and covered by decaying leaves and puddles of water. The humidity and heat were impossible to ignore. Mindanao is a vast tropical expanse of 36,700 square miles — the second-largest island among the more than seven thousand making up the Philippines — with high mountains, majestic waterfalls, swamps complete with crocodiles, pythons, kalaw birds (a type of hornbill), and monkeys. In the sixteenth century, Mindanao harbored a variety of localized kin-based groups known as *barangay.* Some of these communities had converted to Islam in the previous century and begun to coalesce into larger sultanates. The arrival of the Spanish set the stage for a showdown between Muslims and Christians that would rage for centuries, even after the United States took over in 1898. Yet on that first day in the Davao Gulf, the voyagers did not see anyone. They spent the time quietly filling up seven or eight casks of water before going back to the *San Lucas* for the night.[2]

The following morning, the crew woke up to human calls coming from the top of a nearby hill, "and we replied even though we could not see the people," said the ship's captain, "because they were hidden by the forest." There were three callers. Lope Martín and four sailors got into the rowboat, went ashore, and signaled to the people in the hills to come down for a parley. They did. Unlike the Micronesian islanders, who went about almost naked, these three men wore clothes made of cotton, carried wooden shields that Don Alonso referred to as "tablachinas," or "Chinese boards," and had daggers dangling from their belts. The three men curtly asked the Spanish to stay at that cove and then left. In the afternoon, they came back reinforced by about thirty or forty warriors as well as a headman. On seeing this contingent gathering at the beach across from the ship, the Spanish captain, the pilot, and a few others got into the rowboat, but before they had even reached the shore, "the headman waded into the sea, took some water in one hand, and made the sign of the cross." Evidently he had dealt with Christians before.[3]

When the two groups finally came together, the Spaniards embraced the islanders, a ritual of friendship requiring close — potentially fatal — proximity. Mediterranean peoples have been hugging for millennia, as is clear from biblical stories and medieval paintings. But other cultures around the world have been suspicious of the practice. The people of Mindanao tolerated the embraces but immediately responded with a ritual of their own. "To seal the peace, the principal man took a dagger from his belt," Don Alonso wrote, "and he made signs that he wanted to cut himself in the stomach or the arm to draw blood, as is the custom among these natives." A common peace ceremony throughout the Philippines, it called for one leader to shed blood into a cup and offer it to the other one to drink (either straight or mixed with water or liquor) and then for a reciprocal bloodletting of the other leader. But before the headman from Mindanao was able to cut his body, Don Alonso took the dagger from his hand and signaled that they were friends without having to drink each other's blood.[4]

In spite of this shortcutting of the ritual, the people of Mindanao appeared satisfied. They passed around bamboo canes filled with a brown liquor, "like the color of cinnamon." To show that it was not poisoned, Vibán (as the leader was called, according to the Spanish sources) took a big gulp, "and we also drank this wine many times, it was sweet and burned with a taste of ginger." Cinnamon and ginger are common today, but for sixteenth-century Europeans who had never seen the bark of the cinnamon tree or chewed on a stubby ginger root, the drink was like a foretaste of paradise and profit. The hosts "were delighted to see that we drank from their wine without disgust," the *San Lucas* captain reported, "and they also gave us sugarcanes and boiled yams, and we gave them of what we had, and presented their leader with a piece of iron that he held in great esteem." It was getting dark after all the drinking and gift-giving, so the islanders left, "very happy for having negotiated a peace with us, and we were even more contented because we had found a people of such good understanding and secure anchoring with wood and fresh water where we could wait for the rest of the fleet."[5]

The men of the *San Lucas* spent all of February 1565 at that cove, making repairs to the vessel. Yet the warm relationship they had initially enjoyed with the islanders cooled off markedly. One reason may have been the limited goods for trade that they had. In exchange for what few nails they could spare, the men of the *San Lucas* got oranges and lemons (excellent against scurvy), bananas "of three different kinds," sugarcanes "as thick as an arm," dogs "like foxes" (for protein), chickens "like those of Castile," and so on. They even obtained ginger "that is green and big when just dug out of the ground" and cinnamon "with which these natives clean their teeth." But as the Europeans ran out of trade goods, their presence became a nuisance. During that month, they went from honored visitors, to guests who had outstayed their welcome, to intruders. Vibán stopped talking to the visitors, and an attack from land became a distinct possibility.[6]

In the meantime, the men of the *San Lucas* began quarreling among themselves, a feature of many early voyages of exploration. Columbus, Magellan, and many other captains across the Atlantic and the Pacific had endured a variety of mutinies and plots. This penchant for insurrection on the part of many early crews may have been a learned behavior, passed from one to the next, as well as a survival strategy. When following orders seemed wrongheaded or suicidal, it was only natural to revert to a small group of like-minded individuals. The men of the *San Lucas* were no exception. They disagreed over how to proceed. Was it wise to spend an entire month in a godforsaken cove making repairs? Wouldn't it be better to try locating the rest of the fleet? Yet other expeditionaries wanted to go to the Spice Islands, where greater riches could be found, or where they could always consider surrendering to the Portuguese as previous Spanish expeditions had done. These alternatives produced deep divisions that threatened the peace among men facing great uncertainty and forced to live in unbearably close proximity.

A major rift opened between the *maestre* (similar to a boatswain) Juan "the Greek" on the one hand and Don Alonso and Lope Martín on the other. The captain and the pilot had ordered the Greek boatswain to take some men ashore to chop down trees and make lumber for repairing the *San Lucas*. Yet the assigned men became defiant. "They had not come to China to cut down trees but to load up on gold," they said, and Juan the Greek resolutely sided with them. To act on their wishes, the disgruntled men waited for a few days until Don Alonso and Lope Martín went ashore themselves. During their absence, they opened a box where Martín kept his nautical charts—highly confidential and usually kept under lock and key—and reportedly "studied the charts for some time to figure out the whereabouts of the Malucos [Spice Islands] because that is where they intended to go." Trouble was brewing.[7]

In the strict hierarchy of a sailing vessel, a *maestre* was third in command after the captain and pilot. Nonetheless, someone like Juan the Greek was well positioned for a mutiny because he transmitted the orders from the higher-ups to the mariners and cabin boys. A *maestre* was often a father figure to the sailors or, conversely, a taskmaster who assigned jobs and punishments. A challenge from such a well-positioned officer was always dangerous, especially aboard the *San Lucas,* where the captain was an aloof nobleman. Don Alonso had been appointed at the last minute on account of his exalted lineage rather than any relevant experience, as everyone knew. Indeed, this may have been his first ocean passage, so his ability to

make sound decisions was questionable at best. By default, Lope Martín
had assumed responsibility for the safety and navigation of the *San Lucas,* and thus had to contain the insurrection of Juan the Greek and his
men. Like all veteran mariners, Lope Martín must have seen a fair share of
plots and counter-plots during his lifetime. In fact, he excelled at them.
An upwardly mobile mulatto in a world of white officers, he had to be
exceptionally discerning and nimble, knowing when to stay discreetly in
the background, how to form alliances, and when to pounce mercilessly.
An insubordinate Greek boatswain and a few sailors were indeed no match
for Lope Martín.[8]

At first the pilot only gathered information and passed some of it to Don
Alonso, impressing on the captain the fact that the mutineers constituted
"an even greater threat than the Indians." The *San Lucas* leadership could
have ordered the execution of Juan the Greek and his co-conspirators.
This, however, would have required a violent clash and the decimation of
an already minimal crew. Instead, the savvy pilot worked on the *maestre.*
No one knows what Martín told Juan, but the Greek man began wavering
after some time. Fearful that they were being betrayed and would be left
on their own to take the fall, the remaining plotters turned desperate.[9]

Four of them escaped in the rowboat in the middle of the night, taking some harquebuses and the only flint stone aboard the *San Lucas.* The
rowboat itself was a great loss, the only means to get from the ship to
the shore and back, but the flint stone was even more important, not just
for cooking but because "without fire the Indians would gain the upper
hand over us at any time they wanted," as Don Alonso recalled. Tracking down the four escapees thus became the expeditionaries' overriding
concern. One evening, the men of the *San Lucas* spotted a campfire in the
distance. The four runaways were boldly moving inland toward the closest
settlement, willing to take their chances with Vibán and his people. Lope
Martín offered to lead Don Alonso and three sailors on foot to catch them
by surprise. For hours the posse moved quietly through extremely thick

vegetation, skirted a cliff, and crossed numerous streams in pitch darkness, losing sight of the campfire for long stretches. At last the pursuers were close enough to see one of the mutineers keeping guard, moving from one side of the encampment to the other, and adding wood to the fire while the other three slept. Without being noticed, "the pilot approached the encampment and came so close to the man keeping guard that only one tree separated them," the captain recalled, "and he lit his harquebus and shot the guard in the chest with twenty-seven pellets." At that instant, the captain and mariners fell on the sleeping mutineers. Everything was over in a minute. Fortunately, the man who had been shot sustained only minor injuries. All four were tied up and marched to the ship. As they were to be hanged, Don Alonso ordered pulleys and ropes to be set up on one side of the *San Lucas*. With nooses already around their necks, Lope Martín finally intervened. He told Don Alonso "that it would be impossible to leave that port without these four men, because the crew was insufficient and many were ill." It was almost certainly a lie to save their lives. Yet Lope Martín emerged from this episode with gratitude from the rebels, an intact crew, and even more influence than before over the captain.[10]

Having temporarily sorted out their internal problems, the men of the *San Lucas* decided to leave the Davao Gulf. They erected crosses in the cove where they had stayed for a month, "and underneath one of them placed a jar with letters, so the armada would know what had happened to us and where we were going next." On Sunday, March 4, 1565, they pulled up anchor and continued rounding the immense island of Mindanao. During this passage, two events would have lasting consequences. First, at an unspecified site, the voyagers found a good place to wash their clothes. An officer and two cabin boys were dispatched ashore with everyone's dirty garments. The two servants had just started washing when they spotted several islanders closing in on them and thus had to run for their lives, abandoning a mountain of clothes that the voyagers would miss sorely when the weather turned extremely cold later in their adventure.[11]

The second consequential event was an encounter with a Filipino long-
boat that pulled up right alongside the *San Lucas*. "The Indians aboard
spoke many Spanish words," Don Alonso recalled, "and they asked us
if we had come from Malacca [the Portuguese base in Malaysia] or were
going to the Malucos [Spice Islands]." The rowers rattled off words like
"capitán" (*capitão*) and "señores" (*senhores*) to show that they had dealt with
Portuguese merchants before, "but when we told them that we had come
from the east [i.e., across the Pacific], they were shocked because we had
come from so very far away." The voyagers were able to barter for porce-
lains, blankets, "painted textiles" (possibly silk), and some powdered gold
that they would carry back to the Americas as incontrovertible proof that
they had been to Asia.[12]

Almost casually, the Filipinos mentioned that they had seen three other
European vessels. Although they could have been referring to a previous
expedition, in reality the *San Lucas* had come tantalizingly close to the rest
of the fleet. As they sailed slowly through the heart of the archipelago
within sight of thousands of islands, a reunion of all four vessels became
a distinct possibility. A friar named Gaspar de San Agustín, writing more
than a century after the fact, affirmed that from the crow's nest of the *San
Lucas,* some crew members caught glimpses of the other ships but refused
to join them. A close examination of all the vessels' trajectories shows that
this could not have been possible, as we shall see.[13]

Legazpi's fleet arrived in the Philippines two weeks after the *San Lucas,* on
February 13, 1565. The three galleons first touched land on the original Isla
Filipina, present-day Samar, just to the north of Mindanao. Legazpi and his
men were delighted to have reached their intended destination. Yet Samar
was disappointing. They found no suitable ports or even people willing to
talk to them, as the islanders took off in their canoes at the mere sight of
the Spaniards. The mystery deepened as the visitors rounded Samar and
explored the neighboring islands. In stark contrast to their experience in

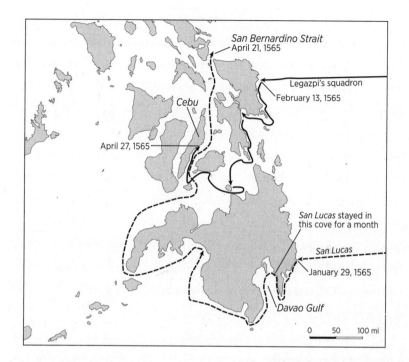

Guam with the highly engaged Chamorros, the people of the Philippines tried to avoid any contact. The expeditionaries were thus forced to sail blind until they finally stumbled on an unlikely source of information. On March 19, 1565, Legazpi's ships were close to the island of Bohol when they spotted a well-armed junk that was "much larger than the ones used by the Indians of these lands." As the Europeans approached to investigate, a cannonade and a shower of arrows and lances greeted them. The naval engagement left heavy casualties on both sides, but the Iberians eventually seized the large junk along with six or seven of its crew members, including the pilot. The large vessel belonged to the sultan of Brunei, who had sent it to trade in the Philippines. The entire crew consisted of Muslims, or "Moros," as Spaniards referred to the Muslims of northern Africa.[14]

The captured pilot spoke Malay, the lingua franca of the region, and communicated readily with Father Urdaneta, who still remembered the language from the eight years he had been marooned in Southeast Asia in the 1520s and 1530s. The Muslim pilot seemed unusually knowledgeable, "not just about the Philippines," the expedition commander observed, "but about the Spice Islands, Borneo, Malacca, Java, India, and China, as he had sailed and traded in all of these places." Tuasan, as this great navigator was called, did not take long in making himself indispensable. He described each of the Philippine islands in detail and listed the products of each of them, such as gold, wax, or slaves. After seeing the European goods aboard the galleons, Tuasan also commented that "such merchandise was not suitable for these islands and would take ten years to sell, but it would require less than a week in Brunei [where he had been employed], Siam [Thailand], or Malacca." The astute pilot was evidently pursuing his own agenda. Commander Legazpi drily responded that he had no authority to range into such places.[15]

Next, the Muslim pilot explained the reticence of the Filipino Natives toward the Spanish. "Two years earlier, eight *paraos* from the Spice Islands appeared with many pieces of artillery," Tuasan recounted, "and they came to Bohol and were received in peace until the Spanish suddenly started robbing, killing, capturing many people, and causing great damage in the islands." Legazpi immediately protested that the perpetrators had been Portuguese based in the Spice Islands rather than Spanish. The pilot replied that "he knew well that they belonged to two separate kingdoms but that the Indians of these islands did not know the difference, especially because the Portuguese themselves had said that they were Castilians." This is how Commander Legazpi finally understood "why the Spanish were so hated in the islands and the inhabitants hid and refused to trade, and the kingdom of Castile enjoyed so little credit and esteem in these parts."[16]

As the fleet commander pondered more seriously where in the Philippines to establish a Spanish base, Legazpi relied on Tuasan's experience and knowledge. The Muslim pilot recommended Cebu (or Zubu) and offered to lead the visitors there—still angling for a job, which he finally got. Within the Visayan Islands (Panay, Negros, Cebu, Bohol, Leyte, and Samar) in the central part of the Philippines, Cebu was quite likely the best choice. Cebu had a long history of interaction with the Spanish going all the way back to Magellan. It was well populated, with a port boasting some three hundred well-built houses as well as many other settlements. According to Tuasan, the Cebuanos possessed "rice by the load." But there was a major inconvenience: Chinese merchants generally bypassed the Visayas because their ships were too large to maneuver there. Instead, they went to the more northerly islands of Mindoro and Luzon. Six years later, the Spanish had to move to Luzon (the large island where Manila is located) to participate in this lucrative trade. Yet, having just arrived in the Philippines and running low on food in the spring of 1565, Commander Legazpi, after a brief conference with his highest-ranking officials, decided to settle down in Cebu. They would first try to barter with the Cebuanos, but if they refused, the voyagers would seize what they needed by force. They even produced a legal justification for such an eventuality. During Magellan's visit in the spring of 1521, almost exactly forty-four years earlier, the people of Cebu had converted to Christianity and formally pledged loyalty to the Spanish monarchy, but they had subsequently "abandoned the Christian faith that they had accepted of their own volition and reverted to their malevolent rituals and ancient ceremonies." The people of Cebu had become renegades and apostates, and therefore the Spanish were within their rights to use force.[17]

Legazpi and his men arrived in Cebu on April 27, 1565, and issued the *requerimiento,* a specious text employed by sixteenth-century Spaniards in conquests all over the Americas, urging Native Americans to accept Christianity and Spanish domination or face the consequences of a violent conquest. The principal leader in Cebu agreed to reach a peace accord with the strangers but shrewdly sent word that it would take him some time to arrive at the place where the Spanish were waiting for an answer. In the meantime, the villagers started to evacuate. "They hurriedly gathered their belongings and placed them in their boats," according to one testimony, "and those who had goats and chickens came out of their houses to collect them, even killing them if they could not carry them in any other way." Legazpi's men also noticed the arrival of "ten or twelve *paraos* with armed people that hid behind a finger of land behind the Spanish flagship." The expeditionaries persisted in reading the *requerimiento* "one and two and three times," even as it became clear that the Cebuanos were preparing for war.[18]

Early the following morning, Legazpi's artillerymen were ordered to train their cannons on the sizable settlement right across from their ship, the first time they would use their heavy weapons since arriving in the Philippines. In a matter of seconds, the attackers inflicted tremendous damage. More than one hundred houses were burned down—about a third of the village—"and if the wind had blown the other way, everything would have been consumed." The coconut trees surrounding the village, "the thing that they value the most," were also destroyed. Soon after that initial blow, Spanish soldiers went ashore to quell any remaining resistance.[19]

The cannonade had started at eight in the morning on Saturday, April 28, 1565. The soldiers gained complete control of the village in short order and had all day to search the place, house by house. They found little of use, "mostly pots, some millet, and very little rice." One man, however, made an astounding discovery. "He went into a very small and poor house and, inside a wooden box, he found a statue of a Christ Child," reads the soldier Juan de Camuz's third-person deposition under oath, "and his right hand with two extended fingers, as if about to make a blessing, and with the other hand he held the world." The Christ Child as *salvator mundi,* or savior of the world, was a popular theme in European iconography of that era. Even Leonardo da Vinci painted Christ as *salvator mundi* around 1500, a work that recently fetched the highest price ever paid for a painting at public auction. The statue found by Camuz had been carved in the Low

An example of the Christ Child as *salvator mundi* by the engraver Martin Schongauer. Christ has his right hand raised in blessing with two fingers extended, and with the other hand holds an orb to signify that he is the savior and master of the world, as is typical of *salvator mundi* iconography.

Countries in the 1510s and given by Magellan to the Cebuanos as a present in the spring of 1521. For reasons that will always remain unclear, the dwellers of that humble house in Cebu decided to preserve it for nearly four and a half decades.[20]

Sixteenth-century Europeans could scarcely interpret such a discovery on the other side of the world as anything other than an omen. When the wooden statue was brought into Legazpi's presence, he "fell to his knees and took it with great veneration, kissing its little feet and looking at the sky." Whatever doubts he and his officers may have harbored about staying in Cebu, they melted at that instant. The fleet commander ordered a solemn procession with the statue, so everyone could see it. The procession would end at a plot of land set aside for a church where the *salvator mundi* Christ Child would remain on display, and his appearance would be marked every year. Thus the Spanish founded their Villa de San Miguel on the island of Cebu on an extraordinary day of war, fire, and a miraculous find.[21]

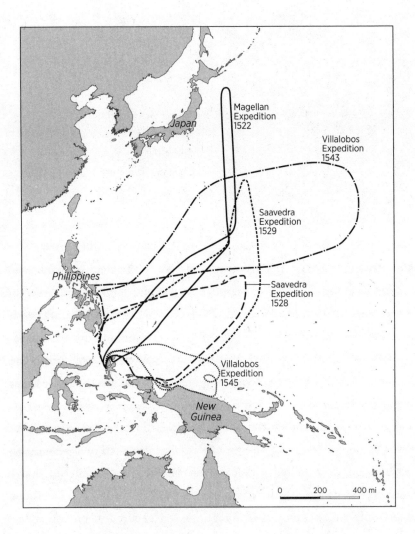

9

Vuelta

*U*ntil April 1565, the Legazpi expedition had accomplished nothing that had not been done before. Magellan, Loaísa, Saavedra, and Villalobos had all journeyed across the Pacific and explored portions of Southeast Asia. The next step, however, was quite literally uncharted. Between 1521 and 1545, Spanish navigators had mounted five valiant attempts at returning to the Americas by re-crossing the Pacific Ocean but had failed every time. A plot of these attempted *vueltas,* five irregular loops in the western Pacific, tells us nothing about the courage of the crews involved, the overwhelming elements they faced, the anguish at having to give up after months of suffering, and the dashed hopes of two generations of navigators attempting to open a new commercial route to the Orient. Nonetheless, they show a clear grasp of the Pacific gyres. Magellan's pilots already knew that they had to steer far to the north of the Philippines — in their case as high as forty-two degrees, around northern Japan and the Oregon coast — to get out of the contrary currents and winds in order to reach the northern side of the North Pacific Gyre and find more favorable conditions for a return. About fifty men aboard Magellan's flagship *Trinidad* persisted for six months in a dramatic passage that ultimately claimed the lives of all but eighteen, as we have seen. Dwindling food stores and progressively colder temperatures forced the survivors, wearing only thin shirts and pants, to turn back.[1]

Later expeditionaries kept trying to find an elusive patch of ocean where the winds and currents flowed toward the Americas. About twenty men on a small craft of the Villalobos expedition came closest to succeeding in 1543. Departing in August from Mindanao, they went farther east than any previous European expedition. Yet a very late start in the sailing season and an inadequate supply of water forced this intrepid crew to turn back after having reached the halfway point between the Philippines and Hawai'i, or about a quarter of the way to Mexico. Iberian pilots were getting closer to solving the puzzle of the *vuelta,* but they were still missing one final piece.[2]

On Easter Sunday, April 22, 1565, the *San Lucas* began the most improvised *vuelta* ever attempted on the Pacific. This epic voyage would include mutiny, marvelous sightings, unforeseeable dangers, and a near shipwreck. It would be the first west-to-east crossing of the Pacific in recorded history, and it jump-started a continuous transpacific flow of germs, plants, animals, peoples, ideas, and products that endures to this day. This voyage, so consequential and still so little known, would be accomplished thanks almost entirely to the skills of the Afro-Portuguese pilot Lope Martín.[3]

The men aboard the *San Lucas* reached the grave decision to attempt the return to the New World after having failed to establish contact with the rest of the fleet. For two months they had rounded Mindanao and navigated through the central Philippines. They had also stopped at "Magellan's Island," as they called Cebu, the one place in the entire archipelago where they were most likely to run into the other Europeans. But as fate would have it, they narrowly missed the rest of the fleet there. The *San Lu-*

cas reconnoitered Cebu sometime around the middle of April and reached the northern edge of the Philippines on April 21. Meanwhile, the other three vessels under Legazpi did not arrive in Cebu until April 27. Had the *San Lucas* lingered in the middle of the archipelago for an extra week or two, the story would have been vastly different. In actuality, although the four vessels converged, they were never close enough for a reunion. When Friar Gaspar de San Agustín affirmed in the seventeenth century that the crew of the *San Lucas* "caught glimpses" of the other vessels but "refused" to rejoin them, he was patently mistaken. Instead, believing they were on their own, the *San Lucas* voyagers began to contemplate excruciating choices: continue to search for the other vessels, all the while consuming their dwindling food supplies; go to the Spice Islands and surrender to the Portuguese; or attempt the *vuelta* by themselves.[4]

Nature intervened in the end. On April 21, the men of the *San Lucas* reached an opening between the islands of Samar and Luzon, now called the San Bernardino Strait. After passing through the strait, they could see no more islands ahead. They had come to the end of the archipelago. The currents are notoriously strong along the San Bernardino Strait, and there was hardly any wind that day, so the *San Lucas* started drifting into the open ocean. Returning to the labyrinth of shoals, narrow passages, and hostile villages from which they had emerged would have required everyone to paddle. "I thus told the pilot to consider carefully our best course in the service of God, His Majesty, and to save everyone aboard," Don Alonso recalled, "and the pilot looked at his chart for some time and thought about all the drawbacks of returning." Lope Martín's exact words have reached us to reveal his awareness of the last major piece of the maddening puzzle of the *vuelta*. He thought "it was best to return to New Spain [Mexico] because the summer season was about to start and, if we could gain enough altitude toward the north, we would find very favorable conditions, and that would be better than being captured by the islanders or the Portuguese."[5]

The pilot's insight is unassailable. To catch the northern portion of the North Pacific Gyre, it was not enough to go north from the Philippines; one had to do so at the right time of year to benefit from the monsoon, a dramatic seasonal reversal of the winds. Although most people associate the monsoon with the Indian Ocean, it extends into the western Pacific, including the Philippines and the China Seas. This 180-degree shift in wind direction stems from the cooling and warming of the Asian landmass. During the winter months, the air above East Asia cools off, becoming more dense than usual, as cold and dry air is heavier and more tightly packed than warm and moist air. This creates a high-pressure zone, forcing the air — like any other fluid — to equalize by moving from high-pressure to low-pressure zones. If we could add artificial coloring to our atmosphere, we would see this heavier mass of continental air at the edge of Asia initially spilling southward into the Pacific Ocean. Because of Earth's spinning and the Coriolis effect, a circulation pattern would soon take hold around this high-pressure zone, with the ocean winds moving from the northeast toward the southwest and all across the Philippines, where this season is called Amihan or the northeast monsoon (meaning that the dominant winds are coming from the northeast). Thus, during November through April, cool and dry air blows from the depths of the Pacific all across the Philippines. Attempting to sail *toward* the depths of the Pacific at this time would have been foolish. By late April, however, Amihan is over and, after a brief period of unsettled winds, the direction is entirely reversed. As the Asian landmass warms up, it creates a low-pressure zone that attracts oceanic air. Blasts of warm and humid air, known in the Philippines as the southwest monsoon or Habagat, thus move from the southwest and continue deep into the Pacific, precisely where the expeditionaries wished to go.[6]

How Lope Martín was able to anticipate this dramatic shift in wind direction is unknown. He may have learned about it from local navigators,

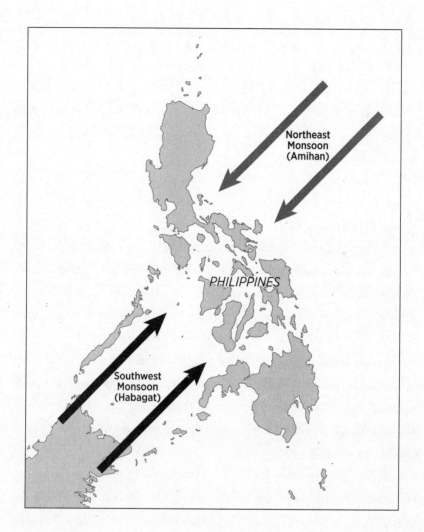

perhaps during the stay in Mindanao or in one of the chance encounters with Filipino canoes. As we saw, Legazpi gleaned precious information from a Muslim pilot he captured in a naval battle. Although Lope Martín may have similarly tapped into the reservoir of local knowledge, it is just as likely that he knew about the monsoon before arriving in the Philippines. Pilots trained in Europe, Africa, and the Americas would have been utterly unfamiliar with the rhythms of the monsoon. But friar-mariner Urdaneta, who, as we know, had lived as a castaway in Southeast Asia for eight years, would have gained a deep understanding of the monsoon seasons. Decades later, when the Augustinian friar became the guiding spirit of the Legazpi expedition in the early 1560s, it would have been only natural for him to discuss the monsoon at length with the expedition pilots, including Lope Martín.[7]

Regardless of how he knew to do it, the pilot's plan to start the *vuelta* in late April was inspired. All five previous return attempts had in fact launched between April and August, well within the southwest monsoon, as doing anything else would have been nearly impossible. The precise timing, however, made a difference. The first return attempt aboard the *Trinidad* during the Magellan expedition had begun even earlier, in the first days of April. The precocity of Magellan's pilots is remarkable, and their early start paid off handsomely. In the first few weeks of the voyage they made excellent progress, sailed sufficiently north to catch the gyre, and would have succeeded had they carried warmer clothes, brought more food and water, and not encountered a freak storm that broke the mast and sails of the *Trinidad*. At the other end of the spectrum, in 1543 the Villalobos expedition waited to start its *vuelta* until August, too late in the season. Although the *San Juan de Letrán* was able to go farther east than any prior return attempt, by the middle of October the ship still had a long way to go when the southwest monsoon was near its end. It turned back eventually. The three other return attempts were doomed from the start because, instead of heading immediately to the northeast to catch the gyre, these vessels meandered along the coast of New Guinea, wasting precious time. The elements drove them back to Asia as they negotiated the immensity of the Pacific far too late in the season.[8]

Lope Martín's proposed start for the return was ideal—not only for his plan to ride the monsoon winds but also for another crucial reason.

This full-length portrait of Philip II by the Flemish painter Antonis Mor (or in Spanish, Antonio Moro) was originally done in 1557, the very year when the young monarch ordered his viceroy in Mexico to conquer his namesake Philippine islands. Philip is dressed in armor for the Battle of Saint-Quentin against France on August 10, 1557.
Patrimonio Nacional, 10014146.

Viceroy of Mexico Don Luis de Velasco in 1549, one year before his arrival in Mexico. *Reproduction authorized by the Instituto Nacional de Antropología e Historia.*

D, Ludouicus D Velasco. 2.ª Prorrex Ct Vniuersalis dux Año 1549

No contemporary painting of Andrés de Urdaneta has survived, so this is an idealized rendition by Víctor Villán de Aza from 1895. Urdaneta appears in the habit of the Augustinian order surrounded by geographic and nautical equipment. *Alamy Stock Photo. Used by permission of Real Monasterio de San Lorenzo de El Escorial.*

No image of Lope Martín survives, but this sixteenth-century drawing of two slaves filling up water barrels provides an idea of the milieu from which he came. *Illustration by Christoph Weiditz, c. 1530. Courtesy of Germanisches National-museum, Digitale Bibliothek. Image 189.*

Several pataches, or dispatch boats, not very different from the *San Lucas,* are visible in this painting of the naval battle of Ponta Delgada in 1582. Dispatch boats had two masts for sails, but they were small enough that rowing was also possible. *Patrimonio Nacional, 10014921.*

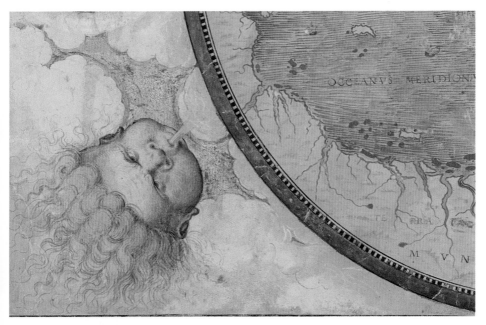

One of four wind heads blowing from the corners of Lopo Homem's 1519 *mappa mundi.* Sixteenth-century navigators understood that there was a stable pattern of winds in the world, represented by these four fascinating heads blowing from different directions. The mapmaker added the inscription: "This is the map of the entire globe now known that I, cosmographer Lopo Homem, drew with great effort, having compared many other maps both ancient and modern, in the illustrious City of Lisbon in the year of Our Lord 1519 by order of Manuel, eminent King of Portugal." *Bibliothèque nationale de France.*

Notice the elaborate attire, jewelry, and dagger of this royal couple from the Philippines, circa 1590. The color red denotes their exalted position. As the drawing was done in ink on Chinese paper, it is likely that the artist may have been Chinese, under commission by the Spanish governor of the Philippines Gómez Pérez Dasmariñas. *Courtesy Lilly Library, Indiana University, Bloomington, Indiana.*

The bay of Acapulco was spacious, with a sandy bottom, and deep enough to accommodate even the largest and heaviest galleons. Practically all transpacific voyages between Mexico and the Philippines during the colonial period began and ended there. *Courtesy of the Benson Latin American Collection, University of Texas at Austin.*

The western North Pacific is the most active tropical cyclone region in the world. Typhoons develop in the warm waters to the south of the Philippines and curve northward toward the coasts of China and Japan, often passing through the Philippines. Over the years, Spanish navigators left ample testimony of this tempestuous part of the Pacific Ocean. A Spanish galleon in 1601 had to overcome eighteen storms in a single passage, and a few years later a ship named the *San Andrés* had to endure no fewer than eleven. During the 250 years of Spanish transpacific trade, forty galleons were lost to typhoons and storms. The Italian circumnavigator Giovanni Francesco Gemelli Careri—a Phileas Fogg of the seventeenth century who recounted his journey in his *Giro del Mondo*—pronounced the voyage from the Philippines to the Americas "the most dreadful and longest of any in the world," singling out "the terrible tempests, one on the back of another." Although typhoons can develop at any time of the year, they are more common in the warmer months of June through November, and thus an early start in April or May is much better.[9]

Lope Martín's timing was unerring, and Don Alonso supported his pilot. "I would rather die at sea in the service of His Majesty than among these peoples [Filipinos]," the captain recalled saying to the crew, "and my determination was to complete the voyage or die in the attempt." After watching Lope Martín perform for the better part of five months, Don Alonso had grown so confident that he was willing to put his life in the pilot's hands. When word about re-crossing the Pacific spread through the *San Lucas,* however, several crew members revolted. The *San Lucas* was a dispatch boat meant to explore coves and inlets in shallow waters, not a vessel intended for the *vuelta*. The plan all along had been to attempt the return aboard one of the two largest ships in the fleet, the *San Pedro* or the *San Pablo,* weighing four or five hundred tons and built at an outrageous cost for this very purpose. Urdaneta had been quite explicit about this. "The main obstacle preventing the return voyage," he had written to the viceroy during the planning stage, "is that it has been attempted with small and miserly vessels." Among such "small and miserly vessels" were Magellan's *Trinidad*, at 120 tons, and the *San Juan de Letrán*, at sixty tons. At a mere forty tons, the *San Lucas* was even smaller.[10]

Another circumstance made the *San Lucas* unsuited for an attempt at the *vuelta*. When the captain and the pilot reached their fateful decision, the vessel had not been stocked for the return voyage. Unable to make landfall at the northern edge of the Philippines, the *San Lucas* had drifted away with only the provisions that it carried at the time. An inventory revealed that there were eight *pipas,* or barrels, aboard the *San Lucas* "and all of them were missing between four and five *arrobas* of water each." (In sixteenth-century usage, a *pipa* consisted of 27.5 *arrobas,* and each *arroba* was equivalent to 4.36 gallons, for a total of 761.19 gallons.) In other words, each of the twenty crew members would have to make do with 38.24 gallons of water to cross the entire Pacific. On a voyage lasting seventy days—the time that it took the *San Lucas* to go from Mexico to the Philippines—this would be a daily ration of 8.7 cups. Before our era of hyper-hydration, the American Food and Nutrition Board would have approved. Eight cups of water was the recommended ration in 1945, a bit of wisdom that endured for decades without much scientific backing. In this case, however, two circumstances made such water intake inadequate. First, the men aboard the *San Lucas* would necessarily spend time in tropical and semitropical regions, where sweating causes greater loss of fluids than normal, especially among active individuals forced to climb ratlines, trim sails, and operate bilge pumps. In very hot temperatures, an active person can lose up to eight cups of fluid in an hour through sweat and urination—the entire daily ration. Second and most important, there was no way to count on a return voyage of a mere seventy days. Any leaks in the casks, a very real possibility, as we shall see, would spell disaster. Modern sailors, especially around-the-world racers, carry as little water as possible to reduce the weight and improve the performance of their vessels. But carrying such limited quantities is possible only because of water makers (desalination equipment) and rain-collecting systems not available to sixteenth-century mariners. Attempting the return voyage with eight partially filled casks of water was suicidal.[11]

The food situation was hardly better. The inventory conducted by Lope Martín and a "gentleman" named Pedro de Rivero showed that the *San Lucas* carried "some fava beans and garbanzos along with twenty *quintales* of *mazamorra*." Seamen were all too familiar with the unappetizing, often revolting, *mazamorra:* hardtack crumbs combined with leftovers such as dry fish or meat left at the bottom of the barrels. This pulpy mess had been rotting away for nearly five months by then, collecting mold and cobwebs, and being nibbled by rats. Twenty *quintales* divided among twenty people works out to less than one pound (0.93) of *mazamorra* per person, plus an unknown amount of fava and garbanzo beans. Given our lack of knowledge about the legumes, it is not possible to calculate an exact daily ration. The calories must have been extremely limited, however, because after the inventory, Don Alonso ordered additional precautions for dispensing food rations, since, as he put it, "our very lives depended on them."[12]

The small size of the *San Lucas,* the only partially filled casks of water, the exiguous provisions, and the danger of a passage that had never succeeded before gave pause to several crew members, who threatened another mutiny. With ample reason, they argued that "discovering the *vuelta* was impossible because of the lack of provisions and also considering everything they had heard from previous armadas, and thus going to the Malucos [Spice Islands] would be so much better." Indeed, a Portuguese fort lay about eight hundred miles away, three weeks of leisurely sailing. Persuading the discontented men to agree to the far riskier plan of voyaging twelve thousand miles to the coast of America must have been difficult in the extreme. The mutinous atmosphere persisted. Yet in a fit of resignation, the voyagers of the *San Lucas* somehow "left everything in the hands of the Lord and his Holy Mother" and began the *vuelta* on Easter Sunday, April 22, 1565.[13]

The first few days were dishearteningly slow, a feeling that any sailor will immediately recognize. In light wind, the sails go unfilled and the vessel barely moves or spins out of control. The *San Lucas* needed to climb from around twelve degrees of northern latitude to more than thirty-five or forty, comparable to ascending from the coast of Nicaragua to Oregon. In late April, however, the southwest monsoon had not yet become fully established, and the conditions were variable. Unable to make progress, the *San Lucas* voyagers spent the time discussing their first objective, a place that they referred to as "Pago Mayor" and described as "a large island at thirty degrees of latitude, surrounded by four or five islands to the south and mainland China to the north." They were referring in all likelihood to Japan. The most southwesterly of the four main Japanese islands, Kyushu, reaches all the way to thirty degrees and is indeed surrounded by smaller islands to the south (including Okinawa) and China to the north. Marco Polo had referred to Japan as "Zipangu," Hispanicized as "Cipango" or "Cipago," and therefore "Pago" may have been a shortening of the name with the added "Mayor" to underscore its great size.[14]

The idea of stopping in Japan to resupply the *San Lucas* may have been immensely comforting to the voyagers. But it rested on misleading geographic information. Lope Martín possessed a chart of the North Pacific that has since been lost. To approximate the expeditionaries' geographic understanding of the region, I use Giacomo Gastaldi's map—first published in 1554 as part of Giovanni Battista Ramusio's great collection of voyages, *Delle navigationi et viaggi,* and re-released as a standalone map in 1564, the very year of the fleet's departure. At first glance, Gastaldi's map is confusing because its orientation is opposite to ours: north is down. Nevertheless, it has the great merit of incorporating the discoveries of Magellan, Loaísa, Saavedra, and Villalobos, supplemented by additional insights

Giacomo Gastaldi's 1554 map of East Asia.

from Portuguese explorers who had reached China in the 1510s and Japan in the 1540s.[15]

Toward the middle of the map, one can see the "Mare de la China," or China Sea. At the top, various Philippine islands are represented: Mindanao is called "Vendanao," Cebu appears twice as "Cyābu" and "Zubut," Samar is identified as "Filipina," etc. At the left-hand margin, between

thirteen and seventeen degrees, the north-to-south chain of the Mariana Islands, then known as "las Islas de los Ladrones" or "Li Ladroni,"
are easy to spot. Finally, below the Marianas, between twenty-four and
twenty-seven degrees, looms "Cympagu," or Japan. Anyone armed with a
map like this and contemplating a passage from the Philippines to America
would have been inclined to call at "Cympagu." In reality, Japan is farther north and much closer to the Asian mainland, thus requiring nearly a
straight northward climb from the Philippines. In later centuries, Spanish
ships returning to the Americas sailed far out from Japan, as their intention
was not just to go north but also to begin making headway east toward the
New World.[16]

In their quest for "Pago Mayor," the *San Lucas* voyagers climbed for
weeks, eventually overshooting their intended target until thirty-one degrees of northern latitude. Japan was nowhere in sight. Yet they did find
a bizarre but majestic column emerging straight out of the ocean. "It was
very narrow, no more than a small house," the captain recalled, "but it was
so tall that I don't believe there is a higher tower anywhere in the world."
The men aboard the *San Lucas* could practically touch its sheer sides, but
there was no place to land. Rising 325 feet above the waterline, this soli-
tary pillar, called Sōfu Gan or "Widow's Crag" by the Japanese and "Lot's
Wife" by British sailors, was the only speck of land the voyagers would
behold between the Philippines and the American continent. Sōfu Gan is
actually an underwater volcano with a single andesite pillar sticking out,
like a candle on top of a birthday cake. It allows us to place the expeditionaries four hundred miles due south from Tokyo. The *San Lucas*'s trajectory
from the Philippines to Sōfu Gan makes clear that, however much the pioneers wished to make landfall in Japan or on the Asian mainland, they were
drifting eastward into the enormity of the North Pacific, one of the most
forbidding regions on Earth.[17]

Not everything, however, was against the *San Lucas* expeditionaries. By

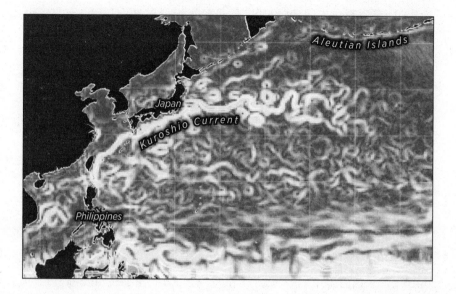

paralleling the coast of Japan, they were riding the most powerful current in the Pacific Ocean. The Japanese call it Kuroshio, or "Black Current," owing to its characteristic cobalt-blue color. An integral part of the North Pacific Gyre, the Kuroshio Current is an enormous ribbon of warm water that starts in the Philippine Sea, brushes against the coast of Taiwan, and moves rapidly up the eastern side of Japan, snaking and pushing against the cold waters coming from the Bering Sea. After veering off from Japan, the current continues eastward for about a thousand miles as a free jet stream known as the Kuroshio Extension, eventually feeding into the larger North Pacific Gyre. This explains why historically some Japanese ships disabled in storms have washed up in North America. This may have occurred prior to 1492, although no hard evidence has surfaced. More convincingly, scholars have estimated that between the sixteenth century and the middle of the nineteenth, more than a thousand Japanese vessels were swept out to sea. Among them, a handful are known to have made landfall in the Americas. A rice cargo ship called the *Tokujômaru,* for instance, ran into a storm that broke its rudder, causing it to drift for sixteen months until running aground in 1813 near Santa Barbara, California, with only the captain and two crew members still alive. Nearly twenty years later, a similar incident occurred when a merchant ship bound for Tokyo, the *Hojunmaru,* was knocked off course by a typhoon, only to reappear after fifteen months, rudderless and dismasted, in Cape Flattery, the most northwesterly point in the continental United States.[18]

The *San Lucas* voyagers reported an unexpected abundance of life in that part of the ocean, an observation that confirms their whereabouts. The collision of the warm Kuroshio Current with subarctic water produces eddies of plankton that are visible even in satellite images. In turn, the plankton attract a variety of animals. The Spanish expeditionaries saw "pig fish as large as cows" and marveled at the "dogs of the sea with their paws and tails and ears . . . and one of them came aboard and barked at us"

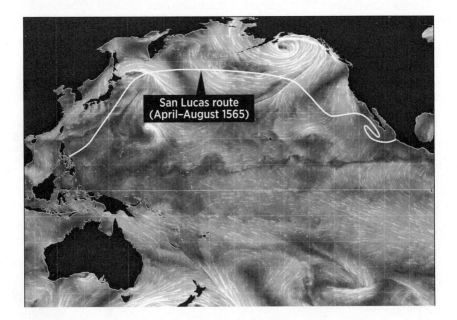

San Lucas route
(April–August 1565)

(almost certainly sea lions, with external ear flaps and very vocal, in contrast to true seals). Quite fittingly, the men of the *San Lucas* also crossed paths with the greatest migratory species of all. "Black shearwaters followed us, shrieking all day and night," Don Alonso recalled, "and their cries were very unsettling because no sailor had ever heard them like that." Sooty shearwaters pursue a breathtaking figure-eight migration spanning the entire Pacific. As they range from New Zealand to Alaska and from Chile to Japan, these noisy birds dive for food in some of the most productive regions of the Pacific, including the plankton-rich eddies off the coast of Japan, where some must have spotted the *San Lucas* slowly making its way in a northeasterly direction.[19]

Climbing to forty degrees and up to forty-three degrees of northern latitude, the pioneers overshot the warm waters of the Kuroshio Current. They had journeyed farther north into the great ocean than any other Europeans, sailing through frigid waters coming from the Bering Sea. Only Magellan's *Trinidad* had plied this part of the Pacific more than forty years earlier, where a storm had dismasted it and forced the last survivors to turn back. Extreme cold—that old nemesis of previous return attempts—became a serious concern for the crew members of the *San Lucas,* especially because they were missing most of their clothes after the washing party had to abandon them in Mindanao months earlier.[20]

The *San Lucas* voyagers now faced "the greatest cold of winter," as the captain put it, "even though it was the middle of summer in June and July." For thirty days the sky turned so dark and stormy that they were unable to see the Sun or the stars. On June 11, snow fell on the deck and did not melt until noon. Lamp oil became so frozen that the bottle in which it was kept had to be warmed over a fire, "and it still came out in pieces like lard." Modern historians have sometimes seized on such unlikely details to discount the veracity of Don Alonso's account. "Porpoises as big as cows present no difficulty," wrote one of these skeptics, "but it is unlikely that

cooking oil would freeze in mid-summer." Lamp oil freezes at around fifteen degrees Fahrenheit, and the process can start even at higher temperatures. Sailing by the Aleutian Islands in June, especially during the Little
Ice Age, would force such doubters to amend their opinions.[21]

Dark and stormy conditions persisting for a month not only threatened
death by exposure but also posed a serious navigational challenge. Since
the men could not see the Sun or the stars, they were unable to establish
their position. Lope Martín's chart reached up to forty-three degrees of
northern latitude. The *San Lucas* expeditionaries were navigating right
along the map's top margin and even venturing off the chart, "and we
could not pinpoint our location because there was no more sea left." As
they were sailing blind, the men of the *San Lucas* pinned their hopes on
their imagination. "We believed [ourselves] to be close to China," Don
Alonso stated, "and understood that the China coast continued and came
close to that of Mexico." In the 1540s, Spanish expeditionaries based in
Mexico had attempted to reach Asia by walking far into North America,
but to no avail. Two decades later, still no one knew how far America was
from Asia. In fact, it would not be until the eighteenth century that the
Danish explorer Vitus Bering finally reconnoitered the region. Yet in the
1560s, two centuries earlier, the lives of the *San Lucas* pioneers depended
on how the two continental landmasses fit together.[22]

It is likely that Lope Martín chose to go all the way to forty-three degrees of northern latitude in the hope of finding land, if not in Japan then
in China. But after reaching the top of his chart, experiencing the bitter
subarctic cold, and failing to see any coasts, the pilot opted to continue
east until striking what he and his crew members vaguely and wishfully
referred to as "the Californias." The only way forward was by running
with the wind, and "thus the pilot picked a path little by little and based
on his experience."[23]

During this long passage, the plight of the expeditionaries worsened.

The sails began to shrivel. They needed to get across the ocean before it became too late in the season, yet every day the wind, sun, and seawater battered their only means of propulsion, tearing it to pieces. The *San Lucas* carried no extra sails or mending equipment, so the crew had to hand-sew the tears with fishing line and repurpose the bonnets (sail extensions) to keep the mainsail and foresail working. Eventually they would have to part with their blankets and even their clothes to patch the holes. The men of the *San Lucas* would not be the first to wash up in the New World naked.[24]

But the most dangerous enemy was not the wind or the sea but the rats. After two months at sea, the large rodent population became thirsty, aggressive, and ready to do anything. "We had to chase after them with sticks," Don Alonso recalled, "because so many had been breeding aboard." During the string of storms, the rats must have been able to drink rainwater. After the weather cleared, however, the only available water aboard the *San Lucas* was sealed in the eight casks, "and in desperation they turned to gnawing on the barrels." The thirsty creatures perforated two barrels in as many hours, spilling all their contents. Disaster had struck. There were only three casks of water left, "and they were not full but missing four or five *arrobas*." In other words, by then the *San Lucas* was carrying a maximum of 294 gallons of water—less than fifteen gallons per person. Such an amount would be appropriate for an extended camping trip but surely not for crossing the largest ocean in the world. To defend what little water they still had, the expeditionaries kept a four-man guard by the casks below decks day and night, "and this gave us so much work, that it could not have been any worse." The guardsmen lit fires to keep the rodents at bay, especially at night, a necessary but extremely dangerous precaution that threatened to burn down the entire ship. Yet the rodents kept attacking, "and we killed between twenty and thirty every night."[25]

With shriveling sails, little water, and a raging war with the rats, the pressure on the pilot became almost unbearable. Where exactly in that immense ocean could they be? How far was it still to "the Californias"? During much of the crossing, Lope Martín had kept the *San Lucas* at around forty degrees of northern latitude, ten to fifteen degrees below the necklace of volcanic islands hanging between Russia and Alaska, the Aleutian Islands. Present-day sailing manuals recommend crossing the North Pacific farther south, at around thirty-five degrees of latitude, to avoid the unsettled weather closer to the Aleutians. The pilot's more northerly trajectory explains the cold and stormy month that the voyagers experienced. On the positive side, however, a more northerly crossing meant less distance between one continent and the other. In mid- to late June, the wind began to shift. It had been blowing toward the Americas, but now the strong breeze started bending southward, an indication "that it was being forced in that direction by the land," as the pilot astutely noted.[26]

Lope Martín was a practical navigator with extensive experience and enormous natural talent. But we know he was also well versed in the cutting-edge technologies of his time. Every day he calculated latitude by measuring the noontime angle of the Sun with respect to the horizon and using a declination table. The other ships in the fleet had the luxury of multiple pilots and instruments. Aboard the *San Lucas,* Lope Martín had to do everything by himself and could not compare his results with anyone else's. Far more impressive, he was capable of calculating longitude, or east-west distance, by measuring the difference between magnetic and true north, a specialized knowledge that put him among the very best pilots in the world. We know this from an offhand comment by Don Alonso: "The pilot reckoned that we were about one hundred leagues from the coast of New Spain and said that there was a certain variation of the compass needle, and thus he adjusted by one-quarter to the northeast." Such a passing statement by a nobleman with no nautical training can be interpreted in more than one way. If we understand that the "certain variation of the compass needle" was in fact "one-quarter to the northeast"—that is, 11.25 degrees to the east of true north—then at the time of the measurement the *San Lucas* would have been at a spot on the Pacific slightly more than one thousand miles due west of Point Reyes, California.[27]

A few more days of agonizing sailing in a southeasterly direction brought the voyagers ever closer to the continent until the evening of July 16, when the North American coastline became faintly visible in the far distance. "The next day before daybreak," Don Alonso recalled, "the pilot rose and told me to come out and behold the land of New Spain, and after looking at it for some time, we thanked Our Lord Jesus Christ for having given us such a blessing." It was the first return from Asia to America ever achieved. Lope Martín estimated their latitude at twenty-seven degrees and three-quarters, around the middle of Baja California in front of a large island now called Isla de Cedros.[28]

From that point onward, the *San Lucas* voyagers must have expected a comparatively safer coastal passage to Navidad. In fact, the most dangerous moment occurred not in the middle of the ocean but right before reaching the continent. On the night of July 28 they were running fast, with the mainsail and foresail all out and a strong breeze pushing from behind. We can infer from all the near accidents that befell the *San Lucas* since departing from Mexico that Lope Martín was something of a daredevil who pushed his vessel to the limit. With just a few hundred miles left, the pilot must have been highly motivated to go fast. As the wind continued to strengthen, however, the pilot finally gave the order to shorten the mainsail. Unfortunately, it was too late. A few sailors climbed up the mast and started gathering the sail, but as Don Alonso recalled, "we were suddenly hit by a blast of wind, sea, and rain, and the blow was so hard that the sail tore away from the hands of the sailors, knocking open two or three heads and flinging two men onto the deck." Out of control, the *San Lucas* turned abeam to the wind and the large waves, heeling violently with the mast almost touching the water and the men hanging on to anything to stay inside the vessel. Everything above and below decks became pandemonium, "and we could not tell if it was land or sea."[29]

Although a great deal of water had flooded into the *San Lucas* during that first knockdown, the vessel began righting itself as if by miracle. Yet a second large wave washed across the deck at that moment. "This one took the compass and everything else, and the fire that we were keeping, and also the helmsman himself," the captain said, "and thus we remained without heat, with the ship sideways to the waves, and half sunk and buried underneath the sea." As the mainsail emerged in tatters, the only way to regain control of the *San Lucas* was with the foresail. The pilot immediately turned his full attention to it, shouting orders, "but the crew members were dazed and no one came, and it was so dark that they could not find any ropes." They had to expend great energy to contain the sail and bail out the water, "yet everyone was extremely weak from hunger and thirst, and even if there had been food, they could not eat because their gums had grown so large that they covered the teeth," an unmistakable characteristic of scurvy at a very advanced stage. It must have taken a long time before the exhausted men finally got the foresail properly positioned. In the meantime, the *San Lucas* was swept off course.[30]

The expeditionaries had to find a way to save themselves aboard a sinking vessel, navigating with no compass or helmsman, with a few blankets and clothes for a sail, and a crew so enfeebled that they could barely stand. At least they still had their extraordinary pilot, who seemed to know instinctively what to do at every turn. "We begged Our Lady of Guadalupe to keep us safe, and all of us promised to take the makeshift foresail to her shrine in Mexico City," recalled Don Alonso. Mercifully, the elements held during the last few days of navigation. Light morning breezes pushed the pioneers gently forward while the evening rains came accompanied by moderate wind. They would never have survived another storm. Naked, thirsty, hungry, and with alarming symptoms of scurvy, the pioneers of the *San Lucas* pulled into the perfect horseshoe bay of Navidad on August 9, 1565. It had taken them three months and twenty days to connect the two sides of the great ocean.[31]

Copia de vna carta venida de Se-

uilla a Miguel Saluador de Valencia. La qual narra el ventu-
rofo defcubrimiento que los Moxicanos han hecho, naue-
gando con la armada que fu Mageftad mando hazer en
Mexico. Con otras cofas marauillofas, y de gran
prouecho para toda la Chriftiandad: fon
dignas de fer viftas y leydas
¶ En Barcelona, Per Pau Cortey, 1566.

Efto de la China ay dos relaciones, y es, que a los
dezifiete de Nouiembre del año de mil y quinie
ros y feffenta y quatro, por mandado de fu Mago.
fe hizo vna armada en el puerto de la Natiuidad o
la mar del Sur, cient leguas de Mexico, de dos naues, y dos
patayfos, para defcubrir las yslas dela efpeeieria, que las lla-
man Philippinas, por nueftro Rey, coftaron mas de feyfcien
tos mil pefos de Atipufque hechas a la vela.

¶ Partieron el dicho dia del puerto, y nauegaron feys dias
¶ juntas·y a los fiete les dio vna barrufca, que fe aparto dellas
el Patays, que era de cincuenta toneladas, y lleuaua venyte

First page of a letter published in Barcelona in 1566 recounting the "venturous discovery" of a new navigation to Asia "along with other marvelous things of great
advantage to Christendom that are worth knowing and reading about."

10

Fall from Glory

*T*he bold passage of the *San Lucas* caused a burst of excitement in Mexico. America was poised to become the *axis mundi,* the bridge between East and West. Don Alonso, Lope Martín, and their shipmates had finally turned the largest ocean on Earth into a vital space of human contact and exchange. After 1565, for two and a half centuries Spanish galleons sailed yearly from the coast of North America to the Philippines, carrying silver to Asia and returning with silk, porcelain, spices, and other wondrous products. They also transported Asian slaves to America. In a few short years, the Philippines became a major hub where merchants from China, Japan, and elsewhere in Asia gathered to trade with the Americas, and the round trip across the Pacific became not just possible but, in fact, routine. "It is like the return from the Americas to Spain," explained the Jesuit savant José de Acosta in 1590, "as those going from the Philippines or China to Mexico sail far to the north until they reach the latitude of Japan, and then they sight the Californias." By the eighteenth and nineteenth centuries, British and especially American merchants built on these early linkages to launch their own transpacific ventures. As the

Spanish empire in the Americas crumbled in the early nineteenth century, American ships replaced the old galleons. Eventually the United States seized Hawai'i, Guam, and the Philippines, tapped into markets in Japan and China, and established a network of interests that is now once again remaking the world.[1]

The men of the *San Lucas* could not have imagined all the consequences of their odyssey. Yet even at that early date, there were some inklings. At the port of Navidad, the voyagers enjoyed a heroes' welcome. They paused there for a few days to regain some strength before continuing to the viceregal capital of Mexico City and on to Spain, where they hoped to get an audience with Philip II. Wherever they went, the captain of the *San Lucas,* its Afro-Portuguese pilot, and the others were recognized and celebrated, "and everyone rejoiced at the news from those lands and the samples of cinnamon that they had brought."[2]

Their moment of glory ended swiftly, however. Two months after the arrival of the *San Lucas,* another ship of the Legazpi expedition washed up in Acapulco. It was the flagship *San Pedro.* The largest vessel in the fleet had also returned by means of an arc across the Pacific similar to that of the *San Lucas* but more southerly and lasting four months. The *San Pedro* had been loaded with enough provisions to last for eight months at sea and had carried two hundred casks of water. Yet the human toll still had been alarming. Sixteen men had died along the way, including the *piloto mayor* Esteban Rodríguez. Out of nearly two hundred crew members, only eighteen or so "could do any work whatsoever" when they finally pulled into Acapulco on October 8, 1565. Scurvy had wreaked havoc during the passage. Among the survivors were Felipe de Salcedo, Legazpi's eighteen-year-old grandson, who had served as ship's captain during the return voyage, and the resilient Andrés de Urdaneta, who at the age of fifty-seven had circumnavigated the globe, sailed from America to Asia twice, and returned once. Legazpi himself had remained behind in command of the Spanish settlement in the Philippines.[3]

The men of the *San Pedro* had every reason to feel proud, especially Urdaneta. Since the start of the secretive venture to find the *vuelta,* the friar-mariner had projected supreme confidence, often quipping that he would return "not on a ship but on an ox cart if necessary." He had finally made good on this promise, although it had not been easy. As we saw, the Audiencia of Mexico had betrayed the friar, leading him to believe that the fleet was going to New Guinea, only to change the destination to the Philippines in mid-ocean. Yet Urdaneta had regained his composure and served well. He had identified Guam correctly when all the other pilots thought they were much farther along, helped the fleet navigate through the Philippines, communicated in Malay with the captured Muslim pilot, and above all guided the *San Pedro* back across the great ocean with a sure hand. When he arrived in Acapulco, one of the first things he did was draw a chart "with all the winds, directions, coasts, and peninsulas." It remained in use for decades, "and not a single thing has been added," commented an Augustinian chronicler nearly sixty years later. Friar Urdaneta was evidently a man of uncommon vitality, utterly dependable, an extraordinary navigator, and a towering figure in the annals of the early navigation of the Pacific.[4]

Yet the friar-mariner and his companions had not been the first to return. When they heard of the *San Lucas*'s earlier arrival, they must have been skeptical. Was it even possible for such a small and poorly provisioned dispatch boat to sail to Asia and return? The claim was all the more suspicious because the *San Lucas* had become separated from the rest of the fleet a mere ten days after departing from Navidad and not too distant from the American coast. Nonetheless, the *San Lucas* voyagers had reappeared months later bearing porcelain, silk, cinnamon, and other products from Southeast Asia, proving that they had indeed crossed and re-crossed the Pacific. Thus the greatest mystery always came back to the matter of their separation.

Many expedition members, beginning with Commander Legazpi back in the Philippines, had a clear answer to this question. On November 7, 1565, Legazpi's legal representative in Mexico City formally accused the captain of the *San Lucas,* Don Alonso de Arellano, of "absconding and becoming absent from the fleet under the cloak of night, without cause, and when the sea was calm and the weather was good." The document went on to demand that "the said captain, his pilot, and their soldiers appear before their general [Legazpi himself] to answer for their conduct"—all the way back in the Philippines! It was a very serious charge, potentially amounting to treason, thus triggering an investigation against the pioneers of the *San Lucas.*[5]

Yet Don Alonso's initial impulse was to brush aside the accusation and carry on with his preparations to cross the Atlantic and seek an audience with the Spanish king. As a nobleman with many allies in high places, he was not about to change his plans on account of what he must have viewed as a specious allegation. Anyone wishing to travel to Spain needed to secure written permission before being allowed to board a ship in Veracruz, so Don Alonso paid a visit to the Audiencia and had no difficulty getting their approval. If anyone wanted to stop him, it would have to be at the highest levels of the royal bureaucracy in Madrid.[6]

Yet Gabriel Díaz, Legazpi's representative in Mexico City, was nothing if not persistent. Díaz was a treasurer at the Minting House, a high-ranking royal official in his own right, and a longtime Legazpi colleague and friend. On hearing that "Don Alonso and some of his soldiers were getting ready to depart for the kingdoms of Castile," treasurer Díaz went into legal overdrive. He lodged a second complaint four days after the first one, a third one two days later, and a fourth one three days after that. Díaz also made contact with crew members of the *San Lucas,* some of whom had arrived in Mexico City with Don Alonso, or perhaps they were in the middle of a pilgrimage to the shrine of the Virgin of Guadalupe to present the tattered sail, as they had promised when they had nearly capsized. What is certain is that treasurer Díaz met at least one of the *San Lucas's* men and obtained sufficient information to level an additional accusation against Don Alonso and Lope Martín of "throwing a Spaniard into the ocean while still alive and a second man who was an Indian."[7]

Although murdering two crew members in cold blood may seem very serious to our sensibilities, in the sixteenth century ship's captains had considerable latitude in disciplining their men. Crew members could be thrown overboard for even minor infractions like falling asleep twice during their watch, as happened during the Villalobos expedition. Why these two luckless crew members of the *San Lucas* were executed and at what stage of the voyage is unknown, but most likely it was when they were at the border of the Philippines arguing over whether to attempt the *vuelta*. Regardless of the exact circumstances, such a brutal punishment was within the scope of Don Alonso's authority.[8]

Thus, "becoming absent" from the fleet "when the sea was calm and the weather was good" remained the only serious accusation. The Audiencia had to consider the case no fewer than four times, prompted by treasurer Díaz's vigorous legal offensive. Given what we know today, it is almost certain that the charge was unfounded. First, on the night of the separation, December 1, 1564, no pilot of the expedition reported a "calm" sea and "good" weather, as Díaz insisted. Aboard the flagship *San Pedro,* one of Legazpi's own pilots recorded "a downpour in the early evening," while the other pilot wrote in his logbook that he could not measure the latitude that day "because of the many rains," implying that the bad weather had started in the morning. Indeed, not a single pilot in any of the four vessels was able to establish latitude between December 1 and December 3 and again on December 5, evidently because during those days of rain and storms, they could not see the Sun to measure its altitude with respect to the horizon. This is entirely consistent with the testimony given by Don Alonso, Lope Martín, and other men of the *San Lucas* before the Audiencia of Mexico on November 22, 1565. "We had rough weather coming from the northeast," they declared, "and on December 1 at night, the wind became so strong that it pushed us toward the southwest, and we were taking on water and could not turn sideways because the vessel is small and very low." Without having been there, it is impossible to know for certain if there was anything that the *San Lucas*—by far the smallest and lowest ship in the fleet—could have done to remain within sight of the others. But the fact is that bad weather in the middle of the ocean, especially in the pitch darkness of a stormy night, sometimes resulted in unintended separations among sixteenth-century squadrons crossing oceans.[9]

Precisely because this was a real possibility, Commander Legazpi, as we have seen, had issued detailed orders. The stray ship would go immediately to nine degrees of latitude and "proceed due west toward the Philippines" looking for the "Islands of the Kings" and the "Islands of the Corals," and then go up to ten degrees toward the "Islands of Reefs" and "Matalotes." On finding any of these islands, the lone vessel would wait ten days for the rest of the fleet to catch up. If still no contact had occurred, the separated voyagers would continue on to the Philippines after leaving a sign in the form of a large cross with a bottle buried at its foot containing a letter. The men of the *San Lucas* had followed these orders to the extent possible. They had navigated between eight and nine degrees but could not stop in Micronesia for the same reason that the rest of the fleet had not paused there either, as it consisted of minuscule atolls and islets rimmed with jagged edges, and sitting atop pillars of coral with no place to anchor. If anyone had deviated from this contingency plan, it had been not the *San Lucas* but the rest of the fleet. For a month and a half, the three ships under Legazpi had sailed at around nine or ten degrees of latitude, as agreed. Yet after a mid-ocean gathering of all the captains and pilots, Commander Legazpi had suddenly changed course and ordered the squadron to ascend to thirteen degrees in order to call at Guam, thus making the separation permanent.[10]

Once the *San Lucas* arrived in the Philippines, the activities of the men reveal not an absconding crew with a devious plan but a group of survivors facing a hostile environment and attempting to save themselves. They waited, as we have seen, at an exposed cove on the Davao Gulf in eastern Mindanao for one month — hardly the best way to avoid detection — where they built several crosses and buried a jar containing letters "so the armada would know what had happened to us and where we were going next." They then rounded Mindanao, navigating right through the middle of the archipelago, within sight of countless islands. They had also visited Cebu, where the chances of finding the rest of the fleet were greatest and where indeed they came close to doing so. The general impression one gets is of an accidental separation followed by clear attempts to rejoin the fleet.[11]

Don Alonso and Lope Martín chose to return to Navidad, overcoming immense hurdles and suffering greatly along the way. If they had been pursuing a nefarious plan of illicit enrichment, why had they not acted on it? From the Philippines, the most natural continuation would have been to the Spice Islands, and indeed many crew members wanted to go there. Such a course would have been especially beneficial to Lope Martín, who could have expected a favorable reception or at least an accommodation with his Portuguese compatriots there. Actions speak louder than words. Ultimately, the *San Lucas* expeditionaries carried out their orders, found the *vuelta,* and performed a service of incalculable value to the Spanish crown.

One final piece of evidence has a bearing on the pilot's guilt or innocence and exposes the ruthless wheeling and dealing prevalent in the early years of Pacific exploration, a time when a single cargo of spices or silk could bring immense wealth to a plucky crew. While the investigation of Don Alonso and Lope Martín was running its course in Mexico City in the fall of 1565, on the other side of the world, in the Philippines, General Legazpi uncovered a dangerous conspiracy while settled on the island of Cebu. Several crew members had planned to steal a cache of weapons and trade goods and make off with them on one of the moored ships. The plotters intended to barter for spices in Southeast Asia and then sail to France, getting there either "by way of the Strait of Magellan . . . or by way of Malacca, where the Portuguese would receive them well." More than forty men were reportedly implicated in this ambitious scheme, mostly foreigners but some Spaniards as well.[12]

Legazpi received timely intelligence about the plot and had the leaders apprehended, questioned, and executed. The investigation revealed that their plan had been conceived even before the expedition's departure from Navidad a year earlier, "and it was understood that the men involved would flee on the *San Lucas,* pursuing a different course from the flagship and becoming separated." It would take two years for this information to reach Mexico, so the Audiencia in Mexico City considering the cases of Don Alonso and Lope Martín in November of 1565 did not have these facts at their disposal. Nonetheless, we can make some educated guesses. Although Lope Martín was never mentioned by name, and the evidence is circumstantial at best and extracted under duress, it is likely that the pilot was involved at least to some extent, given that the plotters were primarily non-Spaniards and that their initial plan had been to flee aboard the *San Lucas.* As we have seen, Lope Martín was extraordinarily well adapted to the cutthroat world of the early voyages of exploration, and thus at the very least he must have been aware of this intrigue, may have been present in the initial conversations at Navidad, and may well have been one of the ringleaders. But regardless of the extent of his initial involvement, for some reason he reconsidered, attempted to rejoin the rest of the fleet, and ultimately stayed true to his mission and sailed back to Mexico.[13]

The Audiencia threw out all the charges, clearing Don Alonso and Lope Martín. But the cabal of elderly men ruling Mexico — prone to secret orders, tortuous dealings, and blatant manipulation — could not refrain from playing one final trick. They allowed Don Alonso to proceed to Spain to request an audience with the king but retained Lope Martín's services.

The Audiencia members would soon be dispatching another expedition to the Philippines with supplies for Legazpi, and what better pilot than the extraordinary Lope Martín? Left unsaid was an ulterior motive. Sending the Black man back to Cebu meant that he would have to appear before Commander Legazpi, who would finally get the satisfaction of bringing to justice at least one crew member from the wayward *San Lucas*. At a distance of nearly five centuries, it is impossible to tease out all the reasons for this unequal treatment of Don Alonso and Lope Martín, but the vast social differences between a nobleman captain and a mulatto pilot surely mattered.[14]

Lope Martín knew well what awaited him in the Philippines. As he would later explain, "The very hour that the general [Legazpi] saw me there, he would hang me on the spot." Yet the Audiencia would not take no for an answer. To persuade Lope Martín, the rulers of Mexico gave him eleven thousand ducats to purchase a large ship and hire a crew to his liking. It was an enormous sum of money. Even after accepting the commission, it is likely that Lope Martín did not intend to follow through. He traveled from Mexico City to the Pacific coast with a small entourage, ostensibly to examine vessels and sign up crew members. The pilot actually selected a vessel at the port of Huatulco, but it was much too small. In reality, Lope Martín and his group of friends were living in the moment and in a mood to celebrate. "The road seemed too long to them," the Spanish ambassador in Portugal commented, "and they squandered the money and for this were thrown in jail." Embezzling royal funds was a time-honored tradition in the early transpacific fleets. Just a year earlier, the man who had raised Legazpi's fleet — the larger-than-life adventurer and bigamist Juan Pablo de Carrión — had become the target of a similar accusation. The Audiencia members must have known that it was risky to entrust eleven thousand ducats to a group of seamen who had just experienced months of extreme privation and near-death adventures across the Pacific.

It is impossible to know whether this had been a deliberate ploy. Yet now that Lope Martín was in jail for defrauding the royal treasury, they could exert a great deal more pressure on him.[15]

The rest of the story unfolded with the precision of a Shakespearean play. The Audiencia procured an old ship for the follow-up expedition to the Philippines, appointed a captain—a man named Pero Sánchez Pericón from Málaga in southern Spain, described as a "miserable, melancholic enemy of friendship, and who delighted in solitude"—and released Lope Martín from jail on the condition that he serve as lead pilot. The Audiencia members also made a final decision about Lope Martín's fate, "writing to General Legazpi to hang the pilot as soon as he got there [the Philippines] as a reward for his services, and putting the letter in a sealed envelope that would be carried by the ship's secretary." There was only one problem with this plan. Secretary Juan de Zaldívar leaked the sealed document's contents, and Lope Martín's talent as a pilot was surpassed only by his skill at plotting and conspiring. He would now do everything within his power to stay alive and exact revenge.[16]

11

Survival and Revenge

*T*he voyage that began in Acapulco in May 1566 was unconventional. A ship named the *San Jerónimo* would dash across the Pacific steered by a pilot who had no reason to reach his destination. As one of the travelers put it, "If Homer and Virgil had come, they would have needed to summon all of their abilities to convey the hunger, destruction, deaths, cries, sighs, imprisonments, travails, delays, afflictions, and all the calamities and shipwrecks that we experienced." Trouble began even before casting off, when "a swirl of wind and rain" demolished several houses in Acapulco and tossed the *San Jerónimo* about while lying at anchor, causing the stern to hit land and threatening to sink the vessel. In all likelihood, 1565–66 was an El Niño year that brought earlier and more intense tropical storms than usual to Acapulco, where the hurricane season normally begins in May.[1]

Lope Martín first tried to bring Captain Pero Sánchez Pericón to his side. "You are making a mistake if you think that I will take you to Cebu," he said to the captain, "because the very hour that the general [Legazpi] saw me there, he would hang me on the spot." As alternatives, the pilot laid out a world of possibilities. "I could take you to Japan, where you could get more than 200,000 ducats to add shine to your lineage," the Afro-Portuguese proposed, "or to the Cape of Cinnamon in Mindanao . . . and I could then take you through the Strait of Magellan to Spain." Although these were far-fetched schemes, the captain of a well-supplied galleon with a pilot of Lope Martín's caliber could not dismiss them entirely. Pericón gave few hints about his true intentions. His twenty-five-year-old son, however, Diego Sánchez Pericón de Mesa, was talkative, opinionated, and reckless. Serving as a junior officer aboard the *San Jerónimo,* Diego was "a lot younger in discretion than in years," a mercurial presence who thought himself on top of the world thanks to his father's appointment as sea captain. The overall effect of the Pericóns on Lope Martín was to embolden him.[2]

Somehow the pilot came to conceive of this voyage less as a death sentence and more as a dangerous opportunity. In the weeks before departure, he even hurried the captain to finish the preparations, as the sailing conditions were becoming more challenging by the day. Lope Martín was right. Modern sailing guides suggest starting from the coast of Mexico either before June or after October to avoid the summer tropical storms. During April, while Captain Pericón rushed to get all the supplies loaded, the pilot put together a crew, "choosing those who were best suited for his purposes, particularly the ones who came from the municipality where they said he had been married and others from Portugal inasmuch as they say he comes from there." This is the only shred of evidence that Lope Martín had a wife in Ayamonte on the Spanish-Portuguese border.[3]

By the end of the month, about 130 men, more or less evenly split between sailors and soldiers, boarded the *San Jerónimo.* As the pilot had handpicked the sailors, he enjoyed broad support from them. Some were mulattos like Lope Martín, or hailed from the Spanish-Portuguese border region, or had traveled together before and knew one another well. Juan

Yáñiz, for instance, was a fellow Portuguese mariner, a *San Lucas* veteran, and "Lope Martín's intimate friend." All of this made for a cohesive crew.[4]

In contrast, the soldiers had come together through greed. Earlier in the year, word had spread in Mexico City that the *vuelta* had been discovered and a follow-up expedition to the Philippines would be departing soon. Wishing to gain access to the riches of the Orient, many men had volunteered, so many indeed that only those with connections, or who had signed on "through favors," had secured spots. In the previous transpacific voyage, each soldier had been paid 175 pesos. This time, owing to the excessive enthusiasm, and at Captain Pericón's suggestion, each soldier was offered merely one hundred pesos. Essentially, these so-called soldiers —even though they were closer to entrepreneurs or agents of wealthy and influential patrons—would be forgoing much of their compensation for the opportunity of going to Asia to seek their fortune.[5]

Two sergeants, Juan Ortiz de Mosquera and Pero Núñez de Solórzano, were in command of the military men. Their undisguised contempt for the Pericóns injected great uncertainty into the venture. Mosquera was "an old soldier, able, courageous, and too much of a man," who loathed Diego Sánchez Pericón because of the captain's son's complete lack of discipline and military training. Solórzano, the more junior of the two commanding officers, had been in an actual "brawl" with him. Unclear lines of authority may have been at the root of this conflict. Both Mosquera and Solórzano outranked the younger Pericón and gave him orders even though he was the ship captain's son. Yet the two sergeants repeatedly complained about their junior officer's unruliness. Also contributing to the antagonism may have been Captain Pericón's avaricious ways. The older Pericón had suggested the drastic salary reduction for the soldiers and had extorted an additional fifty pesos to transport each soldier, boasting that he "would have made them serve for free." Whatever the actual reason for the conflict between the Pericóns and the top military commanders, it gave Lope Martín ample room to maneuver by inserting himself between them.[6]

On the morning of May 1, the *San Jerónimo* cleared the capacious bay of Acapulco and entered "the true sea that makes all others appear like rivers and puddles," as soldier Juan Martínez, the Homer and Virgil of this voyage, referred to the Pacific. Over the next ten days, the ship descended toward the equatorial region to a latitude of nine degrees, where "the excessive heat, fatigue, and lack of winds held us back," Martínez recalled, "and caused the bodies to be altered to the point of illness." The atmosphere became uneasy and electric when two soldiers fell sick and died. A story began circulating about three *naos* that had departed from Mexico earlier in the year bound for Peru. Without any wind in the middle of the ocean, they had been trapped for weeks and the men had perished, "and nothing had remained, not hair nor bones." The *San Jerónimo* voyagers prayed fervently and collected alms to avoid a similar fate. A "deformed comet" appeared like an unmistakable omen of "the great difficulties that we would experience and the evil thoughts some among us were having." By then, many soldiers wanted to return to the Americas to load more fresh water before attempting the Pacific crossing, while others would have remained on dry land if given a chance. Lope Martín was in his element now.[7]

This was also a moment of reckoning for the pilot. As Pericón would never deviate from his orders to go to the Philippines, with each passing day Lope Martín found himself closer to the gallows. The pilot's predicament was brutally simple. To survive, he would have to find a way to eliminate the ship's captain. Thus he talked more openly about his circumstances, made promises, forged alliances, and finally began agitating against the prickly Pericón. The captain's principal object of affection was a horse that he kept in a sling below decks. The beast, however, drank too much water at a time when the precious liquid was becoming scarce, and many crew members noticed. The pilot "did not hold his tongue and said that it was better to kill it," a pronouncement that Pericón took as an affront. The captain went so far as to post guards by the animal — drawing complaints from the soldiers thus tasked, who felt demoted to horse

Typical horse transport
system in the Spanish
fleets according to a
drawing from the 1530s.

grooms—yet on the morning of May 25, Pericón's beloved horse was
found dangling over a puddle of blood. A sailor had slipped through the
night and sunk a dagger into its heart, "from where the blood flowed as if
out of a drainage pipe," Martínez noted drily, "and everything was done
so subtly that the guards could not see anything."[8]

Pericón became incensed. The perpetrators' identity was hardly a mystery. They had openly criticized the captain for days, "losing all sense of
shame in word and deed and showing very little respect." At the top of
the list was Lope Martín, but it extended to about two dozen individuals,
"particularly from among the sailors." The mutiny was also starting to
spread to the military men. A soldier named Felipe del Campo had joined
forces with Lope Martín and served as go-between with the two military
leaders, Sergeants Mosquera and Solórzano, whose hatred for the Peri-

In the nautical world, the forecastle, or *alcázar* in Spanish—a term of Arabic origin meaning "fortress"—referred to a storeroom on a raised deck at the front of the ship. The men of the *San Jerónimo* stored their weapons in a room like this one. Notice the hatch leading below decks, similar to the one used during the first mutiny.

cóns remained undiminished. The captain needed to act urgently. As he could not proceed solely on rumor, he drafted a decree and had it read aloud throughout the ship, accusing "certain people who were conspiring against His Majesty and his [Pericón's] person." Captain Pericón also offered one thousand pesos in gold for information about the conspirators as well as a separate reward of four hundred ducats for leads about the horse killer. In the cramped quarters of a sixteenth-century sailing vessel, the tension must have been unbearable. If it came to open violence in the middle of the ocean, the consequences would be fatal for everyone. Yet no one came forward. The captain and his son became more isolated than ever. Their few remaining allies counseled them to stay alert and to move about the *San Jerónimo* with guards. But Captain Pericón was "a very devout man, given to praying and keeping to his own opinions."[9]

Meanwhile, the plotters were well coordinated. Some broke into the *alcázar,* or forecastle (a depot or storeroom on top of a raised deck in the forward part of the ship), and retrieved many weapons kept there under lock and key. Six days after the horse killing, a sailor named Bartolomé de Lara created another provocation. He complained to the younger Pericón about the "wretched food and drink." As the exchange escalated, the captain's son pulled out a whip to put Lara in his place, but the mariner drew out a dagger, forcing the young officer "to retreat in a great commotion and go down to his quarters to fetch some soldiers." It took several men to disarm Lara and lock him up below decks. Only two days later, however, his friends released the feisty sailor. He strolled around the deck as if nothing had happened in yet another display of blatant disregard for the captain's authority.[10]

The end came that very night, in the wee hours of Monday, June 3, 1566, Pentecost. Fresh out of the brig and ready for vengeance, Lara put himself at the head of a very tight group consisting of the military commander Sergeant Mosquera and two soldiers. Late in the evening they made their way quietly to the stern of the *San Jerónimo,* opened a hatch, and descended through a passageway that ended in front of the captain's quarters, where the Pericóns were sleeping. Daggers drawn, Lara and Mosquera stepped in front while the two soldiers stayed a few paces behind for support. The two ringleaders burst into the cabin and killed father and son, but not without loud screams and groans. Like the horse, the Pericóns died in total darkness and with a profusion of blood. Lope Martín and several sailors stood close by with shields and swords drawn in case anyone came, while other mutineers were posted where many of the soldiers were sleeping, "and those who stirred and attempted to get up were tamped down with the flat part of the sword and told, long live the king, nothing is happening."[11]

The morning unveiled a gruesome scene. To dispose of the corpses, the mutineers had to bring them up on deck. One of the soldiers who had participated in the killing held his bloody dagger like a trophy. He had plunged it completely into the captain's dead body and intended to keep it unwiped, "to claim the reward that he deserved." Sergeant Mosquera took full responsibility. The top military officer of the *San Jerónimo* was indeed "courageous and too much of a man," as soldier Martínez had described him. But even he had been shaken by the night's events. Both sailors and soldiers were still struggling to comprehend what had happened when a corporal acclaimed Sergeant Mosquera and urged everyone to name him captain. The military commander demurred, however. "There are men of greater courage aboard this vessel," he countered. Yet the soldiers pressed their commanding officer "twice and three times" until Sergeant Mosquera accepted. He asked them only "not to address him as captain but continue to call him as before." The gravity of the crime he had committed a few hours earlier must have weighed heavily on Mosquera. He had suddenly become the most visible leader of a bloody mutiny. Yet he might be able to justify his actions against the Pericóns (still universally despised) if he completed the mission. The new captain thus made clear his intention to take the *San Jerónimo* to the Spanish camp in the Philippines, as was the original plan. These "sweet words" reassured many men aboard the *San Jerónimo*—but not Lope Martín.[12]

Sergeant Mosquera was popular with his men and therefore much harder to eliminate than Pericón. His supporters consisted of a majority of the soldiers, almost all the royal officials, some sailors, including the *maestre,* or boatswain, and the chaplain. The new captain was also a prudent man. On pain of death, he ordered all the sailors to give up the weapons they had squirreled away in sea chests and dark corners of the ship during the run-up to the mutiny. Mosquera also knew what Lope Martín was capable of and kept a close eye on him. For the next two and a half weeks, a series of realignments, conspiracies, and counter-conspiracies unfolded in hushed voices aboard the *San Jerónimo*. To survive, the pilot had to use all his powers of persuasion. He retained the support of many sailors, the ship's secretary Juan de Zaldívar, who had leaked the pilot's death sentence in the first place, and a few discontented soldiers like Felipe del Campo. At this time, Lope Martín also added Sergeant Solórzano to his camp, the highest-ranking military officer aboard except for Mosquera. This would prove decisive.[13]

Two-thirds of the way to the Philippines, by the middle of June time was running short for the pilot. Sergeant Mosquera must have suspected that Lope Martín was up to something because he considered hanging the pilot preemptively. This would have left even more blood on his hands. But what gave the new captain pause was the difficulty of maneuvering the galleon and bringing it safely into port in Cebu without the pilot. Mosquera had asked the *maestre,* a man named Rodrigo del Angle, if he felt sufficiently confident in his sailing abilities to take over the *San Jerónimo*. Boatswains possessed some nautical training and oversaw all the sailors, so in theory they could act as substitute pilots. Angle had replied to Mosquera that he felt perfectly qualified, a "presumption" that Lope Martín would never forgive. In spite of Angle's assurances, Sergeant Mosquera chose to do nothing, a costly mistake. "It must have been divinely ordained," declared the soldier-chronicler aboard the *San Jerónimo,* waxing philosophical, "that someone as able and discreet as Mosquera would in the end become blind."[14]

At midnight on Friday, June 21, Mosquera was at the *alcázar* talking with the two soldiers involved in the killing of the Pericóns. As the new captain had been worrying about the royal investigation that would ensue on arrival, it was only natural to agree on a single version of events with his accomplices. Unbeknownst to Mosquera, however, these two soldiers had joined the pilot's faction. Their mission was to keep the substitute captain occupied in the forecastle. In the meantime, Sergeant Solórzano, the second-highest-ranking officer aboard the *San Jerónimo,* went below decks, where many soldiers were sleeping, and, "adducing sophistic reasons," ordered them to turn over their weapons immediately. Keeping only "the odd knife," the soldiers had no choice but to obey their commanding officer. The ploy nearly came undone when Mosquera heard a noise from below. He started to go down to investigate, but the two soldiers called him back to the forecastle and then blocked his way. Not wanting to appear excessively mistrustful or fearful, the captain returned, although he must have suspected something.[15]

The conversation continued until well into the morning of June 22, when Lope Martín and others joined Mosquera in the *alcázar*. They were having a lively exchange over breakfast "with much bacon and wine." Without warning, some sailors entered the room and unceremoniously tied Mosquera's hands behind his back and snapped a pair of shackles on his feet. The merriment and laughter continued a little longer. "What kind of child's play is this?" the captain inquired while pretending to be amused. They marched him down to the deck and made him sit on a box close to the yardarm. The prisoner was still smiling and putting on a brave face. At last, Lope Martín pronounced his sentence. "Confess yourself, you are about to die," the pilot said, "because you have killed the captain." Mosquera had worried all along about his participation in the killing of the Pericóns, and now he was getting swift justice in the manner of the sea. The pilot also accused the sergeant of attempting to murder him, a charge that Mosquera vehemently denied. The priest rushed to the scene and pleaded with the pilot, telling him to think carefully about what he was poised to do, but Lope Martín turned his back on the cleric and gave a signal. Instantly, some mariners hoisted Mosquera, "without giving him time to confess or say Jesus," as the soldier Martínez later recalled, "and threw him into the sea with the shackles and still half alive." Not content with having executed him, they also made it known that he was "a sodomite who had practiced this abominable sin in Italy where he had lived and had tried the same in New Spain."[16]

The sailors were now in full command of the vessel, and Lope Martín had turned into something of a Lope de Aguirre of the Pacific, a renegade explorer beyond the pale of imperial control. He may have considered going to Japan, the Spice Islands, or perhaps to the "Cape of Cinnamon" in Mindanao. Any of these destinations offered products that would have made the pilot and his supporters rich. For the soldiers, those were dark days when "no one trusted one another" and "a melancholy silence reigned over the deck."[17]

On June 29, 1566, after surviving two mutinies and two months of sailing, and one week after Mosquera's execution, the men of the *San Jerónimo* began to sight land. Some of the sailors had passed by the Marshall Islands before and knew what to expect. The soldiers, however, more eager than ever to get off the *San Jerónimo,* were disappointed by the tiny low-lying islands fringed by coral, with no good anchorages, and sometimes populated by "the Bearded Ones," or "los Barbudos." "Instead of our much-desired motherland," Martínez ruminated, "we could call this our stepmother land."[18]

For a week the *San Jerónimo* skirted atolls and reefs. As they appeared to reach the end of the Marshalls, those in command of the ship let out all the sails and pushed hard. Yet one night, "in an instant, we found ourselves completely surrounded by islands and capes," Martínez recalled, "and they were so close to us that they caused great alarm among the mariners, let alone the soldiers, and the helmsman asked whether he should steer toward the land." As the favorable winds and currents propelled the *San Jerónimo* furiously forward, it was preferable to run aground close to an island rather than smashing into a reef far from land. Lope Martín barked some orders to the contrary. The sailor Lara became so agitated that he pushed the helmsman aside and took the wheel himself. After a few violent turns and scrapes against coral and rock, "God decided to take us through a channel that was not even a stone's throw wide." This narrow passage mercifully opened into a perfectly calm and limpid lagoon—as is typical in many ring-shaped atolls — protected from the open sea by massive reefs all around. Here the pilot and his faction hatched one last scheme to rid the vessel of unwanted cargo.[19]

The *San Jerónimo* had come to rest in the interior lagoon of Ujelang Atoll, the westernmost of the Marshall Islands. While the Ujelang lagoon is quite large, about twenty-five square miles, the land area is less than 0.7 miles, consisting mostly of exposed promontories of sand and coral on its rim. Only on the south side was there a more substantial strip of land. "It was flat and fertile," as Martínez described it, "and there were four huts but no people because they live on other islands." The travelers counted about 150 palm trees. Instead of subsisting on moldy hardtack, they would have immediate access there to coconut meat and milk. With some luck, they could find some birds' eggs and catch fish. They also discovered a small pond of fresh water, a godsend as they were running dangerously low.[20]

The pilot ordered almost everyone ashore, saying that the *San Jerónimo* needed repairs. The vessel would have to lie on its side at low tide so the caulkers could scrub the exposed parts of the hull and fix damaged areas.

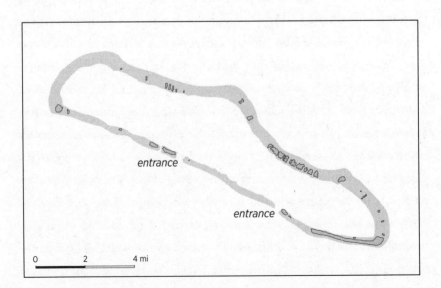

Naturally, the soldiers became suspicious. The allure of getting off the ship, eating some coconuts, and sleeping on the soft sand must have been considerable. Yet the fear of being marooned must have been overwhelming. In the end, there was no choice. Soldiers and sailors alike had to bring down their sea chests and spread out around the palm trees, setting up camp close to relatives and friends. There were three distinct groups: the mutineers, the loyalists, and the vast majority whose allegiance was unknown or uncertain. The mutineers had all the weapons, so they could have sailed away at any moment. This is exactly what Lope Martín's closest military collaborator, Felipe del Campo, proposed. The pilot, however, had a different idea. He needed time to probe the loyalties of all the men at Ujelang. To reach a destination other than the Philippines, Lope Martín would require many sailors and soldiers. Therefore he spent days trying to win over the undecided, promising them all manner of riches. With surprising speed, Lope Martín had made the transition from dead man walking to ringleader of a major transpacific venture. Meanwhile the loyalists were reduced to waiting. "We were troubled men, domesticated and disarmed," Martínez recalled, "and there were secrets passed among these evil men that we didn't know about." A rumor had it that they were going to spend the winter—still nearly six months away!—at Ujelang. Others overheard the pilot saying that "only later, at the Island of the Thieves [Guam], would the selection of the men take place."[21]

According to Martínez, Lope Martín likened his situation to that of Hernán Cortés, giving us some insight into his frame of mind. Forty-seven years earlier, the great conqueror of Mexico had similarly faced a grave moment of decision upon landing on the coast of Veracruz, at the head of a renegade expedition, and on hearing about the fabulous riches of the Aztec Empire. As the pilot himself explained one night at Ujelang, Cortés had delivered a speech to his soldiers, asking them whether they preferred to return to Cuba or proceed inland toward the city of Tenochtitlán. Cortés promised to surrender the ships and some provisions to those who wished to go back while he would continue with the others. According to the pilot's version, the conquistador asked his men to form two camps so there would be "a record" of their choice. Cortés thanked those who had thrown their lot in with him, reiterating his promise to make them rich, and then ordered his ships destroyed, forcing all the others to go inland as well but under a cloud of suspicion. Many lessons can be drawn from this story. Martínez, our soldier-chronicler, to his own mind was merely chiding the mulatto for the hubris of likening himself to the great Cortés. Most of the men probably dwelled on the obvious inference that it was much better to volunteer rather than be forced into the pilot's venture. Some may have found some solace in the thought that even a suicidal plan like Cortés's had ended up well for many of the men involved. Lope Martín himself evidently appreciated Cortés's ingenious method of distinguishing between friend and foe.[22]

Over a period of a few days, the pilot was able to lure some additional men into his camp. To show their acceptance — like an initiation ritual into piracy — they were required to swear before a crucifix and take a consecrated wafer from the chaplain, promising absolute loyalty to the group "beyond king and nationality." Of course, some men could never be brought into the fold. One of them was boatswain Rodrigo del Angle, who had committed the capital offense of offering to replace Lope Martín as pilot of the San Jerónimo during the second mutiny. At Ujelang, Angle felt as though "he was already dragging a rope around his neck." The boatswain sent intermediaries to try to make peace with the pilot but without success. Another man on the outside was Santiago de Garnica, who had served as alguacil del agua, or constable in charge of distributing the water aboard the San Jerónimo. Garnica was widely believed to have kept the late Captain Pericón abreast of the plotters' movements and was therefore beyond redemption. A more surprising late dissenter was Bartolomé de Lara. The feisty sailor had killed the Pericóns with his own hands, thus doing Lope Martín's bidding to the point of serving as his enforcer and executioner. At Ujelang, however, Lara had a falling-out with the pilot and reportedly stayed at the ship, "sulking and weeping like a child after a scolding from his mother." These three men formed a nucleus of resistance that would grow to include a handful of soldiers, a Flemish gunner, the chaplain, and a few others. At great peril, they broached the possibility of seizing the *San Jerónimo*.[23]

The counter-plotters faced long odds. As the soldiers were not permitted aboard the *San Jerónimo,* they would have to swim to it. The only loyalists able to come and go as they pleased were Lara, another sailor named Morales, the Flemish gunner (Juan Enrique Flamenco), and the boatswain Angle, who, in spite of being considered hostile to the mutineers, had legitimate work to do aboard the *San Jerónimo*. These few loyalist crew members would have to overpower the guards posted at the vessel, gain access to the weapons locked in the storeroom, and make them available to their supporters. They also had to overcome one final obstacle. Lope Martín had taken ashore all the compasses and charts as well as the two principal sails (the mainsail and the forward sail). The nautical equipment privately owned by boatswain Angle, the man who would pilot the ship should the plan succeed, had also been removed from the ship. To leave Ujelang and have even the slightest chance of reaching the Philippines, the counter-plotters would thus have to find a way to retrieve the sails and at least some of the instruments. They tried their luck on Wednesday, July 16.[24]

Lara, Morales, the Flemish gunner Juan Enrique, and Angle armed themselves as best they could, took the small boat, and rowed toward the *San Jerónimo*. They entered "with their weapons gleaming and blazing, giving forward and backward strokes." The assailants promptly slashed a mulatto, one of Lope Martín's closest allies, who was guarding the ship. Although wounded, this man "jumped into the water and went to take this bitter news to his friends." The *San Jerónimo* must have been about one hundred yards from the beach, so the assailants had only a moment to look for the firearms. A Galician boy held the keys to the depot where they were kept, "but because he did not find the key fast enough, Rodrigo del Angle gave him a bad cut in the head." The attackers then hurried to bring the weapons onto the deck and distributed them liberally to friends and allies, including some who had been kept in shackles aboard the ship, such as the secretary Juan de Zaldívar, who, like the sailor Lara, had once supported Lope Martín but had subsequently quarreled with him. The coup was over in minutes. With relatively little resistance, the loyalists had taken command of the ship.[25]

On land, confusion prevailed. Lope Martín believed that his supporters aboard the *San Jerónimo,* perhaps drunk and incapacitated for a few hours, would eventually regain control. He was also certain that without sails and navigational instruments, the *San Jerónimo* would be as good as a sitting duck. Many men in the camp nevertheless feared that the *San Jerónimo*'s departure from Ujelang was imminent. Four or five soldiers saw no other recourse but to swim out to the ship. They were running a great risk, as they had made a very public choice and had left all of their possessions behind. Their reception at the other end was uncertain. Their gamble paid off, however. They were immediately welcomed and provided with weapons. Even then, doubts persisted as to the true state of affairs aboard the ship. It was only after the ever feisty Lara came to the side of the *San Jerónimo* and called loudly for Felipe del Campo to come aboard on account of their old friendship that the dramatic shift that had taken place on the vessel became obvious to the men on land. Del Campo replied to Lara that he would "gladly go to the ship to punish him and the other scoundrels that were there."[26]

At last, Lope Martín ordered his followers to swim out to the *San Jerónimo* and retake it, even though it would be nearly impossible, with well-armed soldiers standing guard on the deck who could easily capture those who reached the ship. Perhaps seizing the rowboat would have been easier, but the Flemish gunner was standing on it, preventing anyone from even getting near. As more and more sailors dashed into the water, the boatswain Angle lost his nerve. He cut the two anchor cables and had the few sails available aboard set up. Very slowly, the *San Jerónimo* turned and began to move toward the narrow channel through which it had entered the lagoon. From the beach, the men watched in astonishment. As our soldier-chronicler remarked, they were "leaving behind cruelly and miserably their enemies as well as their friends, guilty and not guilty alike."[27]

Yet the *San Jerónimo* could not go far. Missing the two principal sails and facing light winds and a contrary tidal current (atolls are notoriously tidal), the ship lost momentum well before reaching the channel, was driven back by the strong current, and came to rest somewhat farther away from the encampment than before. Intense negotiations unfolded over the next four days. The terms of a possible agreement were quite straightforward. The people aboard the *San Jerónimo* needed the two sails and some nautical equipment while the people on land—accepting that they could not recapture the *San Jerónimo*—wanted food. During the negotiations, scores of soldiers as well as many sailors were able to reach the galleon. Finally, on July 21 at dawn, the *San Jerónimo* slipped out of the lagoon. Left behind were twenty-seven men, among them the pilot and his closest friends and associates. They were seasoned navigators in possession of firearms, with plenty of food and water, and on an atoll visited from time to time by Micronesians. Tantalizing evidence suggests that they survived.[28]

12

At the Spanish Court

W hile Lope Martín and his men struggled to stay alive, Friar Andrés de Urdaneta spent the last few months of his life wrestling
with the imperial bureaucracy. The friar-mariner had arrived in Acapulco
on October 8, 1565, and promptly made his way to the viceregal capital,
Mexico City, where he was greeted as "something of a miracle." Carrying
ginger, cinnamon, gold dust, jewels, and "some objects of witchcraft and
other good things," Urdaneta and his companions represented the start of
a new era. Mexico was poised to become the meeting point between East
and West, "the heart of the world," as one flattering chronicle put it.[1]

Yet there was little time for celebration. The transpacific pioneers were
bearing important letters from the Philippines as well as petitions for reinforcements and provisions. A ship was prepared immediately for a voyage
to Spain so Urdaneta could report directly to Philip II. There was reason
for the haste. As we have seen, Don Alonso de Arellano, the nobleman
captain of the *San Lucas,* had left for Europe a few days earlier, perhaps
to claim a reward for having discovered the *vuelta* and "usurp the glory
of others," as some feared. Urdaneta would have to neutralize this unex-

pected rival at court. Therefore, around the middle of December 1565, still recovering from the ravages of the voyage across the great ocean, Urdaneta and a few fellow travelers boarded a ship in Veracruz. This Atlantic passage through a well-established route to Sanlúcar de Barrameda in southern Spain at least gave the friar-mariner some time to organize his thoughts.[2]

Yet this reprieve ended abruptly on arrival. In Seville, Urdaneta must have been thoroughly debriefed about the technical details of the *vuelta*. During his stay in Spain, the friar-mariner met such luminaries as Francisco Faleiro, a leading authority on longitude; the *maestro* Pedro de Medina, author of the celebrated *Arte de navegar* (1545); and Alonso de Santa Cruz, the empire's most influential cosmographer of his time. Santa Cruz had tutored Philip II in geography and devoted decades of his life to elaborating an atlas of all the coasts and islands known in the world, a massive work deemed so sensitive that Philip had forbidden its publication.[3]

It should have been a time of scholarly exchange and renewal. Instead, Urdaneta became embroiled in a major controversy. As one of his main goals in Spain had been to advocate on behalf of his former comrades who remained at great peril in the Philippines, the friar-mariner appeared before the Council of the Indies to do so. His petition, however, only succeeded in reviving the decades-old debate over whether the Philippines lay on the Spanish or the Portuguese side of the world. Before the councilors could act on Urdaneta's request for reinforcements, they needed an unequivocal answer to this question. So did the Spanish king. Spending his time in the summer palace at the Bosque de Segovia some forty-seven miles north of Madrid, the never-sleeping Philip II yearned for clarity. "Tell them to gather all the papers and nautical charts [about the Philippines]," a frustrated monarch ordered his councilors. "I believe that I have some of them; the other day I looked in Madrid and, if I have them, they must be there. You, Eraso [secretary Antonio de Eraso], may have some." The search was in vain, however. The mighty empire now spanning the entire world possessed no good maps of the Philippines.[4]

As we have seen, Spain and Portugal had divvied up the world, first
with a meridian line running from pole to pole through the Atlantic—
according to the 1494 Treaty of Tordesillas—and then by extending the
Tordesillas line to the other side of the world. Yet estimating east-west
distance was extraordinarily difficult in the sixteenth century, so no one
knew exactly where to draw the antimeridian line. To avoid a costly war
in the distant Pacific, the two Iberian rivals had thus reached an agreement
in 1529 that held the key to whether Spain could legally occupy the Philippines. As Portugal was already in control of the Spice Islands, the Spanish
negotiators consented to surrendering an additional slice of the world in
exchange for a cash payment. The Treaty of Zaragoza of 1529 thus adjusted the antimeridian, shrinking the Spanish area of exclusive control
and expanding the Portuguese hemisphere to accommodate all Lusitanian
possessions in Asia. From then on, the antimeridian would be drawn seventeen degrees to the east of the Spice Islands (a much easier measurement
than extending the line all the way from the Atlantic). As compensation,
Spain would receive 350,000 ducats. Spanish officials thus began referring
to this slice of the world given up to Portugal as *el empeño,* or the "pawned"
territories"—the assumption being that Spain could always recover such
territories by returning the money. In the meantime, many in Spain won-
dered whether the Philippines were included in the "pawned territories."[5]

When Friar Urdaneta began petitioning for reinforcements for the
Spanish encampment in the Philippines in the fall of 1566, the Spanish
crown had to settle the matter. Philip thus summoned all major cosmographers to Madrid to respond to two disarmingly simple questions: First,
were the Philippines included in the territories "pawned" to Portugal according to the 1529 Treaty of Zaragoza? Second, with regard to the original antimeridian, were the Philippines on the Spanish or the Portuguese
side of the world? Alongside Faleiro, Santa Cruz, and other prominent
cosmographers, Urdaneta gave his considered opinion on October 8, 1566.
His text reveals a man of deep convictions. The friar-mariner dispensed

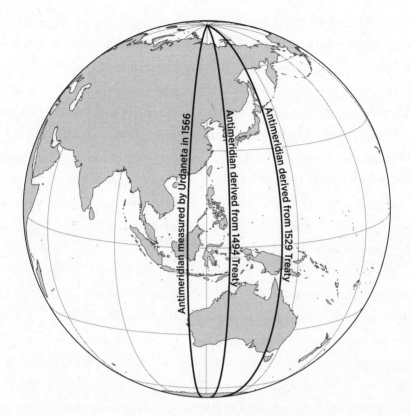

with the first question summarily—almost dismissively. Without a doubt, the Philippines lay on the Portuguese side. "I sailed in that gulf in the year of 1526," the Augustinian elaborated briefly by way of explanation, "and resided there for eight years in the service of His Majesty the Emperor, may God hold him in his glory, and I also went there last year of 1565 from the port of Navidad." No other Spaniard alive could claim as much familiarity with that region. He had seen it with his own eyes.[6]

The second question, about the Philippines in relation to the original antimeridian, was far more difficult to answer. To tackle it, Urdaneta employed two methods. First, with the help of Portuguese charts that had come into his possession, he worked out the length of each passage from the Tordesillas line, around Africa and India, and all the way to the Pacific

Ocean. This method was akin to a land surveyor measuring the boundary of a large property by pacing from one tree to a nearby stream to a large rock farther along the way. Once he had retraced the better-known Portuguese route to the other side of the world, Urdaneta used basic trigonometry to disaggregate north-south and east-west distances for each segment, and finally added the latter until reaching the equivalent of 180 degrees to determine the precise location of the antimeridian. In addition to aggregating the errors of the different segments, this procedure had the further disadvantage of requiring knowledge of Earth's size to establish an equivalence between degrees of longitude and distances, a vexing problem that was far from resolved in Urdaneta's time.[7]

Therefore, the friar-mariner used a second and far more parsimonious approach based on astronomical observations. As we have seen, one of Urdaneta's fellow Augustinians, Friar Martín de Rada, had carried to the Philippines "an instrument of medium size" to derive east-west distances with respect to the Spanish city of Toledo. The details of this instrument and the nature of Rada's calculation are unknown. In theory, it would have been possible to approximate longitude through astronomical means. (Rada could have measured the angle between the Moon and a star in the background to establish an absolute clock of sorts, because it would have been the same time wherever this angle was visible from Earth. Compare it to the local time, and thus calculate east-west distance.) In practice, however, this would have required extremely accurate angular measurements seemingly impossible with the astrolabes, cross-staffs, and other instruments available in the sixteenth century.[8]

Regardless of the difficulties, Urdaneta became convinced that the two methods yielded consistent results. According to the friar-mariner, the antimeridian passed through the island of Borneo, "all of which shows that the Spice Islands are within the demarcation of His Majesty," Urdaneta reported happily, "as well as a small part of Java, the better part of China, and other islands." Spain would thus be able to colonize the Philippines legitimately if the crown could repay Portugal and thus regain the "pawned territories."⁹

Urdaneta's mixed opinion did not please the Spanish monarch. This probably explains why Philip II did not grant an audience to Urdaneta and offered him only a modest stipend for food and lodging during his stay in Spain. The king's displeasure would have been even greater had he known the real answer: the Philippines had *never* been in the Spanish hemisphere according to either the 1494 Treaty of Tordesillas or the 1529 Treaty of Zaragoza. None of this mattered, however. Philip was determined to add his namesake islands to the already unwieldy Spanish Empire. At least this would justify his sending reinforcements for the men stranded in the Philippines.¹⁰

Even while mired in this cosmographical disputation, Urdaneta also must have sought intelligence about his rival Don Alonso de Arellano. Very little is known about the activities of the nobleman captain of the *San Lucas,* who, together with Lope Martín, had beaten the friar-mariner

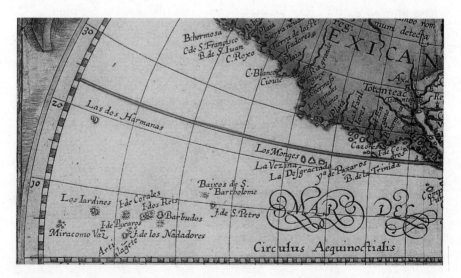

Petrus Plancius's 1594 *Orbis Terrarum* with some of the islands visited by the *San Lucas.*

to the *vuelta*. The Augustinian chronicler Gaspar de San Agustín categorically affirmed that Don Alonso had appeared in court "to request a reward from His Majesty, and a great prize would have been given to him had it not been for Father Andrés de Urdaneta, who arrived just in time to reveal the true version of events." San Agustín was also certain that, after Urdaneta's decisive intervention, Don Alonso had lost all credibility and been thrown into jail, "where he had languished for a long time." No record of any of this exists, however.[11]

On the contrary, scattered information suggests that Don Alonso was able to meet with leading cartographers and nautical experts of that era, all of whom would have been extremely interested in the information the nobleman had to offer. Intriguingly, the trail leads away from Spain and in the direction of Holland and England, upstart empires in the process of challenging the Iberians in the Far East. In 1594 a Dutch-Flemish astronomer and clergyman in Amsterdam named Petrus Plancius published a map of the world which includes some islands that only the *San Lucas* had visited up to that time. Near the lower-left corner of Plancius's *Orbis Terrarum,* one can see the "I. de los Nadadores," or "Island of the Swimmers," a name bestowed by Don Alonso himself because so many locals had swum out to the *San Lucas,* nearly overwhelming it. Plancius's map also features the island of "Miracomo Vaz," or "Watch How You Go," thus called by Lope Martín because, as he had said, "it would be convenient for later navigators passing near there to know." Don Alonso must have approached English mapmakers as well. Richard Hakluyt, the famous writer and booster of English colonization of North America, spent several years collecting nautical information. The 1599 edition of *The Principall Navigations, Voiages, Traffiques and Discoueries of the English Nation* contains a rare and very valuable map, one of the first to use Mercator's novel projection. This map shows the so-called "I. de don Alonço," giving us another clue about the activities of the *San Lucas* captain.[12]

Don Alonso may indeed have fallen out of favor in Spain. To obtain

some compensation for having risked his life crossing the Pacific, the nobleman, evidence indicates, sought out Dutch and English mapmakers.
Ironically, to lure them, Don Alonso may have used the deposition that he,
Lope Martín, and others had given in Mexico City to defend themselves
against the charge of having abandoned the rest of the fleet deliberately,
a testimony that explicitly mentions the "Isla de los Nadadores," "Miracomo Vaz," and others. Spain's loss was Holland's and England's gain. Little else is known about Don Alonso's fate.[13]

As for Urdaneta, he yearned for a simpler life in his Augustinian monastery in Mexico City. After wrestling with the Spanish imperial bureaucracy for nearly a year, he requested permission to return to the Americas.
By the summer of 1567, he was back in his old cell. He may have planned
to continue on to the Philippines "to achieve the spiritual conquest of
their inhabitants," as some sources indicate. Yet his condition "not only
due to his age [fifty-nine years] but also to his continuous and lengthy pil-
grimages through the world" made such a project unfeasible. Urdaneta's
superiors reportedly persuaded him to remain at the monastery, where he
died a year later, on June 3, 1568.[14]

Epilogue

*M*arooned at Ujelang Atoll, Lope Martín and twenty-six of his men remained on the westernmost of the Marshall Islands for an indefinite amount of time. They were all seasoned navigators, well armed and determined to stay alive. Although no Marshallese resided permanently at Ujelang, nearby islanders visited the atoll from time to time. Indeed, a few days before their marooning, on July 21, 1566, the men of the *San Lucas* spotted "three *paraos* with their sails headed for us, and they still came straight at us even though they knew we were there and saw our ship." The pilot's plan had been "to catch them and bring them to where we were, so they would fish for us." They even tried to ambush one of the Marshallese vessels, but it slipped away.[1]

The stranded men also found an abandoned *parao* in a state of near completion in one of the nearby islets of the atoll around the lagoon. It was a substantial vessel, "with space for about thirty men," more than enough to accommodate Lope Martín and his party. As they were all expert seamen and not afraid to venture into the Pacific, it is perfectly plausible that Lope Martín and his men used it to reach another island or even a mainland.[2]

The trail goes almost completely cold after the marooning in late July 1566, except for some indirect but nonetheless suggestive evidence. Two years later, in 1568, another Spanish expedition passed through the Marshall Islands, probably a little to the east of Ujelang Atoll. The fleet commander, Álvaro de Mendaña, as well as his pilot, Hernán Gallego, reported how, on approaching one of the islands, they spotted a vessel leaving in a great hurry. The explorers had dispatched a boat ashore to investigate, but the villagers had deserted the place. Yet the investigating party found "a chisel made of a nail" and a piece of rope. Mendaña and Gallego believed that Lope Martín and his men had been there, "and perhaps thinking that Mendaña had come to punish them, they had fled in that vessel that they had probably built and gone to New Guinea." Exactly why these later explorers thought that the pilot and his comrades had chosen New Guinea as their refuge is unclear.[3]

Another Spanish expedition, this one in 1606, captured a Marshallese man. When the Europeans questioned their prisoner about nearby lands, he intriguingly "pointed to several places on the horizon, counted on his fingers several times, and ended by saying, 'Martín Cortal.'" He may have been alluding to Lope Martín.[4]

More than a century later, a missionary in the Carolines named Juan Antonio Cantova became quite puzzled by the skin color and physiognomy of the locals, some of whom appeared to be "pure Indians," the Jesuit noted, "while there can be no doubt that others are mestizos, born of Spaniards and Indians." As the peoples of the Carolines and Marshalls had very seldom been in contact with Europeans up to that time, Father Cantova surmised that they were descendants of Lope Martín and his men.[5]

If so, Lope Martín may have avoided execution and found a new life in the tiny islands in the middle of the Pacific. Although he may not have achieved his grand design of taking a shipload of spices to Europe, his Pacific life would have been a fitting end for the man who first learned to navigate the largest ocean in the world.

With their voyages, Lope Martín and Andrés de Urdaneta wove together all the major landmasses of the world for the first time in history. Plants, animals, products, and ideas began flowing across the Pacific nearly half a millennium ago, a process that reshaped the world. Yet only one of them has received credit for this great maritime feat. "The first and true discoverer of this navigation and return is Father Andrés de Urdaneta," fellow Augustinian Gaspar de San Agustín proclaimed as early as 1698, "and not Captain Don Alonso de Arellano nor his pilot Lope Martín." The laudatory writings of the Augustinian order over the centuries have cemented this selective interpretation. Modern scholars continue to hold more or less the same view. The famous French historian Pierre Chaunu, for instance, considered Lope Martín's voyage "merely anecdotal" while granting to Urdaneta the honor of "having found the immutable line of fifteen thousand kilometers through water that the galleons would follow until 1815." Others concede that Arellano and Lope Martín may have been the first to return but minimize the significance of their accomplishment. "It is only on the basis of Urdaneta's passage," the Spanish scholars Amancio Landín Carrasco and Luis Sánchez Masiá argue, "that we know with precision the route that would enable the Spanish presence in the Philippines."[6]

Regardless of who deserves more credit, there is no doubt about their monumental accomplishment. A natural barrier that for millions of years had prevented the movement of almost all organisms on Earth finally came down with the *vuelta*. Regular transpacific contact has ushered in far-reaching biological, demographic, economic, political, and cultural changes. Just as Columbus's voyages triggered a transatlantic transfer of plants, animals, germs, goods, and ideas beginning in 1492, Lope Martín and the more immediately storied Urdaneta launched the same process for the lands around the Pacific.

Among other things, the newfound transpacific connection led to a population boom in Asia, driven by the introduction of New World crops, especially sweet potatoes, corn, and peanuts. Today, China is the second-largest producer of corn in the world, after only the United States; China and India are the top two producers of peanuts; and New Guineans obtain more calories per person from sweet potatoes than anyone else in the world. Corn, for example, was domesticated in the Americas at least nine thousand years ago but spread across the Pacific only in the sixteenth century. In China, this New World crop made inroads along the Yangtze and Han River valleys, where rice had been cultivated for millennia. Rice requires flooded fields of arable land, so cornfields sprang up at higher elevations and in drier conditions, where rice cultivation was marginal or impossible, thus extending China's agricultural frontier and transforming what had once been forested hills into cornfields. Roughly speaking, corn produced the same number of calories per hectare as rice, but with far less irrigation and labor. This led to a significant population boom. Although the precise timing and magnitude of this demographic expansion varied from one Asian nation to another, all of them benefited from the incorporation of New World crops. A full accounting of this vast energy transfer from the Americas to Asia has yet to be made, but the preliminary information shows that it was enormous.[7]

Regular transpacific contact also created the first global trading system recognizable to us even today. Economic activities in the Americas came to depend not just on colonial-metropolitan relationships across the Atlantic but on supply and demand around the world—especially in Asia. Excellent examples are the great silver mines of Peru and Mexico, which constituted a mainstay of the economy of the Americas in colonial times and structured life for hundreds of thousands of Native Americans who directly or indirectly, forcibly or not, became a part of the silver economy. Traditionally, this is told as a story of European empires extracting valuable resources from their American colonies. Left unsaid is that the most important end-market customer by far was not Europe but China, where a major tax reform known as "the single lash of the whip" replaced paper money with silver in the sixteenth century. With this tax reform, China instantly became a worldwide magnet for the white metal, absorbing the silver production of neighboring Japan and then turning to the New World mines, which produced upwards of eighty percent of the world's silver between 1500 and 1800. Without China's massive and persistent demand for silver, the mines on the American continent would never have attained the scale they did, nor would their profits have spilled over into other colonial enterprises and affected so many lives throughout the hemisphere. The sixteenth century gave rise to the first truly global economy, in which Asia's relative demographic and economic weight was significant and at times paramount. This feature of our world economy has become familiar to us, as China has continued to demand global resources such as soybeans, copper, and steel, affecting markets all around the world.[8]

By the end of the eighteenth century, British and especially American merchants began building on these earlier transpacific linkages to launch their own ventures. As the Spanish empire in the Americas crumbled in the early nineteenth century, American ships came to replace the old Spanish galleons. The story of the United States' expansion through the Pacific is well known, as the nation took control of Hawai'i, Guam, and the Philippines, opened direct trade with Japan and China, and forged a vast network of transpacific interests. As we live in a world increasingly centered on the Pacific, it is imperative that we understand how we got here. The voyages of Urdaneta and of Lope Martín, the Black pilot who now takes his place in world history, were at the dawn of this transformation.

Note About Dates and Measurements

Today, travelers flying from San Francisco to Tokyo or New York to Beijing notice how their phones and computers add one day after crossing the International Date Line—an imaginary line running through the middle of the Pacific from the Arctic to the Antarctic which marks the change from one calendar day to another. Magellan's crew members were probably the first to notice. When the remnants of that first circumnavigation venture reached the Cape Verde Islands in the middle of the Atlantic and compared the calendar aboard the ship with one kept by the islanders, the survivors realized that they were off by one day. The pioneering voyagers in this book crossed that same imaginary line but, like Magellan's crew, failed to adjust their calendars. From the middle of the Pacific onward, their logbooks and diaries are therefore one day off with respect to ours. I have retained their uncorrected dates because they make more sense as lived experience.

Spanish seamen measured distance in *leguas,* or nautical leagues. To make the experience of sixteenth-century explorers accessible to modern readers, I have chosen to convert this arcane unit into statute miles like those commonly appearing on road signs throughout the United States (and as opposed to modern nautical miles, representing minutes of arc around the sphere of the Earth). This is easier said than done, however. *Leguas* could be equivalent to either three or four Roman miles, or some other length, depending on the context. Columbus once helpfully noted that pilots generally used the four-mile Roman league to measure distances at sea. I thus assume that one *legua* is equivalent to 3.67 miles. This may not hold in every case, but it gives us a rough sense of scale. Converting sixteenth-century Spanish *leguas* into modern miles is convenient. Yet the question remains: How accurate were their sixteenth-century measurements? At that time, no one knew Earth's actual size. Lope Martín and Andrés de Urdaneta assumed that each degree of Earth's circumference measured 17.5 *leguas*. This would make Earth's circumference 23,121 miles, somewhat smaller but relatively close to the real value of 24,901 miles.

Acknowledgments

The intellectual debts that I have incurred while writing this book are considerable and too many to list here. The endnotes give a good idea, but I still need to single out a few individuals. Joaquim Alves Gaspar at the Universidade de Lisboa fielded some of my initial questions about charts, latitudes, and longitudes and graciously read chapters and offered detailed comments and suggestions. Ryan Crewe provided many bibliographic leads and sound advice. Alison D. Sandman saved me from embarrassing errors. Ricardo Padrón shared some of his vast cartographic knowledge with me. Omaira Brunal-Perry at the Richard F. Taitano Micronesian Area Research Center, University of Guam, was immensely helpful. A. Katie Stirling-Harris, my Iberianist colleague at the University of California, Davis, kindly inquired on my behalf and conveyed a wealth of bibliographic leads from Pedro Pinto and Bill M. Donovan. A number of friends and colleagues read portions (or the entirety) of the manuscript, including Ari Kelman, Eva Mehl, Jaana Remes, and Chuck Walker. I am very grateful to Susan Rabiner, my literary agent, and Deanne Urmy, my editor at Houghton Mifflin Harcourt, for their excellent advice and unflagging support. Over the years, I have presented chapters and various materials from this book in conferences, symposia, invited talks, archival visits, casual hallway encounters, coffees, and just querying colleagues in person or by e-mail. In particular, I thank the participants of the UC Davis History Writing Seminar in the winter of 2018 and the members of the Latin American History Workshop in the winter of 2019. My wife, Jaana Remes, our children, Samuel and Vera, my mother, María Teresa Fuentes, my brother Mauricio and his fiancée, Vania, my *primos* and *tíos* in Mexico, my family in Finland, and several friends—including the Colmecas, the Broken Tiller Crew, the Spice Cadets, the UWCers, and others—have sustained me over the years. I cannot thank them enough.

Notes

Preface

1. The total area of Earth's landmasses is 148,434,000 sq. km, while that of the Pacific Ocean is 161,760,000 sq. km. The volume of water contained in all oceans is 1,335,000,000 km³, while the volume of water in the Pacific Ocean is 660,000,000 km³, or 49.4 percent. All of these figures and the boundaries of the different oceans used to calculate surfaces and volumes come from the National Oceanic and Atmospheric Administration (NOAA), http://www.ngdc.noaa.gov/mgg/global/etopo1_ocean_volumes.html. The swimming comparison assumes a speed of two miles per hour. For the unfortunate angler, see Jonathan Franklin, *438 Days: An Extraordinary True Story of Survival at Sea* (New York: Atria Books, 2015), passim. For the experiment with the buoys, see Alan Dotson et al., *A Simulation of the Movements of Fields of Drifting Buoys in the North Pacific Ocean* (Honolulu: Hawai'i Institute of Geophysics, 1977), 12.

2. Erasmus Darwin, *The Botanic Garden* (New York: T. & J. Swords, 1798), 1.1.73–79.

3. The quote is from George Howard Darwin, "On the Precession of a Viscous Spheroid, and on the Remote History of the Earth," *Philosophical Transactions of the Royal Society of London* 170 (1879): 535–36. For an excellent discussion of the development of Darwin's ideas, see Stephen G. Brush, "Early History of Selenology," in *Origin of the Moon,* ed. William K. Hartmann, Roger J. Phillips, and G. Jeffrey Taylor (Kona, HI: Lunar and Planetary Institute, 1986), 2–15.

4. The quote is from Osmond Fisher, "On the Physical Cause of the Ocean Basins," *Nature* (January 12, 1882): 243–44. On the continuing popularity of the Darwin-Fisher theory about the origin of the Moon, see Alfred T. DeLury,

"Sir George Howard Darwin," *Journal of the Royal Astronomical Society of Canada* 7 (1913): 114–19. Present-day astronomy textbooks still make it a point to criticize this theory, once so widely accepted. See H. Karttunen et al., eds., *Fundamental Astronomy* (New York: Springer, 2009), 195.

5. The quote comes from a letter that Wegener wrote in 1910 to Else Köppen, in David M. Lawrence, *Upheaval from the Abyss: Ocean Floor Mapping and the Earth Science Revolution* (New Brunswick, NJ: Rutgers University Press, 2002), 34.

6. The quote is from Alfred Wegener, *The Origin of Continents and Oceans* (New York: Dover Publications, 1966), 75.

7. The quotes appear in Lawrence, *Upheaval from the Abyss,* 51 and 58–59.

8. See D. G. van der Meer et al., "Intra-Panthalassa Ocean Subduction Zones Revealed by Fossil Arcs and Mantle Structure," *Nature Geoscience* 5, no. 2 (February 26, 2012): 215–19.

9. True dinosaurs emerged some 230–240 million years ago, a time when the lands of the world were still relatively close together. For a popular treatment, see Steve Brusatte, *The Rise and Fall of the Dinosaurs: A New History of a Lost World* (New York: William Morrow, 2018), 34–35. For the original paper advancing the theory that an asteroid killed the dinosaurs, see Luis W. Alvarez et al., "Extraterrestrial Cause for the Cretaceous-Tertiary Extinction," *Nature* 208, no. 4448 (June 6, 1980): 1095–1108. For the likely site of the impact, see Alan R. Hildebrand et al., "Chicxulub Crater: A Possible Cretaceous/Tertiary Boundary Impact Crater on the Yucatán Peninsula, Mexico," *Geology* 19 (September 1991): 867–71. For the most complete and accessible account of this remarkable discovery written by one of the protagonists, see Walter Alvarez, *T. Rex and the Crater of Doom* (Princeton: Princeton University Press, 1997).

10. The quote is from Alvarez, *T. Rex and the Crater of Doom,* 14. My description is based entirely on his reconstruction of events. More recently, some scientists have posited that massive volcanic eruptions in what is today India—the so-called Deccan Traps—may have contributed significantly to the mega-death. The debate rages as of this writing. See Paul Voosen, "Did Volcanic Eruptions Help Kill Off the Dinosaurs?," *Science,* February 21, 2019.

11. Elizabeth Kolbert, *The Sixth Extinction: An Unnatural History* (New York: Henry Holt, 2014), 72–76 and 86–87; Nicholas R. Longrich, Bhart-Anjan S. Bhullar, and Jacques A. Gauthier, "Mass Extinction of Lizards and Snakes at the Cretaceous-Paleogene Boundary," *Proceedings of the National Academy of Science* 109, no. 52 (December 26, 2012): 21396–401; Nicholas R. Longrich, Tim Tokaryk, and Daniel J. Field, "Mass Extinction of Birds at the Cretaceous-Paleogene (K-Pg) Boundary," *Proceedings of the National Academy of Science* 108, no. 37 (September

13, 2011): 15253–57; Kenneth D. Rose, *The Beginning of the Age of Mammals* (Baltimore: Johns Hopkins University Press, 2006), 4–5.

12. Even though ferns are primitive in the sense that they do not produce flowers like the more evolved land plants, they are nonetheless able to reproduce even when conditions are adverse. Not only are ferns not dependent on a delicate cycle involving pollen, pistils, insects, birds, and so on (all of which were surely disrupted by the impact), but also they have the additional advantage of being able to propagate via spores that form on the underside of their leaves in great quantity and are protected by a strong case, or via their modified stems, called rhizomes, which grow above or below the soil surface. New ferns will grow even from a small piece of rhizome. Not surprisingly, many fern species endured. Ferns are characterized by a bi-generational life cycle, although the details of this cycle vary by species. For the case of mammals, see the introduction to Kenneth D. Rose, *The Beginning of the Age of Mammals* (Baltimore: Johns Hopkins University Press, 2006). Only one cactus was found outside the Americas in ancient times: a spindly species known as mistletoe cactus or *Rhipsalis baccifera*. Originally from tropical America (possibly southern Brazil), *R. baccifera* spread before the Age of Discovery to sub-Saharan Africa, Madagascar, and Sri Lanka. Birds that ate the seed and flew over the Atlantic Ocean likely dispersed it. Other than this very exceptional case, cacti have been (and for the most part remain) New World plants. Edward F. Anderson, *The Cactus Family* (Portland: Timber Press, 2001), 18; J. Hugo Cota-Sánchez and Márcia C. Bomfim-Patrício, "Seed Morphology, Polyploidy and the Evolutionary History of the Epiphytic Cactus *Rhipsalis Baccifera* (Cactaceae)," *Polibotánica* 29 (March 2010): 109.

13. The quote is from Alfred Russel Wallace, *The Geographical Distribution of Animals,* 2 vols. (New York: Harper & Brothers, 1876), 1:14. To be sure, strong-flying birds did not need rafts, and neither did some species like tortoises that simply floated across the ocean while keeping their heads above the water and endured without food or water for up to six months. See Minh Le et al., "A Molecular Phylogeny of Tortoises (Testudines: Testudinidae) Based on Mitochondrial and Nuclear Genes," *Molecular Phylogenetics and Evolution* 40, no. 2 (2006): 517–31.

14. The phrase describing the condition of South America comes from George Gaylord Simpson, *Splendid Isolation: The Curious History of South American Mammals* (New Haven: Yale University Press, 1980), passim. North America became a separate continent about fifty-five million years ago. Nevertheless, because of its proximity to Siberia, the formation of occasional land bridges through Beringia, and the existence of Greenland as a stepping-stone, North America is not a good place to learn about the crossability of the Atlantic Ocean. South America is a

much better gauge. For a useful summary of the African origin of caviomorph rodents and primates, see John J. Flynn, André R. Wyss, and Reynaldo Charrier, "South America's Missing Mammals," *Scientific American* 296 (May 2007): 68–75. On caviomorph rodents, see Céline Poux et al., "Arrival and Diversification of Caviomorph Rodents and Platyrrhine Primates in South America," *Systems Biology* 55, no. 2 (2006): 228–44; Pierre-Olivier Antoine et al., "Middle Eocene Rodents from Peruvian Amazonia Reveal the Pattern and Timing of Caviomorph Origins and Biogeography," *Proceedings of the Royal Society* 1732 (2011): 1319–26. On the oceanic dispersal of primates, see among the sources just cited Flynn, Wyss, and Charrier, "South America's Missing Mammals," 72–73; and Poux et al., "Arrival and Diversification of Caviomorph Rodents and Platyrrhine Primates in South America," 240–41.

15. Geckos and skinks crossed the Atlantic not once but multiple times. No fewer than three different gecko lineages are believed to have crossed the Atlantic on rafts. The details of these momentous journeys will never be known. Nevertheless, their African background coupled with their presence in South America ten, twenty, or thirty million years ago leave little doubt about their movements. Skinks also crossed the Atlantic Ocean several times, and their journeys provide some additional information. Biologists have established that one genus of skink known as *Mabuya* made two separate Atlantic crossings: one to the archipelago of Fernando de Noronha, which lies 225 miles off the coast of Brazil, and another one to the continent. Fernando de Noronha is right on the path of the South Equatorial Current, leading from the Gulf of Guinea to South America, precisely the place where one would expect an errant raft launched from Africa to make landfall. T. Gamble et al., "Coming to America: Multiple Origins of New World Geckos," *Journal of Evolutionary Biology* 24, no. 2 (2010): 231–44; S. Carranza, E. N. Arnold, J. A. Mateo, and L. F. López-Jurado, "Long-Distance Colonization and Radiation in Gekkonid Lizards, *Tarentola* (Reptilia: Gekkonidae), Revealed by Mitochondrial DNA Sequences," *Proceedings of the Royal Society* 267 (2000): 637–49; S. Carranza and E. N. Arnold, "Investigating the Origin of Transoceanic Distributions: MtDNA Shows *Mabuya* Lizards (Reptilia, Scincidae) Crossed the Atlantic Twice," *Systematics and Biodiversity* 1, no. 2 (August 2003): 275–78. See also Emma C. Teeling et al., "A Molecular Phylogeny for Bats Illuminates Biogeography and the Fossil Record," *Science* 307, no. 5709 (January 2005): 583; Le et al., "A Molecular Phylogeny of Tortoises (Testudines: Testudinidae) Based on Mitochondrial and Nuclear Genes"; Nicolas Vidal et al., "Blindsnake Evolutionary Tree Reveals Long History on Gondwana," *Biology Letters* 6, no. 4 (March 2010): 558–61; and Gerald Mayr, Herculano Alvarenga, and Cécil Mourer-Chau-

viré, "Out of Africa: Fossils Shed Light on the Origin of the Hoatzin, an Iconic Neotropic Bird," *Naturwissenschaften* 98, no. 11 (October 2011): 961–66.

16. One hypothesis is that a gecko lineage (the ancestor of *Tarentola*) may have crossed the Atlantic from west to east. Gamble et al., "Coming to America," 238. It is just one among several possibilities, however.

17. See Isabel Sanmartín and Fredrik Ronquist, "Southern Hemisphere Biogeography Inferred by Event-Based Models: Plant Versus Animal Patterns," *System Biology* 53 (2004): 216–43. These authors present a very complex picture in which the breakup of the continents as well as later dispersals played a role in shaping biogeographic patterns. Still, the dispersal episodes they discuss occurred along the South America–Antarctica–Australia corridor rather than through the open ocean. See also Maria A. Nilsson et al., "Tracking Marsupial Evolution Using Archaic Genomic Retroposon Insertions," *PLoS Biology* 8, no. 7 (July 2010): 1–9.

18. Brice P. Noonan and Jack W. Sites Jr., "Tracing the Origins of Iguanid Lizards and Boine Snakes of the Pacific," *American Naturalist* 175 (January 2010): 65; John R. H. Gibbons, "The Biogeography of *Brachylophus* (Iguanidae) Including the Description of a New Species, *B. vitiensis,* from Fiji," *Journal of Herpetology* 15, no. 3 (July 1981): 255–73.

19. Gibbons, "The Biogeography of *Brachylophus* (Iguanidae) Including the Description of a New Species, *B. vitiensis,* from Fiji," 270 and 273. Still, there is at least one competing explanation for the presence of *Brachylophus* in the South Pacific Islands involving an overland dispersal from the New World through either Australia (by way of Antarctica) or Asia (via the Bering Strait), followed by island-hopping along a Melanesian land bridge to Fiji and Tonga. The main problem with this explanation is that *Brachylophus,* or remains of *Brachylophus,* have not been found in Australia or Asia. Nevertheless, it is possible that humans hunted them into extinction in these regions, and some paleontological specimens might still turn up. See Noonan and Sites, "Tracing the Origins of Iguanid Lizards and Boine Snakes of the Pacific," 61–72.

20. Scholars subscribe to different models for the colonization of Polynesia, and many details about population movements across the Pacific and timing remain uncertain. Parsing the different models is beyond the scope of this contextual introduction. I base this broad outline on Peter Bellwood, *First Migrants: Ancient Migration in Global Perspective* (Chichester: Wiley Blackwell, 2013), 191–205; Patrick Vinton Kirch, *On the Road of the Winds: An Archaeological History of the Pacific Islands Before European Contact* (Berkeley: University of California Press, 2000), passim; and recent updating of radiocarbon dates. See especially Janet M. Wilmshurst et al., "High-Precision Radiocarbon Dating Shows Recent and

Rapid Initial Human Colonization of East Polynesia," *Proceedings of the National Academy of Sciences of the United States of America* 108, no. 5 (February 2011): 1815–20. See also Patrick Kirch, "When Did the Polynesians Settle Hawai'i? A Review of 150 Years of Scholarly Inquiry and a Tentative Answer," *Hawaiian Archaeology* 12 (2011): 3–26. For the case of the Marianas, see Mike T. Carson, *First Settlement of Remote Oceania: Earliest Sites in the Mariana Islands* (New York: Springer, 2011), 1–7 and 69–76. The earliest settlers of the Marianas took rice but not pigs or any other animals, a curious exception to the more general pattern of relying on tropical plants and pigs.

21. Bellwood, *First Migrants,* 191–97; Vicki A. Thomson et al., "Using Ancient DNA to Study the Origins and Dispersal of Ancestral Polynesian Chickens Across the Pacific," *Proceedings of the National Academy of Science* 111, no. 13 (April 1, 2014): 4826–31. Recent genetic work supports Bellwood's initial model linking Taiwan and the Philippines with the Lapita settlers in places like Vanuatu and Tonga. See Pontus Skoglund et al., "Genomic Insights into the Peopling of the Southwest Pacific," *Nature* 538 (October 2016): 510–13.

22. For exciting recent genetic evidence, see Alexander G. Ioannidis et al., "Native American Gene Flow into Polynesia Predating Easter Island Settlement," *Nature,* July 8, 2020. From this study, it is not possible to tell whether Native Americans traveled to these islands or, alternatively, Polynesians reached the coast of South America and then traveled back with Native Americans or Native American DNA. On sweet potatoes, see Jon Hather and P. V. Kirch, "Prehistoric Sweet Potato (*Ipomoea batatas*) from Mangaia Island, Central Polynesia," *Antiquity* 65 (December 1991): 887–93. Scholars have considered the Pacific golden plover a possible carrier. See the discussion in Richard Scaglion and María-Auxiliadora Cordero, "Did Ancient Polynesians Reach the New World? Evaluating the Evidence from the Ecuadorian Gulf of Guayaquil," in *Polynesians in America,* ed. Terry L. Jones et al. (Lanham, MD: Altamira Press, 2011), 174–75. See also D. E. Yen, *The Sweet Potato and Oceania: An Essay in Ethnobotany* (Honolulu: Bishop Museum Press, 1974), 331–40; R. C. Green, "Sweet Potato Transfers in Polynesian Prehistory," in *The Sweet Potato in Oceania: A Reappraisal,* ed. Chris Ballard et al. (Rosebery, NSW: Centatime, 2005), 43–62; D. E. Yen, "Subsistence to Commerce in Pacific Agriculture: Some Four Thousand Years of Plant Exchange," in *Plants for Food and Medicine,* ed. N. L. Etkin, D. R. Harris, and P. J. Houghton (London: Royal Botanic Gardens Press, 1998), 169–70; Caroline Roullier et al., "Historical Collections Reveal Patterns of Diffusion of Sweet Potato in Oceania Obscured by Modern Plant Movements and Recombination," *Proceedings of the National Academy of Science* 110, no. 6 (February 5, 2013): 2205–10; and Monica Tromp and John

V. Dudgeon, "Differentiating Dietary and Non-dietary Microfossils Extracted from Human Dental Calculus: The Importance of Sweet Potato to Ancient Diet on Rapa Nui," *Journal of Archaeological Science* 54 (February 2015): 54–63. A more recent study clarifies the origins of the sweet potato and posits a long-distance dispersal in pre-human times; see Pablo Muñoz-Rodríguez et al., "Reconciling Conflicting Phylogenies in the Origin of Sweet Potato and Dispersal to Polynesia," *Current Biology* 28, no. 8 (April 2018): 1246–56. This last conclusion, however, is based on only one sample. On coconuts, see H. C. Harries, "Dissemination and Classification of *Cocos nucifera*," *Botanical Review* 44, no. 3 (September 1978): 265–319; and Luc Baudoin, Bee F. Gunn, and Kenneth M. Olsen, "The Presence of Coconut in Southern Panama in Pre-Columbian Times: Clearing Up the Confusion," *Annals of Botany* 113, no. 1 (November 2013): 1–5. The case of chickens is more controversial. See Alice A. Storey et al., "Radiocarbon and DNA Evidence for a Pre-Columbian Introduction of Polynesian Chickens to Chile," *Proceedings of the National Academy of Science* 104, no. 25 (June 19, 2007): 10335–39. Although some doubts were raised early on, the authors have addressed them in Alice A. Storey, Daniel Quiróz, and Elizabeth A. Matisoo-Smith, "A Reappraisal of the Evidence for Pre-Columbian Introduction of Chickens to the Americas," in Jones et al., *Polynesians in America,* 139–70. But the results are still not without challenges. See Thomson et al., "Using Ancient DNA to Study the Origins and Dispersal of Ancestral Polynesian Chickens Across the Pacific," 4826–31.

23. For a good introduction, see Ben Finney, "Nautical Cartography and Traditional Navigation in Oceania," in *The History of Cartography,* 3 vols. (Chicago: University of Chicago Press, 1998), 2:443–92; and Ben Finney and Sam Low, "Navigation," in *Vaka Moana, Voyages of the Ancestors: The Discovery and Settlement of the Pacific,* ed. K. R. Howe (Honolulu: University of Hawai'i Press, 2006), 156–96.

24. Paul Rainbird, *The Archaeology of Micronesia* (New York: Cambridge University Press, 2004), 52–62. David Abulafia's expansive treatment of the oceans came too late for the writing of this book. But I wholeheartedly agree with him that it is crucial to document the role of non-Europeans in the early history of the oceans without denying the transformative effect of Europeans in the fifteenth and sixteenth centuries. David Abulafia, *The Boundless Sea: A Human History of the Oceans* (New York: Oxford University Press, 2019), passim.

1. A Global Race

1. On this massive insurrection, see Carlos Sempat Assadourian, *Zacatecas: Conquista y transformación de la frontera en el siglo XVI; Minas de plata, guerra, y evangelización*

(Mexico City: El Colegio de México, 2008); Ida Altman, *The War for Mexico's West: Indians and Spaniards in New Galicia, 1524–1550* (Albuquerque: University of New Mexico Press, 2010), chap. 5; and Alberto Carrillo Cázares, ed., *El debate sobre la Guerra Chichimeca, 1531–1585,* 2 vols. (Zamora: El Colegio de Michoacán, 2000), passim. Navidad had served as the starting port for coastal and transpacific attempts to reach Asia in 1542. Its northerly location made sense for the coastal expedition led by Juan Rodríguez de Cabrillo. See Richard Flint and Shirley Cushing Flint, *A Most Splendid Company: The Coronado Expedition in Global Perspective* (Albuquerque: University of New Mexico Press, 2019), 87–89. Starting from Navidad, however, made far less sense for a purely transpacific expedition.

2. On the long preparations at Navidad, see especially Luis Muro, "La expedición Legazpi-Urdaneta a las Filipinas: Organización, 1557–1564," in *Historia y sociedad en el mundo de habla española,* ed. Bernardo García Martínez et al. (Mexico City: El Colegio de México, 1970), 141–216; and above all the primary sources transcribed in José Ignacio Rubio Mañé, "La expedición de Miguel López de Legazpi a Filipinas," *Boletín del Archivo General de la Nación* (Mexico City), 2nd ser., 5, nos. 3–4 (1964): 755–98.

3. On the tonnage of the ships of discovery, see the discussion in María del Cármen Mena, *Sevilla y las flotas de Indias: La Gran Armada de Castilla del Oro (1513–1514)* (Seville: Universidad de Sevilla, 1998), 241–46.

4. On Lope Martín's life story, as well as that of Friar Andrés de Urdaneta, see the chapters that follow. For the preparations, see especially Muro, "La expedición Legazpi-Urdaneta a las Filipinas," 189–96.

5. The quote is from "Traslado de la Capitulación de Tordesillas," Arévalo, June 7, 1494, in *Colección general de documentos relativos a las Islas Filipinas existentes en el Archivo de Indias de Sevilla,* 5 vols. (Barcelona: Compañía General de Tabacos de Filipinas, 1918), vol. 1, document 6, emphasis added. For the negotiations after Columbus's return, see Antonio Rumeu de Armas, *El Tratado de Tordesillas: Rivalidad hispano-lusa por el dominio de océanos y continentes* (Madrid: MAPFRE, 1992), 99–150. Columbus himself was probably the first to suggest dividing the Atlantic between the two powers, a conclusion that arises from a letter sent by the Catholic monarchs to Columbus dated September 5, 1493, stating that "la raya que vos dijistes que debía venir en la bula del papa." See quote and analysis in Rumeu de Armas, *El Tratado de Tordesillas,* 116. See also Luís Adão da Fonseca and Cristina Cunha, *O Tratado de Tordesilhas e a diplomacia Luso-Castelhana no século XV* (Lisbon: Inapa, 1991), passim; Alfonso García-Gallo de Diego, "Las bulas de Alejandro VI y el ordenamiento jurídico de la expansión portuguesa y castellana en Africa e Indias," *Anuario de Historia del Derecho Español* 27–28 (1957): 461–830; István Szászdi

León-Borja, "Las paces de Tordesillas en peligro: Los refugiados portugueses y el dilema de la guerra," in *Las relaciones entre Portugal y Castilla en la época de los descubrimientos y la expansión colonial,* ed. Ana María Carabias Torres (Salamanca: Universidad de Salamanca, 1996), 117–32; and Antonio Sánchez Martínez, "De la 'cartografía oficial' a la 'cartografía jurídica': La querella de las Molucas reconsiderada, 1479–1529," *Nuevo Mundo* online, 2009, https://journals.openedition.org/nuevomundo/56899, among others.

6. After the War of the Castilian Succession (1475–1479)—in which Portugal backed a rival of Isabella to the throne of Castile and lost—the two Iberian neighbors were eager to let bygones be bygones, guarantee the security of their unpopulated border region in Iberia, and instead channel their energies into the realm of exploration. For instance, according to the Treaty of Alcáçovas (1479), Spain secured possession of the Canary Islands—an excellent base for further exploration on the coast of Africa—while Portugal retained Madeira, the Azores, and Cape Verde, and cunningly negotiated the exclusive right of exploring and colonizing other lands of the Atlantic Ocean south of the Canary Islands. This set the stage for the ensuing competition not only in the Atlantic but also beyond. For one thing, the Treaty of Tordesillas of 1494 drew a meridian line down the middle of the Atlantic but did not address the crucial issue that a similar line on the other side of the world would need to be drawn as well. For a broad context, see Felipe Fernández-Armesto, *Pathfinders: A Global History of Exploration* (New York: Norton, 2006), 196–97.

7. As Juan Gil has noted about Portugal and Spain: "The history of these two nations, so similar and so distinct, so amicable and so rivalrous at the same time, is the result of their common actions." Juan Gil, *El exilio portugués en Sevilla: De los Braganza a Magallanes* (Seville: Fundación Cajasol, 2009), 8. On Portugal's population, see the discussion in Alain Milhou, "América frente a los sueños orientales (1492–principios del siglo XVV)," in *España y América en una perspectiva humanista: Homenaje a Marcel Bataillon,* ed. Joseph Pérez (Madrid: Casa de Velázquez, 1998), 146–47; and Charles Ralph Boxer, *The Portuguese Seaborne Empire, 1415–1825* (Harmondsworth: Penguin Books, 1969), 4–5. For the larger context, see Bailey W. Diffie and George D. Winius, *Foundations of the Portuguese Empire, 1515–1580* (Minneapolis: University of Minnesota Press, 1977), 195–219; and Daviken Studnicki-Gizbert, *A Nation upon the Ocean Sea: Portugal's Atlantic Diaspora and the Crisis of the Spanish Empire, 1492–1640* (London: Oxford University Press, 2007), 17–39. For a slightly higher estimate, see Sanjay Subrahmanyam, "Holding the World in Balance: The Connected Histories of the Iberian Overseas Empire, 1500–1640," *American Historical Review* 112, no. 5 (December 2007): 1366. I thank Ryan Crewe

for his sound bibliographic suggestions. In emphasizing Portugal's initial maritime prowess, I do not mean to imply that Spain did not develop it as well in the
course of the sixteenth century, as will become obvious later on. For a discussion of this, see Brian Patrick Jones, "Making the Ocean: Global Space, Sailor
Practice, and Bureaucratic Archives in the Sixteenth-Century Spanish Maritime
Empire" (PhD diss., University of Texas at Austin, 2014).

8. Demographic numbers for Spain in the fifteenth and sixteenth centuries are
   somewhat speculative. In addition to Subrahmanyam, "Holding the World in
   Balance," see Fernand Braudel, *The Mediterranean and the Mediterranean World in
   the Age of Philip II,* 2 vols. (New York: Harper & Row, 1966), 1:394–95; and more
   recently J. H. Elliott West, *Empires of the Atlantic World: Britain and Spain in America, 1492–1830* (New Haven: Yale University Press, 2006), 53. The difference in
   maritime orientation between Portugal and Spain is one of degree, of course.
   As mentioned, some Spanish kingdoms had explored the Atlantic, particularly
   Andalusia, the Basque Country, the peoples of Mallorca and Barcelona, and even
   Castilians. There is no question, however, as reflected in the Treaty of Alcáçovas,
   that by the late fifteenth century, Portugal's policies of expansion were far more
   oriented toward the ocean. See Rumeu de Armas, *El Tratado de Tordesillas,* 14–85.

9. The quotes are from Bartolomé de las Casas, *Historia de las Indias,* 3 vols. (Mexico City: Fondo de Cultura Económica, 1986), 1:34–35. Columbus's early years
   remain murky. For instance, there are discrepancies about the date when he first
   arrived in Portugal. The documentation places Columbus in Savona and Genoa
   in the early 1470s. He still appears before a notary with his mother and brother
   in Savona on August 7, 1473. After that, the paper trail in Italy disappears, so his
   relocation to Portugal is possible at any date after the summer of 1473. At the
   other end, his arrival in Portugal must have occurred no later than May 1476. For
   the documents in Savona and Genoa, see Juan Pérez de Tudela, ed., *Colección documental del descubrimiento (1470–1506),* 3 vols. (Madrid: Editorial MAPFRE, 1994),
   1:1–13. On Columbus's years in Portugal, see especially Samuel Eliot Morison,
   Admiral of the Ocean Sea: A Life of Christopher Columbus (Boston: Little, Brown and
   Company, 1942), 35–39; and Diffie and Winius, *Foundations of the Portuguese Empire,* 167. See also Francisco de Freitas Branco, "Cristóvão Colombo em Portugal,
   na Madeira, no Porto Santo," *Ibero-Amerikanisches Archiv* 12, no. 1 (1986): 28.

10. The quote is from Andrés Bernáldez, *Historia de los Reyes Católicos Don Fernando
    y Doña Isabel* (Seville: Imprenta de José María Geofrin, 1870), 357. Bernáldez
    met Columbus in Seville and offered him lodging in his house. On the Italian
    community in Portugal, see Carmen M. Radulet, "A política de D. João II e a
    comunidade italiana em Portugal," in *D. João II: O mar e o universalismo lusíada*

(Lisbon: Instituto Hidrográfico, 2000), 65–69; Diffie and Winius, *Foundations of the Portuguese Empire*, 167; and Morison, *Admiral of the Ocean Sea*, 35–37. On mapmaking and the Columbus brothers, see George E. Nunn, "The Three Maplets Attributed to Bartholomew Columbus," *Imago Mundi* 9, no. 1 (1952): 12–14. By "Italian," I mean a community coming from the Italian peninsula, as there was no Italian nation in the fifteenth century.

11. Jerónimo Münzer, *Viaje por España y Portugal* (Madrid: Ediciones Polifemo, 1991), 177. Münzer visited Lisbon in 1494. See also Damião de Góis, *Elogio da cidade de Lisboa* (Lisbon: Lisboa Guimarães Editores, 2002), 145–53. Some authors have identified that large painting in the castle as Fra Mauro's world map. See Roger Crowley, *Conquerors: How Portugal Forged the First Global Empire* (New York: Random House, 2015), 15–16. Although plausible, such an association is far from certain.

12. Some of the shipyards were run by a royal agency called the Armazéns (warehouse or depot) da Guiné e Índia, related to the Casa da Guiné e Índia but somewhat autonomous. In spite of its pedestrian-sounding name, the Armazéns officials were charged with nothing less than organizing and outfitting the royal fleets. The great Lisbon Earthquake of 1755 destroyed the archives of the Armazéns, thus depriving us of much information about their day-to-day activities. See Leonor Freire Costa, "Carpinteiros e calafates da Ribeira das Naus: Um olhar sobre Lisboa de quinhentos," *Penélope* 12 (1994): 37–54; and Leonor Freire Costa, *Naus e galeões na ribeira de Lisboa: A construção naval no século XVI para a Rota do Cabo* (Cascais: Patrimonia, 1997), 264–70.

13. On Columbus's marriage to Felipa, see las Casas, *Historia de las Indias*, 1:35–36; and Ferdinand Columbus, *The Life of the Admiral Christopher Columbus by His Son, Ferdinand*, trans. and annotated by Benjamin Keen (New Brunswick, NJ: Rutgers University Press, 1959), 14. The quote comes from the latter source. See also Morison, *Admiral of the Ocean Sea*, 37–38.

14. These quotes are marginal annotations or postils that Columbus made on a copy of Pierre d'Ailly's *Ymago mundi* (1410). See Consuelo Varela and Juan Gil, eds., *Cristóbal Colón: textos y documentos completos* (Madrid: Alianza Editores, 1982), 90. Columbus's 1478–79 voyage to Madeira is well documented and can be dated with certainty because he was unable to purchase the quantity of sugar agreed to in the contract, so he had to appear in person in a court in Genoa on August 25, 1479. See the court document in Pérez de Tudela, *Colección documental del descubrimiento*, 1:34–41. Columbus's trip to the coast of Ghana is documented in his postils. See also Morison, *Admiral of the Ocean Sea*, 36–37.

15. The quote is from Gomes Eanes de Azurara, *Crónica do descobrimento e conquista da Guiné* (Lisbon: Publicações Europa-América, 1981), 59. See also C. R. Boxer,

The Portuguese Seaborne Empire, 1415–1825, 26. Some authors contend that Cape Bojador was where Cape Juby is now, but its exact location remains uncertain. Strictly speaking, the term "gyre" is used in oceanography to refer to currents. As far as sailing is concerned, however, the winds propelling the currents matter even more. In this book I thus use the term "gyre" to refer to both the winds and the currents.

16. There is precious little research into the Portuguese discovery of the Atlantic gyres. Some of the sources include Avelino Teixeira da Mota, *A evolução da ciência náutica durante os séculos XV e XVI na cartografia portuguesa da época* (Lisbon: Junta de Investigações Científicas do Ultramar, 1961), 7; and [Carlos Viegas] Gago Coutinho, *A náutica dos descobrimentos*, 2 vols. (Lisbon: Agência Geral do Ultramar, 1951), 1:86–88. Coutinho was an admiral who had direct experience in the Atlantic Ocean. He rightly belittles some of the reasons traditionally adduced by historians for the difficulty of rounding Cape Bojador, such as the belief in those days that the sea would become so hot in the more southerly latitudes that the water would boil or that the sea would plunge into an abyss. He also casts doubt on the idea that it was the introduction of the caravel, better able to sail against the wind, that finally allowed the Portuguese to round the cape.

17. Dava Sobel, *Longitude: The True Story of a Lone Genius Who Solved the Greatest Scientific Problem of His Time* (London: Fourth Estate, 1995), 4.

18. Pedro Nunes, *Tratado da Sphera*, 131, quoted in António Barbosa, *Novos subsídios para a história da ciência náutica portuguesa da época dos descobrimentos* (Porto: Instituto Para a Alta Cultura, 1948), 23. Nunes is also quoted in Luís de Albuquerque, "Astronomical Navigation," in *History of Portuguese Cartography*, 2 vols., ed. Armando Cortesão (Coimbra: Junta de Investigações do Ultramar, 1971), 2:227.

19. For the start of this latitude revolution, see Laguarda Trias, *Las más antiguas determinaciones de la latitud en el Atlántico y en el Índico* (Madrid: Instituto Histórico de la Marina, 1963), passim; and Albuquerque, "Astronomical Navigation," 227–28 and 245–73. The relationship between the altitude of the North Star and latitude had already been explained in the *Libros del saber de astrología* commissioned in the thirteenth century by the famous Castilian king Alfonso X, known as "el Sabio," "the Wise." In a broad sense, celestial navigation had been a common practice in many parts of the world since time immemorial. Phoenicians, Arabs, Chinese, Polynesians, and many other seafaring peoples had used stars and constellations to guide their movements. Some of these same peoples had also worked out the mathematics involved in calculating distances by triangulating with the Sun. Yet the Portuguese went well beyond their predecessors in that they effectively combined the practical observations made by pilots with the insights of mathema-

ticians and astronomers. They also surpassed their predecessors in developing a navigational infrastructure that included procuring and adapting instruments to measure angles, sending expeditions to establish the latitudes of various islands and points along the African coast, updating charts and maps according to the new observations, developing navigational manuals that most pilots could use, and commissioning declination tables. This is a great story of technological innovation that has been told largely in the Portuguese language. Some of the key works include Joaquim Bensaúde, *L'astronomie nautique au Portugal à l'époque des grande découvertes* (Bern: Akademische Buchhandlung von Max Drechsel, 1912), passim; and Luciano Pereira da Silva, "A arte de navegar dos portugueses desde o Infante a D. João de Castro," in *Obras completas,* vol. 2 (Lisbon: Divisão de Publicações e Biblioteca Agência Geral das Colónias, 1942), 223–432. Leite Pinto summarized some of his findings in a conference at the Société Astronomique de France in May of 1933 and published under the title *L'astronomie nautique au Portugal, à l'époque des grandes découvertes* (Orléans: H. Tessier, 1933). More substantial are Barbosa, *Novos subsídios para a história da ciência náutica portuguesa da época dos descobrimentos;* Teixeira da Mota, *A evolução da ciência náutica durante os séculos XV e XVI na cartografia portuguesa da época;* and various works by Luís de Albuquerque, including "Astronomical Navigation" and *Curso da história da náutica* (Rio de Janeiro: Serviço de Documentação Geral da Marinha do Brasil, 1971), passim. On the need to reevaluate Iberian science, see Francisco Contente Domingues, "Science and Technology in Portuguese Navigation: The Idea of Experience in the Sixteenth Century," in *Portuguese Oceanic Expansion, 1400–1800,* ed. Francisco Bethencourt and Diogo Ramada Curto (New York: Cambridge University Press, 2007), 460–79; Jorge Cañizares-Esguerra, "Renaissance Iberian Science: Ignored How Much Longer?," *Perspectives on Science* 12, no. 1 (2004): 86–125; and Cañizares-Esguerra, "On Ignored Global 'Scientific Revolutions,'" *Journal of Early Modern History* 21, no. 5 (October 2017): 420–32.

20. It was only in 1500 when a physician and astronomer named João Faras first described the Southern Cross in detail during Cabral's expedition to Brazil. For the description of the Southern Cross, see Faras to the king, Vera Cruz, May 1, 1500, *Revista do Instituto Histórico e Geográfico Brasileiro* 5, no. 19 (1843): 342–44. Even then, Faras expressed the opinion that "the best alternative is to navigate according to the altitude of the Sun rather than any other star."

21. Manuals on the altitude of the Sun began circulating in the fifteenth century, but only later publications survive such as the *Manual of Munich* (circa 1509) and the *Manual of Évora* (1519). See the discussion in Barbosa, *Novos subsídios,* 48–80; and Albuquerque, "Astronomical Navigation," 273–327.

22. The method in question is the *Reportório dos tempos* and is both quoted and explained in Albuquerque, "Astronomical Navigation," 233. I want to express my appreciation to Joaquim Alves Gaspar for improving my explanation.

23. The quote is from João de Barros, *Primeira década da Ásia* (Lisbon: Aillud, 1920), bk. 4, chap. 2. By the nineteenth century, Alexander von Humboldt referred to Behaim as "the great cosmographer of Nuremberg," and in 1890 Behaim's natal city unveiled a statue in his honor. For a broader discussion of this breakthrough, see Bensaúde, *L'astronomie nautique au Portugal,* passim; Pereira da Silva, "A arte de navegar dos portugueses," 326–28; Pinto, *L'astronomie nautique au Portugal, à l'époque des grandes découvertes,* 7–9; Albuquerque, "Astronomical Navigation," 295; and J. Moreira Campos, "Mestre José Vizinho," *Revista Beira Alta* (1955): 3–8; among others.

24. On Zacuto's life and a discussion of his work with extensive samples and running commentary, see Francisco Cantera Burgos, *Abraham Zacut* (Madrid: M. Aguilar, 1935); José Chabás and Bernard R. Goldstein, *Astronomy in the Iberian Peninsula: Abraham Zacut and the Transition from Manuscript to Print* (Philadelphia: American Philosophical Society, 2000); and Bensaúde, *L'astronomie nautique au Portugal,* 22. Zacuto's astronomical tables existed in manuscript form at least since 1478 in his *Ha-hibbur ha-gadol* (The Great Composition) and were known in the Iberian Peninsula. Bensaúde notes that Augustinus Riccios, a famous astronomer in his own right who studied under Zacuto, had the greatest regard for his teacher's astronomical tables. Bensaúde and Albuquerque note that all of Zacuto's declinations assume that Earth's rotation axis is tilted by twenty-three degrees and thirty-three minutes, which is the same tilt used in all Portuguese tables until the 1530s. Bensaúde, *L'astronomie nautique au Portugal,* 23; and Albuquerque, "Astronomical Navigation," 295. For an excellent introduction to the work of Zacuto, see Luís de Albuquerque's introductory essay in Abraão Zacuto, *Almanach Perpetuum* (Lisbon: Imprensa Nacional–Casa da Moeda, 1986), 22–23. There are doubts about the exact date for which that one-year declination table was elaborated. See Fontoura da Costa, *A ciência náutica dos Portugueses na Época dos Descobrimentos* (Lisbon: Comissao Executiva das Comemoracoes do Quinto Centenario da Morte do Infante D. Henrique, 1958), 34–40; and Albuquerque, *Curso de história da náutica,* 108. See also Campos, "Mestre José Vizinho," 3–8; Barbosa, *Novos subsídios,* 48–80; and Albuquerque, "Astronomical Navigation," 288–95.

25. For a fascinating discussion of the navigational methods used in the Indian Ocean by Arab pilots and the similarities and differences with their Iberian counterparts, see J. Custódio de Morais, "Determinação das coordenadas geográficas no

Oceano Índico pelos pilotos portugueses e pilotos árabes no princípio do século XVI," *Boletim do Centro de Estudos Geográficos* 2, no. 18 (1960): 3–49.

26. The quote is from Columbus's marginal annotation to Eneas Silvio Piccolomini's *Historia rerum ubique gestarum*, in Varela and Gil, *Cristóbal Colón*, 91. The latitude of Sierra Leone reported by Columbus was erroneous, as well as some other information. Yet we have to bear in mind that this was just the testing phase of this novel system of navigation, or perhaps erroneous latitudes were deliberately reported for the benefit of spies from other nations. See also Bensaúde, *L'astronomie nautique au Portugal*, 107; Barbosa, *Novos subsídios*, 48–80; Albuquerque, "Astronomical Navigation," 288–95; Chabás and Goldstein, *Astronomy in the Iberian Peninsula*, 158; Diffie and Winius, *Foundations of the Portuguese Empire*, 166–74; and Joaquim Alves Gaspar, "From the Portolan Chart of the Mediterranean to the Latitude Chart of the Atlantic: Cartometric Analysis and Modeling" (PhD diss., Universidade Nova de Lisboa, 2010), 14–17.

27. The quote is from João Barros, *Decades of Asia*, reproduced in Morison, *Admiral of the Ocean Sea*, 71. On Columbus's proposal to the Portuguese, see W.G.L. Randles, "The Evaluation of Columbus' 'India' Project by Portuguese and Spanish Cosmographers in the Light of the Geographical Science of the Period," *Imago Mundi* 42 (1990): 50–64; Diffie and Winius, *Foundations of the Portuguese Empire*, 166–70; Nicolás Wey Gómez, *The Tropics of Empire: Why Columbus Sailed South to the Indies* (Cambridge: MIT Press, 2008), chap. 2; Almirante Teixeira da Mota, "Cristóvão Colombo e os portugueses," in Carlos Araújo, ed., *Lisboa e os descobrimentos, 1415–1580: A invenção do mundo pelos navegadcores portugueses* (Lisbon: Terramar, 1990), 151; and António Brásio, *Monumenta missionaria africana*, 2nd ser., vol. 1 (Lisbon: Agência Geral do Ultramar, 1958), 234–35.

28. Randles, "The Evaluation of Columbus' 'India' Project by Portuguese and Spanish Cosmographers in the Light of the Geographical Science of the Period," 50–64.

29. Manuel I to Ferdinand and Isabella, Lisbon, 1503, in *Carta de El-Rei D. Manuel ao Rei Catholico, narrando-lhe as viagens portuguezas á India desde 1500 até 1505, reimpressa sobre o portotypo romano de 1505* (Lisbon: Academia Real das Sciencias, 1892), 9–31. See also a similar 1501 letter in William Brooks Greenlee, *The Voyages of Pedro Álvares Cabral from Contemporary Documents and Narratives* (London: Hakluyt Society, 1938), 41–52.

30. Geniuses working in isolation seldom conceive the greatest ventures of exploration; these instead tend to spring from incremental technical advances shared by the entire community of pilots, navigators, and explorers. In this instance, the idea of finding a passage between the two oceans as a way to reach the Spice

Islands had been in the wind for at least four years and probably more. Already in 1514 Juan Díaz de Solís had signed a contract with the Spanish to do exactly that, and just a few weeks before Magellan and Faleiro had their audience with the Spanish monarch, a fellow Portuguese pilot named Estevão Gomes had similarly offered to open a new way to the Spice Islands by sailing westward. The time was ripe for such an undertaking. See Jean Denucé, *Magellan: La question des Moluques et la première circumnavigation du globe* (Brussels: Académie Royale de Belgique, 1910), 248; and Tim Joyner, *Magellan* (Camden, ME: International Marine, 1992), 82–83. For a discussion of Juan Díaz de Solís's expedition, see Rolando A. Laguarda Trías, "Las longitudes geográficas de la membranza de Magallanes y del primer viaje de circunnavegación," in *A viagem de Fernão de Magalhães e a questão das Molucas,* ed. Avelino Teixeira da Mota (Lisbon: Junta de Investigações Científicas do Ultramar, 1975), 143–45. It is unclear whether Gomes had initially traveled with Magellan to Spain in 1517 or what prior dealings they may have had.

31. The first quote is from Bartolomé de las Casas, *Historia de las Indias,* 3 vols. (Mexico City: Fondo de Cultura Económica, 1986), 3:174–75. The second quote is from Gonzalo Fernández de Oviedo, *Historia general y natural de las Indias,* 5 vols. (Madrid: Ediciones Atlas, 1992), 2:217. Las Casas and other Spanish sources refer to Rui Faleiro as a *bachiller* in the same way that Portuguese sources such as Damião de Góis refer to him as a *bacharel.* Damião de Góis, *Chronica do felicissimo Rei D. Manuel,* 4 vols. (Coimbra: Universidade da Coimbra, 1949), 4:95. For information about Rui Faleiro's background, see Denucé, *Magellan,* 139–42; F.H.H. Guillemard, *The Life of Ferdinand Magellan and the First Circumnavigation of the Globe, 1480–1521* (London: George Philip and Son, 1890), 95–97; Joyner, *Magellan,* 66–67; Laurence Bergreen, *Over the Edge of the World: Magellan's Terrifying Circumnavigation of the Globe* (New York: William Morrow, 2003), 22–23; and André Rossfelder, *In Pursuit of Longitude: Magellan and the Antimeridian* (La Jolla, CA: Starboard Books, 2010), 46–47, among others. Joyner and others have speculated that Rui Faleiro may well have been among King João's group of mathematical experts in the 1480s and 1490s who famously solved the problem of determining latitude by the altitude of the Sun and also turned down Columbus's proposal. Alongside José Vizinho and Martin Behaim, a certain "Mestre Rodrigo" or "Mestre Rui" is mentioned in contemporary chronicles. See Joyner, *Magellan,* 66. I believe that this is very unlikely on the grounds of age alone. If Rui had been active as a cosmographer in the 1480s in his twenties at the earliest, then he would have been older than sixty by 1518. This in itself is not completely out of the question, but we also know that Rui traveled to Spain with his parents, who therefore must have been in their eighties or nineties, unlikely considering that

lifespans were much shorter in the sixteenth century and travel more difficult. Finally, Rui's brother Francisco would go on to live and work in Spain until the 1570s, so he would have had to be thirty or forty years younger than Rui if the latter had indeed worked as a cosmographer as early as the 1480s, once again quite unlikely. On Rui's younger brother, see Francisco Faleiro, *Tratado del esphera y del arte del marear* (Delmar, NY: Scholars' Facsimiles and Reprints, 1998). The introduction by Timothy Coats offers relevant biographical information. See also A. Teixeira da Mota, "A contribuição dos irmãos Rui e Francisco Faleiro no campo da náutica em Espanha," in Teixeira da Mota, *A viagem de Fernão de Magalhães e a questão das Molucas,* 217–341. On Francisco Faleiro's career as a cosmographer in Spain, see also the luminous essay by Edward Collins, "Francisco Faleiro and Scientific Methodology at the Casa de la Contratación in the Sixteenth Century," *Imago Mundi* 65, no. 1 (2013): 25–36.

32. All quotes are from las Casas, *Historia de las Indias,* 3:175, emphasis added. The possibility that navigators before Magellan knew about a strait between the oceans in South America is crucial and has garnered considerable scholarly interest. Contemporary testimonies by Antonio de Herrera and Antonio Pigafetta establish further that Magellan was confident in finding the strait because he had seen a nautical chart elaborated by Martin Behaim (son of the Martin Behaim discussed earlier). Both of these sources are transcribed and commented on in Avelino Teixeira da Mota, *O regimento da altura de leste-oeste de Rui Faleiro: Subsidios para o estudo náutico e geográfico da viagem de Fernão de Magalhães* (Lisbon: Edições Culturais da Marinha, 1986), 55–56. In addition to Teixeira da Mota, see more recent discussion in Rossfelder, *In Pursuit of Longitude,* chap. 3. On Portuguese and Spanish efforts to find a passage between the two oceans before Magellan, see Rolando A. Laguarda Trías, *El predescubrimiento del Río de la Plata por la expedición portuguesa de 1511–1512* (Lisbon: Junta de Investigações do Ultramar, 1973), 21–23; and Martín Fernández de Navarrete, *Colección de los viages y descubrimientos que hicieron por mar los españoles desde fines del siglo XV, con varios documentos inéditos . . . ,* 5 vols. (Madrid: Imprenta Real, 1825), 4:iii–iv.

33. The quote is from Friar Bartolomé de las Casas, *Historia de las Indias,* 3:175, emphasis added. The Spanish verb that las Casas used was *mostrar,* which means either to show or to demonstrate. I believe that the second meaning is more appropriate, given the subsequent actions by Magellan and Faleiro. Rui Faleiro's initial standing is evident in his appointment as co-captain along with Magellan in the contract drawn up after the audience. Faleiro may even have had an edge over Magellan if we are to judge by the fact that Faleiro's name appears first in the contracts. For the placement of Faleiro's name in the documentation, see the contract

between the king of Spain, Rui Faleiro, and Ferdinand Magellan and appointment
of Rui Faleiro and Ferdinand Magellan as captains, both in Valladolid, March
22, 1518, in Navarrete, *Colección de los viajes y descubrimientos*, 4:116–21 and 121–22,
respectively. The need to extend the line to the other side is already evident in
the years between 1495 and 1503. See "Información sobre el derecho que tenían
los reyes católicos a las indias e islas del Mar Océano y acerca de las diferencias que
tenían con el Rey don Manuel de Portugal por la propiedad de dichas islas," n.p.,
n.d. (but between 1495 and 1503), in *Colección general de documentos relativos a las Islas
Filipinas existentes en el Archivo de Indias de Sevilla*, vol. 5, document 210.

34. Laguarda Trías, "Las longitudes geográficas de la membranza de Magallanes y
del primer viaje de circunnavegación," 148–74; and Joaquim Alves Gaspar, "A
cartografia náutica no tempo de Magalhães," unpublished paper presented at the
Simpósio Viagem de Circum-Navegação e Ciência: Diálogos à Volta do Mundo,
Ponte da Barca, April 27, 2019. I want to express my gratitude to Joaquim Alves
Gaspar for shedding light on the sources of Magellan's conviction about the location of the Spice Islands.

35. Most famously, on September 20, 331 BCE, Alexander the Great and his soldiers
were marching through Arbela (Erbil) in northern Iraq when a lunar eclipse occurred "at the fifth hour." Several men had vivid recollections because eleven
days later they defeated Darius III of Persia and came to regard the eclipse as a
portent of their impending victory. Thousands of miles to the west, in Carthage,
Tunisia, the same lunar event was recorded "at the second hour." Ptolemy estimated that the three-hour difference between Arbela and Carthage represented
forty-five degrees of the globe. This method remained in use for a very long
time. More than fifteen hundred years later, on September 17, 1494, Columbus
witnessed a lunar eclipse while exploring what is now the Dominican Republic
and still resorted to the same logic to figure out how far west he had traveled
since leaving Spain. Although Ptolemy's deduction was entirely correct, the real
difference between Arbela and Carthage is only thirty-four degrees. The problem
was that the eclipse had occurred two centuries earlier, and thus Ptolemy had to
rely on terribly inaccurate reports about the timing of this celestial event. Over
the centuries since Ptolemy, astronomers and navigators learned that timing a
lunar eclipse accurately is not a trivial problem, as such events always start with
a very subtle, almost imperceptible darkening of the Moon when it moves into
the penumbra. The chances of accurate measurements increase when the Moon
passes through the more sharply defined umbra but in a trajectory that often veers
off to one side or the other of the dark circle except in the rare event of a total eclipse. Other than lunar eclipses, many celestial events such as conjunctions,

planetary transits, and solar eclipses could have been used to determine longitude. Nevertheless, conjunctions and transits frequently require a telescope to observe and are extremely difficult to measure with the necessary accuracy. Total solar eclipses are very rare and therefore impractical. For the case of Ptolemy, see the introduction to *Ptolemy's Geography: An Annotated Translation of the Theoretical Chapters*, trans. and ed. J. Lennart Berggren and Alexander Jones (Princeton: Princeton University Press, 2000), 29–30. For Columbus, see Laguarda Trías, "Las longitudes geográficas de la membranza de Magallanes y del primer viaje de circunnavegación," 139–41; and Morison, *Admiral of the Ocean Sea*, 653–55. In 1514, Nuremberg mathematician and astronomer Johannes Werner found yet another solution to the problem of longitude. His method consisted of measuring the passage of the Moon (much closer to us) against a seemingly "fixed" star (much farther away) to establish an absolute clock of sorts, compare it to the local time, and thus derive the east-west difference between two points on Earth. See António Costa Canas, "Longitude," in *Dicionário da expansão Portuguesa*, ed. Francisco Contente Domingues, 2 vols. (Lisbon: Círculo de Leitores, 2016), 1:653–55.

36. My discussion is based on Luís de Albuquerque, "Instruments for Measuring Altitude and the Art of Navigation," in Cortesão, *History of Portuguese Cartography*, 2:412–19; Alves Gaspar, "From the Portolan Chart of the Mediterranean to the Latitude Chart of the Atlantic," 18; and João de Lisboa, *Livro de marinharia: Tratado da Agulha de Marear* (Lisbon: Imprensa de Libânio da Silva, 1903), 20–21. The "north" indicated by the North Star was in fact about three and a half degrees away from exact north.

37. For the Cantino Planisphere, see Alves Gaspar, "From the Portolan Chart of the Mediterranean to the Latitude Chart of the Atlantic," 18. Luís Teixeira drew the first known isogonic chart around 1585. See K. M. Mathew, *History of the Portuguese Navigation in India (1497–1600)* (Delhi: Mital Publications, 1988), 59; and Joaquim Alves Gaspar and Henrique Leitão, "Luís Teixeira, c. 1585: The Earliest Known Chart with Isogonic Lines," *Imago Mundi* 70, no. 2 (May 2018): 221–28.

38. Magnetic declinations for San Francisco and the other cities come from the National Oceanic and Atmospheric Administration website, http://www.ngdc.noaa.gov/geomag-web/#declination, and the values correspond to September 18, 2016.

39. In the 1520s, no one knew that magnetic declinations change over time. I thank Alison D. Sandman for her sound advice. On our erratic magnetic pole, see Alexandra Witze, "Earth's Magnetic Field Is Acting Up and Geologists Don't Know Why," *Nature*, January 9, 2019, https://www.nature.com/articles/d41586-019-00007-1. Magnetic declination was an unreliable and confusing system for establishing longitude. Nonetheless, it was still useful as an aid to navigation and

indeed remained in use until the eighteenth century, when the second Astrono-
mer Royal in Britain, Edmond Halley, was still compiling magnetic charts. See
Alan Cook, *Edmond Halley: Charting the Heavens and the Seas* (New York: Oxford
University Press, 1997), 281–84.

40. Teixeira da Mota, "A contribuição dos irmãos Rui e Francisco Faleiro no campo
da náutica em Espanha"; and especially Teixeira da Mota, *O regimento da altura de
leste-oeste de Rui Faleiro,* passim. Rui Faleiro's text submitted to the Spanish crown
was thought for a long time to have been lost. In 1793, however, Martín Fernández de Navarrete published a document from the Spanish archives in Seville that
turned out to be Rui Faleiro's method. Moreover, as Joaquim Bensaúde was able
to show, a document attributed to Antonio Pigafetta (the most famous chronicler
of Magellan's circumnavigation voyage) at the Biblioteca Ambrosiana in Milan
also proved to be another version of Faleiro's method, or *regimento* as it is called
in Portuguese. Of these two versions, the one from Seville is the more complete.
It discusses three methods of determining longitude: the first two—one by the
latitude of the Moon and the other one by the conjunction and opposition of
the Moon and the stars—are discussed only briefly. The third method, based
on magnetic declination, is the only one described in detail and thus the one expected to be used during the expedition. In the end, Rui Faleiro did not go on the
expedition. The man who replaced him as chief pilot, Andrés de San Martín, was
very competent and was able to make longitude observations in the Spice Islands.
San Martín concluded that Faleiro's system based on magnetic declinations did
not work. He also believed that the Spice Islands were on the Portuguese side of
the world after all. See Laguarda Trías, "Las longitudes geográficas de la membranza de Magallanes y del primer viaje de circunnavegación"; and Alves Gaspar,
"A cartografia náutica no tempo de Magalhães"; and personal communication.

41. Magellan and his contemporaries generally believed that the Pacific was much
smaller than it actually is. For an excellent discussion of the changing images of
the Pacific, see Ricardo Padrón, "A Sea of Denial: The Early Modern Spanish
Invention of the Pacific Rim," *Hispanic Review* 77, no. 1 (Winter 2009): 1–27.

42. The expeditions in question are Gil González Dávila in 1521, Juan García Jofre
de Loaísa in 1525, Sebastian Cabot in 1526, Álvaro de Saavedra in 1527, Pedro de
Alvarado in 1533, Hernando de Grijalva in 1537, and Ruy López de Villalobos in
1542. This last expedition can be best understood as a three-pronged attempt at
reaching Asia: an overland expedition led by Francisco Vázquez de Coronado, a
coastal expedition under Juan Rodríguez Cabrillo, and the transpacific voyage
of Villalobos. See Flint and Flint, *A Most Splendid Company,* 87–89. The expeditions of González Dávila and Cabot did not even make it into the Pacific. For

sketches of the other voyages, see Amancio Landín Carrasco, ed., *Descubrimientos españoles en el Mar del Sur,* 3 vols. (Madrid: Editorial Naval, 1992), passim. Some of the same ground is covered in Henry R. Wagner, "Spanish Voyages to the Northwest Coast in the Sixteenth Century. Chapter V: The Occupation of the Philippines and the Discovery of the Return Route," *California Historical Society Quarterly* 7, no. 2 (June 1928): 132–93; Harry Kelsey, "Finding the Way Home: Spanish Exploration of the Round Trip Route Across the Pacific Ocean," *Western Historical Quarterly* 17, no. 2 (April 1986): 145–68; and Andrew Christian Peterson, "Making the First Global Trade Route: The Southeast Asian Foundations of the Acapulco-Manila Galleon Trade, 1519–1650" (Ph.D diss., University of Hawai'i at Mānoa, 2014), chaps. 2 and 3.

43. The quote is from a letter from Francisco Xavier to Simón Rodríguez, Goa, April 8, 1552, transcribed in Isacio Rodríguez Rodríguez, O.S.A., "Andrés de Urdaneta, agustino, 500 años del descubridor del tornaviaje," in *Andrés de Urdaneta: Un hombre moderno,* ed. Susana Truchuelo García (Ordizia, Spain: Ayuntamiento de Ordizia, 2009), 207. Some of the most useful works on Magellan's voyage include Alfredo Cominges Bárcena et al., "La primera circunnavegación," and Amancio Landín Carrasco and Mario Romero de Pazos, "Gómez de Espinosa y su intento de regreso por el Pacífico," both in Landín Carrasco, *Descubrimientos españoles en el Mar del Sur,* 1:89–160 and 163–86, respectively. For a popular treatment, see Bergreen, *Over the Edge of the World.* For the return attempts in 1528 and 1529, see Juan Génova Sotil and Fernando Guillén Salvertti, "Viaje de Saavedra, desde Nueva España," in Landín Carrasco, *Descubrimientos españoles en el Mar del Sur,* 1:223–68. For the *vuelta* of 1543, see Roberto Barreiro-Meiro Fernández, "Bernardo de la Torre y su intento de tornaviaje," in Landín Carrasco, *Descubrimientos españoles en el Mar del Sur,* 2:361–75; and for that of 1545, see Juan Génova Sotil, "Ortiz de Retes, por aguas australes," in Landín Carrasco, *Descubrimientos españoles en el Mar del Sur,* 2:379–402.

2. Dream Team

1. For Philip's life, see the works cited in the next note. Even though the 1557 order to launch an expedition to Asia came from Philip II, the impetus to cross the Pacific had never ceased in Mexico itself. In particular, Don Antonio de Mendoza, the viceroy of Mexico between 1535 and 1550, embarked on a three-pronged strategy to reach Asia by land, by coastal sailing, and via a transpacific voyage led by Villalobos. See Flint and Flint, *A Most Splendid Company,* 87–89. Although Viceroy Mendoza ultimately failed in opening regular trade with Asia, he dis-

cussed the possibility of finding the return voyage across the Pacific with his successor, Don Luis de Velasco, when the two met in 1550. (For the purposes of this book, I have chosen to use the modern spelling of "Luis," omitting the accent mark.) There is no question that this long-standing Mexican enthusiasm for the Orient—involving conquistadors, the church, and viceregal authorities—influenced Philip's 1557 decision. For this lingering interest in reaching Asia originating in Mexico, see Matthew Restall, *When Montezuma Met Cortés* (New York: HarperCollins, 2018), 274–75; Serge Gruzinski, *The Eagle and the Dragon: Globalization and European Dreams of Conquest in China and America in the Sixteenth Century* (Cambridge: Polity, 2014), passim; and Flint and Flint, *A Most Splendid Company,* passim. I thank Ryan Crewe for his excellent interpretive and bibliographic leads.

2. The first quote is from the bishop of Limoges in Hugh Thomas, *World Without End: Spain, Philip II, and the First Global Empire* (New York: Random House, 2014), 298. Philip's admission is from 1557 and appears in Geoffrey Parker, *Imprudent King: A New Life of Philip II* (New Haven: Yale University Press, 2014), xvii. Parker offers the most insightful portrait. See also Henry Kamen, *Philip of Spain* (New Haven: Yale University Press, 1997), 12–20.

3. The first quote comes from Friar Gerónimo de Santiesteban to Viceroy of Mexico Antonio de Mendoza, Cochin, India, January 22, 1547, transcribed in the *Colección de documentos inéditos relativos al descubrimiento, conquista, y organización de las antiguas posesiones españolas en América y Oceanía,* vol. 13 (Madrid: Imprenta de José María Pérez, 1870), 151–64. The second quote is from Ruy López de Villalobos to Viceroy of Mexico Antonio de Mendoza, n.p., 1545, transcribed in the account written by García de Escalante Alvarado, Lisbon, August 1, 1548, in *Colección de documentos inéditos relativos al descubrimiento, conquista y organización de las antiguas posesiones españolas en América y Oceanía,* vol. 5 (Madrid: Imprenta de Frias y Compañía, 1866), 183. It was too late for Villalobos. A year after writing this letter, he would succumb after suffering from very high fevers on Ambon Island (one of the Spice Islands). The Villalobos expedition of 1542–1548 is well covered in the literature. See especially Roberto Barreiro-Meiro Fernández and Amancio Landín Carrasco, "La expedición de Ruy López de Villalobos," in Landín Carrasco, *Descubrimientos españoles en el Mar del Sur,* 2:319–58; Gaspar de San Agustín, *Conquistas de las Islas Filipinas, 1565–1615* (Manila: San Agustín Museum, 1998), chaps. 6–7. The first news about the expedition reached the Iberian Peninsula only in the summer of 1547, when a Portuguese armada coming from India brought letters from some of the Spanish expeditionaries. The survivors would arrive one year later. Consuelo Varela, *El viaje de don Ruy López de Villalobos a las Islas del Poniente, 1542–1548* (Milan: Cisalpino-Goliardica, 1983), 15–16.

4. On the news trickling into Spain by way of Portugal and the sensitivities around the division of the world, see the information given by Viceroy of Mexico Antonio de Mendoza to Juan de Aguilar to pass on to the Spanish king and the Council of the Indies, Mexico City, 1544, Archivo General de Indias, Seville (hereafter AGI), Patronato, 24, R. 10.

5. For the naming of the archipelago of Saint Lazarus, see Antonio Pigafetta, "Primo viaggio intorno al mondo," in *Magellan's Voyage Around the World,* primary source ed., 2 vols. (Cleveland: Arthur H. Clark Company, 1906), 1:104–5. The exact date of their arrival had been March 16, 1521. Much of the documentation in the Spanish archives during the first half of the sixteenth century uses the term "las Islas del Poniente." The first mention of "las Islas Filipinas" occurs in the account of García de Escalante Alvarado, Lisbon, August 1, 1548, transcribed in the *Colección de documentos inéditos relativos al descubrimiento, conquista y organización de las antiguas posesiones españolas en América y Oceanía,* 5:117–209. For the most succinct and accurate explanation of the origins of the name "las Islas Filipinas" by a sixteenth-century witness, see the writings of geographer Juan López de Velasco, *Geografía y descripción universal de las Indias* (Madrid: Impresor de la Real Academia de la Historia, 1894), 581–82. Gerardo Mercator, the Flemish geographer famous for his novel projection, includes supporting evidence for this usage in his map of the world of 1569. See Barreiro-Meiro Fernández and Landín Carrasco, "La expedición de Ruy López de Villalobos," 340–41.

6. King Philip II to Viceroy of Mexico Luis de Velasco, Valladolid, September 21, 1557, transcribed in Muro, "La expedición Legazpi-Urdaneta a las Filipinas," 208–9. As explained earlier, Viceroy Luis de Velasco had discussed the need to find the return route from Asia with his predecessor in 1550. See Ma. Justina Sarabia Viejo, *Don Luís de Velasco virrey de Nueva España, 1550–1564* (Seville: Escuela de Estudios Hispano-Americanos, 1979), 464. For Philip's accession to the throne, see Parker, *Imprudent King,* 49–56; and Kamen, *Philip of Spain,* 63–71.

7. All the quotes are from King Philip II to Viceroy of Mexico Luis de Velasco, Valladolid, September 21, 1557, transcribed in Muro, "La expedición Legazpi-Urdaneta a las Filipinas," 208–9. The majority of sixteenth-century expeditions were financed with private funds. See Flint and Flint, *A Most Splendid Company,* 61–63. To be sure, the Spanish crown directly organized expeditions such as those of Columbus, Pedrarias Dávila, Loaísa, and some others. Still, as Oviedo wrote in his famous chronicle, "their Majesties almost never risk their wealth and money in these new expeditions of discovery." Gonzalo Fernández de Oviedo, *Historia general y natural de las Indias,* 4:300.

8. The quotes about Don Luis's lifestyle come from a 1589 treatise on life in Mexico

City written by Juan Suárez de Peralta, *Tratado del descubrimiento de las Indias* (Mexico City: Secretaría de Educación Pública, 1949), 99–100. The demand for a raise is in Viceroy Velasco to Emperor Charles V, Mexico City, May 4, 1553, partly transcribed in José Ignacio Rubio Mañé, "Apuntes para la biografía de don Luis de Velasco, el Viejo," *Revista de Historia de América* 13 (December 1941): 61. On Don Luis's dining habits, see also Thomas, *World Without End,* 34. On his passion for horseback riding and bullfighting, see Thomas, *World Without End,* 34–36; and Sarabia Viejo, *Don Luís de Velasco,* 10. On the renovation of Moctezuma's palace, see Rubio Mañé, "Apuntes para la biografía de don Luis de Velasco, el Viejo," 91. This last source includes a complete transcription of Don Luis's last will, which is extremely informative about the state of the viceroy's finances. On the theatrical and performative aspects of being a viceroy, see Alejandro Cañeque, *The King's Living Image: The Culture and Politics of Viceregal Power in Colonial Mexico* (Routledge: New York, 2004), especially chap. 4.

9. For Don Luis's meetings and other activities, see King Philip II to Viceroy Don Luis de Velasco, Valladolid, September 24, 1559, in *Colección de documentos inéditos relativos al descubrimiento, conquista y organización de las antiguas posesiones españolas de ultramar* (hereafter *CDIU*), vol. 2 (Madrid: Imprenta Real, 1886), document 10; and Muro, "La expedición Legazpi-Urdaneta a las Filipinas," 142–43. For Don Luis's feisty reply, see Viceroy Don Luis de Velasco to King Philip II, Mexico City, May 28, 1560, in *CDIU* 2, document 12.

10. For Carrión's recent notoriety, see the comic by Ángel Miranda (author) and Juan Aguilera (illustrator), *Espadas del fin del mundo* (Madrid: María de los Dolores Vicente Martín, 2016).

11. The quotes and a wealth of information about Carrión's life and marriage to Doña María are from the "Proceso contra Juan Pablo de Carrión, natural de Valladolid, vecino de Zapotlán, por casado dos veces," Michoacán, 1572, Archivo General de la Nácion, Mexico City (hereafter AGN), Instituciones Coloniales, Inquisición 61, vol. 93, Expediente 2. For a brief sketch of Carrión, see José Miguel Romero de Solís, *Andariegos y pobladores: Nueva España y Nueva Galicia (Siglo XVI)* (Zamora: El Colegio de Michoacán, 2001), 115. For Juan Pablo de Carrión's activities in Spain, see "Real Cédula a los oficiales de la Casa de la Contratación para que resuelvan y sentencien en el pleito entre Juan Pablo de Carrión con el fiscal y con Diego de Montemayor y otros," Valladolid, February 21, 1554, AGI, Indiferente, 1965, L. 12, F. 98r–v; "Real Cédula a los oficiales de la Casa de la Contratación para que permitan a Juan Pablo de Carrión acabar de cargar su galeón pasadas las hojas del Guadalquivir," Valladolid, September 26, 1554, AGI, Indiferente, 1965, L. 12, F. 220r–v; and above all the "Real Cédula a los oficiales

de la Casa de la Contratación para que envíen al Consejo de Indias relación de lo que ha sucedido con el capitán Juan Pablo de Carrión, acusado de abandonar la conserva," Valladolid, December 19, 1554, AGI, Indiferente, 1965, L. 12, F. 285r–v. From this last document, it is clear that, even while in prison, Captain Carrión was writing to Philip II claiming that he was innocent and seeking to lessen his punishment.

12. Carrión is referred to as a *vecino*—resident or citizen—of Valladolid in the documentation, but it is still possible that he may have been born and spent his formative years in Carrión de los Condes or Palencia. Don Luis's ancestral home in Carrión de los Condes, right along the Camino de Santiago, is well documented.

13. The number of vessels in previous Pacific expeditions is as follows: five with Magellan, seven with Jofre de Loaísa, four with Sebastian Cabot, three with Álvaro de Saavedra, ten with Pedro de Alvarado, two with Hernando de Grijalva, and six with Ruy López de Villalobos. On the initial number of vessels for the expedition, see Philip II to Viceroy Don Luis de Velasco, Valladolid, September 24, 1559, in *CDIU* 2, document 10. For a brief discussion of the nautical challenges posed by crossing the Pacific, see José Ramón de Miguel Bosch, "Las dificultades náuticas del tornaviaje," in Truchuelo García, *Andrés de Urdaneta,* 481–506.

14. The first quote appears in Carrión to the president of the Council of the Indies, n.p., 1565, AGI, Patronato, 263, N. 1, R. 1. See also *CDIU* 2, xxvi–xxvii. See also Philip II to Viceroy Don Luis de Velasco, Valladolid, September 24, 1559, in *CDIU* 2, document 10; Muro, "La expedición Legazpi-Urdaneta a las Filipinas," 143; and "Real cédula concediendo licencia al capitán Juan Pablo de Carrión para pasar a Indias las armas que necesitan para su defensa," Valladolid, September 24, 1559, AGI, Indiferente, 425, L. 23, F. 424r (8). The second quote is from the testimony of Pedro Maldonado in the inquisitorial proceedings against Juan Pablo de Carrión, Michoacán, 1572, AGN, Instituciones Coloniales, Inquisición 61, vol. 93, Expediente 2. Maldonado had known Carrión at least since 1548, when they had both lived in Toledo, traveled together to the Americas, and lived in the house shared by the captain and Doña María. Carrión mentioned Doña María's fear of crossing the Atlantic Ocean in the same proceedings on page 244.

15. The first quote appears in Carrión to the president of the Council of the Indies, n.p., 1565, AGI, Patronato, 263, N. 1, R. 1. See also *CDIU* 2, xxvi–xxvii. The second quote is from the commission given by Viceroy Don Luis de Velasco to Juan Pablo de Carrión, Mexico City, June 14, 1560, from Mercedes in the Archivo General de la Nación (hereafter AGN) and transcribed in Rubio Mañé, "La expedición de Miguel López de Legazpi a Filipinas," 680–82. The timing and reasons for the expansion of the fleet are unclear. See Muro, "La expedición Le-

gazpi-Urdaneta a las Filipinas," 168–70. The third quote and information about Carrión's second marriage come from the inquisitorial proceedings against Juan Pablo de Carrión, Michoacán, 1572, AGN, Inquisición 61, vol. 93, Expediente 2. Leonor Suárez had been previously married to Juan de Almesto (ca. 1498–1563). The timing of Carrión's first meeting with Leonor is uncertain. Their marriage occurred around 1564.

16. On Carrión's anticipation of the role that he would play in the expedition, see his letter to the president of the Council of the Indies, n.p., 1565, AGI, Patronato, 263, N. 1, R.1. See also *CDIU* 2, xxvi–xxvii; and Muro, "La expedición Legazpi-Urdaneta a las Filipinas," 148.

17. The literature on Urdaneta is sizable. A good place to start is Patricio Hidalgo Nuchera, "La figura de Andrés de Urdaneta en la historiografía indiana, conventual, documental y moderna," in Truchuelo García, *Andrés de Urdaneta*, 17–91. Some of the classic works include Fermín de Uncilla y Arroitajáuregui, *Urdaneta y la conquista de Filipinas* (San Sebastián: Imprenta de la Provincia, 1907); José de Arteche, *Urdaneta (el dominador de los espacios del Océano Pacífico)* (Madrid: Espasa-Calpe, 1943); Mariano Cuevas, *Monje y marino: La vida y los tiempos de Fray Andrés de Urdaneta* (Mexico City: Galatea, 1943); and Mairin Mitchell, *Friar Andrés de Urdaneta, O.S.A.* (London: Macdonald and Evans, 1964). For the close relationship between Basque mariners—including Elcano and Urdaneta—during the Loaísa expedition, as well as relations between Europeans and Indigenous women in the Spice Islands, see Juan Gil, "El entorno vasco de Andrés de Urdaneta (1525–1538)," in Truchuelo García, *Andrés de Urdaneta*, 325–90. The distance between Getaria (Elcano's birthplace) and Ordizia (Urdaneta's) is only thirty miles.

18. On Urdaneta's ecclesiastical career and the transcription of his March 20, 1553, oath, see Rodríguez, "Andrés de Urdaneta, agustino, 500 años del descubridor del tornaviaje," 206. See also Cuevas, *Monje y marino*, 149–78; and Mitchell, *Friar Andrés de Urdaneta*, 88–104. The last quote is from Friar Juan de Grijalva, *Crónica de la Orden de N.P.S. Agustín en las provincias de la Nueva España* (Mexico City: Porrúa, 1985), 238. Grijalva's chronicle of the Augustinian order was first published in 1624. For greater context on life in convents for males, as they were called back then—it is only in the nineteenth century that convents became associated exclusively with women and monasteries with men—see Antonio Rubial García, *Monjas, cortesanos y plebeyos: La vida cotidiana en la época de Sor Juana* (Mexico City: Santillana, 2005), 191–93.

19. The first quote is from the "Parecer dado a Antonio de Mendoza: Viaje al Maluco," n.p., April 1573, AGI, Patronato, 46, R. 10. In spite of its present classification and dating, this *parecer*, or opinion, was written by Urdaneta for Viceroy

Don Luis de Velasco sometime before November 1564. The second quote is from Friar Urdaneta to Philip II, Mexico City, May 28, 1560, in *CDIU* 2, document 13. The third quote is from Philip II to Friar Andrés de Urdaneta, Valladolid, September 24, 1559, in *CDIU* 2, document 11. See also Grijalva, *Crónica de la Orden de N.P.S. Agustín en las provincias de la Nueva España,* 238.

20. All quotes come from the "Relación y memoria" written by Friar Andrés de Urdaneta for King Philip II, Mexico City, early 1561, in *CDIU* 2, document 17. The same theme of developing a self-sufficient naval center on the west coast of Mexico appears in a "Parecer dado a Antonio de Mendoza: Viaje al Maluco," n.p., April 1573, AGI, Patronato, 46, R. 10. In spite of its present classification and dating in Spanish archives, Urdaneta wrote this *parecer* for Viceroy Don Luis de Velasco sometime before November 1564. Interestingly, the naval infrastructure of labor and building materials that linked America and Asia ultimately came from the Philippines rather than Mexico. See Peterson, "Making the First Global Trade Route," passim.

21. Viceroy Don Luis de Velasco to King Philip II, Mexico City, May 28, 1560, transcribed in Rubio Mañé, "La expedición de Miguel López de Legazpi a Filipinas," 681. Spanish chronicler Gonzalo Fernández de Oviedo met Urdaneta around 1538–39 and noted these same qualities. Fernández de Oviedo, *Historia general y natural de las Indias,* 1:175. See also Hidalgo Nuchera, "La figura de Andrés de Urdaneta en la historiografía indiana, conventual, documental y moderna," 26; and Rodríguez, "Andrés de Urdaneta, agustino, 500 años del descubridor del tornaviaje," 202.

22. The quote is from Friar Andrés de Urdaneta to King Philip II, n.p., early 1561, in *CDIU* 2, document 17. Urdaneta actually proposed three different trajectories depending on what season the fleet was ready to sail, but it is evident that his main plan was to sail across the equator to New Guinea as described. If departing in October–November, however, Urdaneta contemplated a straight course from Navidad to the Philippines like the one proposed by Carrión. Finally, if casting off in March–October, Urdaneta recommended following the coast of North America up to California before turning west, "reconnoitering the lands between that region and China and all the way to the vicinity of Japan." Such a route would have been very challenging, as the fleet would have had to fight contrary winds and currents while climbing toward California and then face very uncertain conditions crossing the Pacific at that latitude toward China or Japan.

23. All quotes are from Captain Carrión to King Philip II, n.p., n.d., ca. September 1564, about the navigation that the fleet should follow, *CDIU* 2, document 23.

24. The quote is from Captain Carrión to King Philip II, n.p., n.d., ca. September

1564, about the navigation that the fleet should follow, in *CDIU* 2, document 23. See also Carrión to the president of the Council of the Indies, n.p., 1565, AGI, Patronato, 263, N. 1, R. 1; transcription in *CDIU* 2, xxvi–xxvii; and Muro, "La expedición Legazpi-Urdaneta a las Filipinas," 148. Yet another letter by Carrión helps to clarify and corroborate his position. Captain Carrión to King Philip II, Mexico City, September 11, 1564, transcribed in Rubio Mañé, "La expedición de Miguel López de Legazpi a Filipinas," 693–96. Today recreational sailors may consult the *World Cruising Routes* or comparable manuals to identify the best sailing trajectories from North America to Asia. Although various tracks are possible, the fastest route is indeed to start out from the coast of Mexico sometime between November and May—to avoid the hurricane season—and sail directly to the Philippines to make full use of the trade winds. It is remarkable that navigators of the sixteenth century had already figured out the very best path across the northern Pacific. See Jimmy Cornell, *World Cruising Routes: 1,000 Sailing Routes in All Oceans of the World* (London: Cornell Sailing, 2014), 265–300.

25. The first quote is from Friar Urdaneta to King Philip II, Mexico City, May 28, 1560, in *CDIU* 2, document 13. See also Viceroy Don Luis de Velasco to Philip II, Mexico City, May 28, 1560, in *CDIU* 2, document 12. The last quote is from the "Relación diaria de Andrés de Urdaneta," transcribed in Fermín de Uncilla y Arroitajáuregui, *Urdaneta y la conquista de Filipinas,* 371. See also Rodríguez, "Andrés de Urdaneta, agustino, 500 años del descubridor del tornaviaje," 183–84. The five clove-bearing islands were Tidore, Ternate, Motil, Maquian, and Bachan, according to Captain Carrión, who visited the region in the 1540s. Captain Carrión to the Council of the Indies, n.p., n.d., transcribed in the *Boletín de la Sociedad Geográfica de Madrid* (Madrid: Imprenta de Fortanet, 1878), 4:23–26.

26. The quote is from Captain Juan Pablo de Carrión to King Philip II, September 1564, in *CDIU* 2, document 23. The exact timing of Urdaneta's brinksmanship is uncertain. He proposed his routes in 1561, and Carrión objected to them in writing and proposed his own three years later, as shown in this document. It is reasonable to assume, however, that the captain had opposed Urdaneta since 1561 if not before.

27. The first quote is from Viceroy Don Luis de Velasco to King Philip II, February 9, 1561, in *CDIU* 2, document 14. The second quote is from Juan Pablo de Carrión to King Philip II, September 1564, in *CDIU* 2, document 23. Some sources indicate that Urdaneta influenced the viceroy very directly in the selection of Legazpi. See the discussion in Juan Gil, "El primer tornaviaje," in *La nao de China, 1565–1815: Navegación, comercio e intercambios culturales,* ed. Salvador Bernabéu Albert (Seville: Universidad de Sevilla, 2013), 35–36. For Legazpi's background,

see José de Arteche, *Legazpi: Historia de la conquista de Filipinas* (San Sebastián: Sociedad Guipuzcoana de Ediciones y Publicaciones, 1972), 79–85; José Sanz y Díaz, *López de Legazpi: Primer adelantado y conquistador de Filipinas* (Madrid: Gran Capitán, 1950), passim; Uncilla, *Urdaneta y la conquista de Filipinas,* 182–83; and, more broadly, Marciano R. de Borja, *Basques in the Philippines* (Reno: University of Nevada Press, 2005), 15–29.

28. The quote is from Suárez de Peralta, *Tratado del descubrimiento de las Indias,* 114–15. See also Rubio Mañé, "La expedición de Miguel López de Legazpi a Filipinas," 693–96.

29. France V. Scholes and Eleanor B. Adams, eds., "Cartas del licenciado Jerónimo Valderrama y otros documentos sobre su visita al gobierno de Nueva España, 1563–1565," in *Documentos para la historia del México colonial* (Mexico City: José Porrúa e Hijos, 1959), passim. For a partial list of Don Luis's relatives who benefited from either *encomiendas* or cash payments, see "Relación de algunas personas con quienes tiene trabajado deudo don Luis de Velasco, Virrey de esta Nueva España" and "Relación de los pesos de oro que el Virrey de Nueva España don Luis de Velasco mandó pagar de la caja real a personas deudos, amigos y criados suyos," in Scholes and Adams, "Cartas del licenciado Jerónimo Valderrama . . . ," 229–33 and 234–54. The five Audiencia members or *oidores* were Doctors Ceynos, Villalobos, Orozco, Vasco de Puga, and Villanueva. Doctor Francisco de Ceynos was the one who was too old, and the deaf *oidor* remains unnamed. See Visitador Valderrama to King Philip II, Mexico City, February 24, 1564, in Scholes and Adams, "Cartas del licenciado Jerónimo Valderrama," 89.

30. The first quote is from Visitador Valderrama to King Philip II, Mexico City, February 24, 1564, in Scholes and Adams, "Cartas del licenciado Jerónimo Valderrama," 95. For an estimate of the total cost, see Muro, "La expedición Legazpi-Urdaneta a las Filipinas," 206–7. The other quotes are from Visitador Valderrama to King Philip II, Mexico City, February–March 1564, in Scholes and Adams, "Cartas del licenciado Jerónimo Valderrama," 85.

31. The quote is from the Audiencia of Mexico to King Philip II, Mexico City, September 12, 1564, in *CDIU* 2, document 22. See also Visitador Valderrama to King Philip II, Mexico City, August 18, 1564, in Scholes and Adams, "Cartas del licenciado Jerónimo Valderrama," 158–59; and Muro, "La expedición Legazpi-Urdaneta a las Filipinas," 153. Through the course of his inspection, Valderrama had resented the power of the religious orders. As he wrote to Philip, "These friars have been meddling in matters of justice, government, and finance." One flagrant example had been the undue influence Friar Urdaneta had exerted on Don Luis, even resorting to brinksmanship to get his way. See Visitador Valderrama to King

Philip II, Mexico City, February–March 1564, in Scholes and Adams, "Cartas del licenciado Jerónimo Valderrama," 75.

32. Valderrama's opinion of Carrión appears in Visitador Valderrama to King Philip II, Mexico City, August 18, 1564, in Scholes and Adams, "Cartas del licenciado Jerónimo Valderrama," 157. For evidence of Carrión's mismanagement, see Muro, "La expedición Legazpi-Urdaneta a las Filipinas," 161 and 165.

33. For the secret instructions to Legazpi and his oath, see instructions given by the Audiencia of Mexico to Commander Legazpi, Mexico City, September 1, 1564, in *CDIU* 2, document 21.

3. Navidad

1. The number of people who would go on the fleet was set between 300 and 350 according to the instructions given by the Audiencia of Mexico to Commander Miguel López de Legazpi, Mexico City, September 1, 1564, in *CDIU* 2, document 21. The final number was 380, as we shall see. It goes without saying that hurricanes and other natural forces have altered the bay and lagoon in the intervening centuries. For an excellent article addressing early doubts about whether the fleet had departed from Navidad, along with relevant historical and geographic information, see Carlos Pizano y Saucedo, "El puerto de la Navidad y la expedición de Legazpi," *Historia Mexicana* 14, no. 2 (October–December 1964): 227–49.

2. Admittedly, this is based on local lore rather than on any literature.

3. For the foods produced in the port of Navidad and nearby Cihuatlán, see "Suma de visitas," n.p., mid-sixteenth century, in Francisco del Paso y Troncoso, *Papeles de Nueva España*, 8 vols. (Madrid: Impresores de la Real Casa, 1905), 1:84. On the wheat, see the two orders issued by Viceroy Don Luis de Velasco to the Alcalde Mayor of Pátzcuaro Bachiller Alonso Martínez, Mexico City, June 23 and July 2, 1563, both transcribed in Rubio Mañé, "La expedición de Miguel López de Legazpi a Filipinas," documents 36 and 37. On the bacon, lard, cheese, fava beans, and garbanzos, see Muro, "La expedición Legazpi-Urdaneta a las Filipinas," 160.

4. The quote about the illnesses is from the *relación* of the Villa de la Porificación, not far from Navidad, 1585, in *Relaciones geográficas del siglo XVI: Nueva Galicia,* ed. René Acuña (Mexico City: Universidad Nacional Autónoma de México, 1988), 213. Appointment of Father Melchor González by Viceroy Don Luis de Velasco, Mexico City, July 1, 1560, and appointment of Damián de Rivas by Viceroy Velasco, Mexico City, August 30, 1560, both transcribed in Rubio Mañé, "La expedición de Miguel López de Legazpi a Filipinas," documents 3 and 4. For the appointment of Gabriel Sánchez Hernández, see Muro, "La expedición

Legazpi-Urdaneta a las Filipinas," 158–59. The death of Friar Lorenzo Jiménez is chronicled in Cuevas, *Monje y marino,* 188 and 197–98. For a good overview of medical practices at that time, see Linda A. Newson, "Medical Practice in Early Colonial Spanish America: A Prospectus," *Bulletin of Latin American Research* 25, no. 3 (July 2006): 367–91.

5. On the *repartimiento* Indians, see order from Viceroy Don Luis de Velasco to authorities of Tuxpan and Xilotlán, March 5, 1563, transcribed in Rubio Mañé, "La expedición de Miguel López de Legazpi a Filipinas," document 27. On African slaves, see payment receipt for six Black slaves, Mexico City, January 16, 1563, transcribed in Rubio Mañé, "La expedición de Miguel López de Legazpi a Filipinas," document 13; and payment for four Black slaves and a train of mules, April 2, 1563, transcribed in Rubio Mañé, "La expedición de Miguel López de Legazpi a Filipinas," document 28. See also Muro, "La expedición Legazpi-Urdaneta a las Filipinas," 167.

6. The Basque contingent included a carpenter named Gaspar de Arana from Urnieta, a sailor named Martín Urruzuno from Mendaro, and another crew member named Francisco de Astigarribia from Motrico, just to name a few. Other Spanish towns identified in the documentation include Bayona de Galicia, Medina del Campo, Triana (a neighborhood in Seville), Huelva, and Moguer. For these appointments and many others, see the documentation in Rubio Mañé, "La expedición de Miguel López de Legazpi a Filipinas," 749–98. For the broader context, see Antonio García-Abásolo, "Compañeros y continuadores de Urdaneta: Vascos en la nueva ruta de la seda," in Truchuelo García, *Andrés de Urdaneta,* 441–78; and Pablo E. Pérez-Mallaína, *Spain's Men of the Sea: Daily Life on the Indies Fleets in the Sixteenth Century* (Baltimore: Johns Hopkins University Press, 1998), 59.

7. The barrel maker from Belgium was Miguel López, the artilleryman was Francisco Alemán, the carpenter was Juan Inglés, the Venetian crew members included Domingo Hernández and Andrés Domingo, the French pilot was Pierres Plín (or Plún), and the Filipino translators were Gerónimo Pacheco and Juanes de Alzola from Cebu. All of these appointments and others are from Rubio Mañé, "La expedición de Miguel López de Legazpi a Filipinas," 749–98. For estimations of the number of foreigners in other expeditions, see Pérez-Mallaína, *Spain's Men of the Sea,* 55–58. Lope Martín sometimes appears as Lope Martínez in the documentation.

8. For contemporary descriptions of Lagos, see Henrique Fernandes Sarrão, "Historia do Reino do Algarve," in *Duas Descrições do Algarve do século XVI, Cadernos da Revista de História Económica e Social,* ed. Manuel Viegas Guerreiro and Joaquim Romero Magalhães (Lisbon: Livraria Sá da Costa Editora, 1983), 143. On the pi-

lots from Lagos, see João Baptista da Silva Lopes, *Corografia, ou memoria economica, estadistica, e topografica do Reino do Algarve* (Lisbon: Tipografia da Academia R. das Sciencias de Lisboa, 1841), 406 and 473. William Lytle Schurz affirms that Lope Martín took part in the Loaísa expedition. William Lytle Schurz, *The Manila Galleon* (New York: Dutton & Co., 1959), 277. This is surely a mistake. On the ship as a working space and the role of Black people, see Pérez-Mallaína, *Spain's Men of the Sea,* 38.

9. For a characterization of the different ranks, I rely on Pérez-Mallaína, *Spain's Men of the Sea,* 75–79.

10. The quote is from Diego García de Palacio, a well-known writer of naval treatises, quoted in Pérez-Mallaína, *Spain's Men of the Sea,* 37. On Amerigo Vespucci's time as *piloto mayor,* see Felipe Fernández-Armesto, *Amerigo: The Man Who Gave His Name to America* (New York: Random House, 2007), 175–80.

11. On the requirements and training of pilots, see Antonio Sánchez Martínez, "Los artífices del Plus Ultra: Pilotos, cartógrafos y cosmógrafos en la Casa de la Contratación de Sevilla durante el siglo XVI," *Hispania* 70, no. 236 (September–December 2010): 629–32; María Luisa Martín-Merás, "Las enseñanzas náuticas en la Casa de la Contratación de Sevilla," in *La Casa de la Contratación y la navegación entre España y las Indias* (Seville: Universidad de Sevilla, 2003), 667–93; and Alison D. Sandman, "Educating Pilots: Licensing Exams, Cosmography Classes, and the Universidad de Mareantes in 16th Century Spain," in *Fernando Oliveira and His Era: Humanism and the Art of Navigation in Renaissance Europe (1450–1650),* ed. Inácio Guerreiro and Francisco Contente Domingues (Cascais: Patrimonia, 2000), 99–109. On other pilots of African ancestry, the practice of bribing the *piloto mayor,* and the tendency of Portuguese seamen to try to pass as Spanish, see Pérez-Mallaína, *Spain's Men of the Sea,* 40–41 and 57–58. According to regulations issued on August 2, 1547, foreigners could be accepted as pilots if they were married to Spanish women and lived in Spain. As we shall see later on, Lope Martín claimed to have a wife living in Ayamonte. For the regulations concerning foreign pilots, see José Pulido Rubio, *El piloto mayor de la Casa de la Contratación de Sevilla* (Seville: Zarzuela, 1923), 13. Other mariners of the Navidad venture who claimed to come from Ayamonte were Alonso Yáñez and Cristóbal Garrucho. See Rubio Mañé, "La expedición de Miguel López de Legazpi a Filipinas," 749–98. This was a long-standing practice that can be traced back at least to Martín de Ayamonte (or Martinho de Ayamonte in Portuguese), who was a cabin boy on the *Victoria,* one of Magellan's ships. António Baião, "A viagem de Fernão de Magalhães por uma testemunha presencial," *Arquivo Histórico de Portugal* 1, no. 5–6 (1933), 276–81. Indeed, several of Magellan's crew members either hailed from Ayamonte

(cabin boy Francisco de Ayamonte or Luis Alonso, a *vecino* of Ayamonte) or were Portuguese (Fernando Portugués, Álvaro de la Mesquita, Gonzalo Rodríguez Portugués, among others), and many were either African or Afro-Iberian (cabin boy Antón Negro). See *Colección general de documentos relativos a las Islas Filipinas existentes en el Archivo de Indias de Sevilla,* vol. 2, document 84. On the House of Trade and its functions, see Antonio Sánchez Martínez, "La institucionalización de la cosmografía americana: La Casa de la Contratación de Sevilla, el Real y Supremo Consejo de Indias y la Academia de Matemáticas de Felipe II," *Revista de Indias* 70, no. 250 (2010): 715–48; Martínez, "Los artífices del Plus Ultra"; Alison D. Sandman, "Cosmographers vs. Pilots: Navigation, Cosmography, and the State in Early Modern Spain" (PhD diss., University of Wisconsin, 2001), passim; Sandman, "Educating Pilots"; and Alison D. Sandman, "Latitude, Longitude, and Ideas About the Utility of Science," in *Beyond the Black Legend: Spain and the Scientific Revolution,* ed. Victor Navarro Brotòns and William Eamon (Valencia: Soler, 2007), 371–81.

12. The two quotes are from Viceroy Don Luis de Velasco to King Philip II, Mexico City, February 9, 1561, in *CDIU* 2, document 14. The identities of the pilots hired early on by the viceroy and subsequently sent by Philip remain unknown. The other pilots' salaries are also unknown. The three Spanish pilots are Esteban Rodríguez from Huelva, Diego Martín from the neighborhood of Triana in Seville, and Rodrigo de la Isla (or Rodrigo Espinoza). The Frenchman is Pierres Plín (or sometimes Plún). Jaymes Martínez Fortún was also from the neighborhood of Triana according to the log written by pilot Esteban Rodríguez. Andrew Sharp claims that Fortún Martínez was originally from Venice. It is unclear, however, where Sharp got this information. Andrew Sharp, *Adventurous Armada: The Story of Legazpi's Expedition* (Christchurch: Whitcombe & Tombs, 1961), 9. On all the pilots, see also Muro, "La expedición Legazpi-Urdaneta a las Filipinas," 190–91.

13. The quote is from Thomas Cavendish, "First Voyage," in *Voyages of the Elizabethan Seamen: Select Narratives from the "Principal Navigations" of Hakluyt,* ed. Edward John Payne (Oxford: Oxford University Press, 1907), 376. Cavendish was a wealthy young esquire who wished to emulate Francis Drake. He put together a fleet, departed from Plymouth in the summer of 1586, crossed through the Strait of Magellan, and proceeded to attack Spanish ports along the coasts of Chile, Peru, and Mexico. The raid at Navidad occurred in 1587. He was the first English pirate to take one of the Manila galleons involved in the trade between Asia and the Americas. For additional context, see Schurz, *The Manila Galleon,* 305–13.

14. All we know is that the *San Pedro* was around 550 tons. It is possible, however, to estimate its approximate length and width by comparing it to similar vessels

of that era for which we have more information. To derive the size of the *San Pedro*, I have relied on the excellent discussion by Marcelino de Dueñas Fontán, "Medidas de los navíos de la jornada de Inglaterra," in *La batalla del Mar Océano: Corpus documental de las hostilidades entre España e Inglaterra (1568–1604)*, ed. Jorge Calvar Gross et al. (Madrid: Instituto de Historia y Cultura Naval, 1996), 46. In appendix 2, the author includes many examples of vessels, some of which are in the appropriate range of five hundred to six hundred tons. (By "tons," I really mean *toneles machos* for purposes of the calculation, just as I assume *codos de ribera*, or 0.57468 meters, for measurements of length.) For instance, the *San Cristóbal* was 568 tons, with 32.18 *codos* in length and 9.19 *codos* across. The original information about the sizes of various vessels as well as additional insights come from the meticulous work by José Luis Casado Soto, *Los barcos españoles del siglo XVI y la Gran Armada de 1588* (Madrid: Editorial San Martín, 1988), passim. For another calculation with a different result, see Miguel Bosch, "Las dificultades náuticas del tornaviaje," 490–91.

15. I have used the same method to derive the size of the *San Lucas*. There are many examples of pataches of forty tons of remarkably standard lengths and widths in Dueñas Fontán, "Medidas de los navíos de la jornada de Inglaterra," appendix 2. There is no reason to assume that the *San Lucas* would have been any different.

16. The first quote comes from the instructions given by the Audiencia of Mexico to Commander Legazpi, Mexico City, September 1, 1564, in *CDIU* 2, document 21. The second quote is from Commander Miguel López de Legazpi to King Philip II, Navidad, November 18, 1564, in *CDIU* 2, document 24. Some assignments had been made in Mexico City. While some servants were added to the roster, others who had worked in Navidad building the vessels were trying to avoid recruitment. For instance, a very capable carpenter named Gaspar García was fearful that he would be compelled to make the voyage even though he was "old and sick and had a wife in Spain." See order issued by Viceroy Don Luis de Velasco not to compel Gaspar García to go on the ships, Mexico City, July 6, 1563, transcribed in Rubio Mañé, "La expedición de Miguel López de Legazpi a Filipinas," document 38.

17. On the original plan of sending one or two ships back to the Americas, see instructions given by the Audiencia of Mexico to Commander Legazpi, Mexico City, September 1, 1564, in *CDIU* 2, document 21.

18. The first quote about the accommodations is from the instructions given by the Audiencia of Mexico to Commander Legazpi, Mexico City, September 1, 1564, in *CDIU* 2, document 21. Of the quotes about Friar Rada, the first one comes from the opinion or *parecer* of Friar Andrés de Urdaneta, Madrid, October 8,

1566, AGI, Patronato, 49, R. 12; and the second from Juan de la Isla (possibly), "Relación de las Islas del Poniente y del camino que a ella se hizo desde la Nueva España," n.p. 1565, transcribed in *CDIU* 3, document 40. See also Uncilla, *Urdaneta y la conquista de Filipinas*, 264. The Augustinian friars were distributed as follows: on the *San Pedro* were Andrés de Urdaneta, Martín de Rada, and Andrés de Aguirre; and on the *San Pablo*—the second-largest ship—were Diego de Herrera and Pedro de Gamboa. As stated earlier, the sixth friar, Lorenzo Jiménez, died in Navidad. On the pilots and other officials aboard each of the four ships, see Amancio Landín Carrasco and Luis Sánchez Masiá, "El viaje de Legazpi a Filipinas," in Landín Carrasco, *Descubrimientos españoles en el Mar del Sur*, 442–43; and Muro, "La expedición Legazpi-Urdaneta a las Filipinas," 190–93.

19. The quote is from Visitador Valderrama to Philip II, Mexico City, February 24, 1564, in Scholes and Adams, "Cartas del licenciado Jerónimo Valderrama," 95. See also Muro, "La expedición Legazpi-Urdaneta a las Filipinas," 187. Sauz's appointment as military commander had taken place in Mexico City on February 19, 1564, and is transcribed in Patricio Hidalgo Nuchera, ed., *Los primeros de Filipinas: Crónicas de la conquista del archipiélago de San Lázaro* (Madrid: Ediciones Polifemo, 1995), 106. Andrés Hurtado de Mendoza, Marquis of Cañete, was the later viceroy who pardoned Mateo del Sauz.

20. See "Informaciones y otros recaudos del capitán Juan de la Isla," Mexico City, December 14, 1570, AGI, Patronato, 52, R. 4. See also Muro, "La expedición Legazpi-Urdaneta a las Filipinas," 161–63.

21. The quote is from the appointment of Don Alonso de Arellano as captain of the *San Lucas*, Navidad, November 19, 1564, in "Relación del viaje y derrotero de la armada de Legazpi," AGI, Patronato, 23, R. 19. The name of the original captain was Hernán Sánchez Muñoz. On Cortés's family, see María del Carmen Martínez Martínez, "Hernán Cortés en España (1540–1547): Negocios, pleitos y familia," in *El mundo de los conquistadores,* ed. Martín F. Ríos Saloma (Mexico City: Instituto de Investigaciones Históricas/Silex Ediciones, 2015), 577–98; and Robert Himmerich y Valencia, *The Encomenderos of New Spain, 1521–1555* (Austin: University of Texas Press, 1991), 147–48. On Arellano's genealogy, see Amancio Landín Carrasco and Luis Sánchez Masiá, "El viaje redondo de Alonso de Arellano," in Landín Carrasco, *Descubrimientos españoles en el Mar del Sur,* 472–73; Henry R. Wagner, *Spanish Voyages to the Northwest Coast of America in the Sixteenth Century* (San Francisco: California Historical Society, 1929), 118, 350, and 352; and Ricardo Ortega y Perez Gallardo, *Estudios genealógicos* (Mexico City: Dublán, 1902), 21–26. The Counts of Aguilar came from the kingdom of Navarre in northeastern Spain. Hernán Cortés married Doña Juana Ramírez de Arellano y Zúñiga, daughter of

the second Count of Aguilar. Doña Juana's older brother Don Alonso de Arellano became the third Count of Aguilar. He lived out his entire life in Spain and died in 1522. He had both legitimate and illegitimate children. One of his illegitimate sons—by a woman named María de Velasco—was Lope de Arellano, who was born in Arnedo, Spain, but spent much of his life in Mexico and held important posts there. See Romero de Solís, *Andariegos y pobladores,* entry for Lope de Arellano. Alonso de Arellano (the one in the Navidad fleet) appears to have been another illegitimate child of the third Count of Aguilar, possibly also by María de Velasco. This would make him a cousin of Martín Cortés.

22. These procedures and quotes appear in the instructions given by the Audiencia of Mexico to Commander Legazpi, Mexico City, September 1, 1564, in *CDIU* 2, document 21. Although the instructions remained secret until after the fleet's departure, especially with regard to the fleet's course and destination, it is almost certain that similar safety protocols were already in place in previous instructions and indeed in previous expeditions.

23. The quotes are from the instructions given by the Audiencia of Mexico to Commander Legazpi, Mexico City, September 1, 1564, in *CDIU* 2, document 21. The identities of Legazpi's successors are revealed in Visitador Valderrama to King Philip II, Mexico City, August 18, 1564, in Scholes and Adams, "Cartas del licenciado Jerónimo Valderrama," 160. On Guido de Lavezaris's background and earlier involvement in expeditions bound for Asia, see Flint and Flint, *A Most Splendid Company,* passim.

24. Instructions given by the Audiencia of Mexico to Commander Legazpi, Mexico City, September 1, 1564, in *CDIU* 2, document 21.

25. The first quote is from Commander Miguel López de Legazpi to King Philip II, Navidad, November 18, 1564, in *CDIU* 2, document 24. The second and third quotes are from Friar Andrés de Urdaneta to King Philip II, Navidad, November 20, 1564, in *CDIU* 2, document 25.

4. A Disappearance

1. Log of pilot Esteban Rodríguez, 1565, in *CDIU* 2, document 33, entries for November 20 and 21. I also consulted the other version in "Derroteros y relaciones de los pilotos del viaje a Filipinas," AGI, Patronato, 23, R. 16. Exactly what the criers may have said is unknown. This is the version provided by veteran mariner Juan de Escalante de Mendoza while departing for the Indies, transcribed in Pérez-Mallaína, *Spain's Men of the Sea,* 69.

2. For the rations, see the instructions issued by Commander Legazpi to his captains, boatswains, and pilots, Navidad, November 21, transcribed in Muro, "La expedición Legazpi-Urdaneta a las Filipinas," 214. In this example I use the rations for the soldiers, as crew members received slightly different amounts. The equivalences from sixteenth-century Spanish *libras* to pounds and from *cuartillos* to pints are rough approximations but serviceable. See Mariano Esteban Piñeiro, "Las medidas en la época de Felipe II: La uniformación de las medidas," http://museovirtual.csic.es/salas/medida/medidas_y_matematicas/articulos/Capitulo3.pdf. For additional context I have relied on Pérez-Mallaína, *Spain's Men of the Sea,* esp. chap. 4. For concrete evidence of wine in Legazpi's fleet, see payment to Rodrigo de Alcázar for two *pipas* or casks of wine in Rubio Mañé, "La expedición de Miguel López de Legazpi a Filipinas," document 41. On how spirits were used as a tool during bad weather, see Giovanni Francesco Gemelli Careri, *Giro del Mondo* (Naples: Giuseppe Roselli, 1708), bk. 3, chap. 6.

3. The comparison of life on a ship to sharing an urban apartment appears in Pérez-Mallaína, *Spain's Men of the Sea,* 130–31. See also María del Carmen Mena García, *Sevilla y las flotas de Indias: La gran armada de Castilla del Oro (1513–1514)* (Seville: Universidad de Sevilla, 1998), 409–17.

4. The quotes are from the instructions given by Commander Legazpi to the captains, boatswains, and pilots, Navidad, November 22, 1564, AGI, Patronato, 52, R. 4; and "Información de Juan de la Isla," transcribed in Muro, "La expedición Legazpi-Urdaneta a las Filipinas," 212–15. See also the instructions given by the Audiencia of Mexico to Commander Legazpi, Mexico City, September 1, 1564, in *CDIU* 2, document 21. For life aboard ships, see Francisco Contente Domingues and Inácio Guerreiro, *A vida a bordo na carreira da Índia* (Lisbon: Instituto de Investigação Científica Tropical, 1988), 198–99; and José María López Piñero, *El arte de navegar en la España del Renacimiento* (Barcelona: Editorial Labor, 1986), 119–20. On the division of the day, see Fontoura da Costa, *A ciência náutica dos Portugueses na Época dos Descobrimentos* (Lisbon: Comissão Executiva das Comemorações do Quinto Centenário da Morte do Infante D. Henrique, 1958), 60–61. Although these divisions correspond to Portuguese voyages, they were likely the same in Spanish. Columbus, for instance, also mentions the *alva.*

5. The quotes are from the instructions given by the Audiencia of Mexico to Commander Legazpi, Mexico City, September 1, 1564, in *CDIU* 2, document 21. The pilots' logbooks record the mid-ocean meeting on Saturday, November 25, 1564.

6. The quote is from Friar Andrés de Urdaneta to King Philip II, Mexico City, May 28, 1560, in *CDIU* 2, document 13. The second quote is from Commander

Miguel López de Legazpi, "Relación circunstanciada de los acontecimientos y suceso del viaje . . . ," Philippines, May 27, 1565, in *CDIU* 2, document 27, hereafter Legazpi, "Relación circunstanciada."

7. The quote is from the log of pilot Esteban Rodríguez, 1565, in *CDIU* 2, document 33, entry for Sunday, November 26, 1564. See also Legazpi, "Relación circunstanciada."

8. Pilot Rodríguez's log, 1565, in *CDIU* 2, document 33, entry for December 1–2, 1564. For Legazpi's orders to Lope Martín to move ahead, see Legazpi, "Relación circunstanciada."

9. Don Alonso de Arellano, "Relación mui circunstanciada . . . ," Mexico, 1565, transcribed in *CDIU* 3, document 37, hereafter Arellano, "Relación mui circunstanciada"; Legazpi, "Relación circunstanciada"; and the pilot Rodríguez's log, 1565, in *CDIU* 2, document 33, entry for December 1–2, 1564. See chapter 10 for a full discussion of whether the separation was accidental or deliberate. For a brief summary of the case against Martín and Arellano, see Landín Carrasco and Sánchez Masiá, "El viaje redondo de Alonso de Arellano," 474–76.

5. *Mar Abierto*

1. As the crow flies, the distance between the port of Navidad and Mejit Island is 5,629 miles, and easily more than six thousand miles if we allow for the unavoidable deviations from the great circle distance (i.e., the shortest distance between two points on the surface of a sphere). Although Captain Cook is generally regarded as the first European to have made landfall in the Hawaiian Islands, the possibility of earlier European visits is not entirely out of the question. For instance, see Roberto Barreiro-Meiro Fernández and Amancio Landín Carrasco, "El descubrimiento de las Hawaii," in Landín Carrasco, *Descubrimientos españoles en el Mar del Sur*, 405–34. I remain unconvinced.

2. I have to reiterate here that, although oceanographically speaking, a gyre refers solely or primarily to the ocean currents, in this book I use the term more broadly to include both the wind driving the ocean current as well as the current itself. I justify this broad usage because, from a sailing perspective, both currents and winds determine what is possible and what is impossible. For the Coriolis effect, I hasten to add that the ocean currents in a gyre parallel the prevailing zonal winds not directly because of wind drag but because of geostrophic flow—a dynamic balance between Coriolis force and pressure gradient. For the wind-driven ocean currents, the Ekman spiral, and the geostrophic flow, I rely on Paul R. Pinet, *Invitation to Oceanography* (Burlington, MA: Jones & Bartlett Learning,

2016), 188–205. On the impact of ENSO (El Niño–Southern Oscillation) on the Pacific gyres, see William H. Quinn, Victor T. Neal, and Santiago E. Antunez de Mayolo, "El Niño Occurrences over the Past Four and a Half Centuries," *Journal of Geophysical Research* 92, no. C13 (December 1987): 14,449–61. As the authors explain, to determine whether an ENSO event had occurred in the distant past with reasonable accuracy, they looked at various clues and evidentiary strands, the first of which consisted of a significant deviation of normal travel/sailing times along the coast of northern South America related to changes in wind and current patterns.

3. The best discussion of this maneuver (also known as the *volta pelo largo, volta da Guiné,* or *volta da Mina*) is still Gago Coutinho, *A náutica dos descobrimentos,* 11: 197–271. Felipe Fernández-Armesto helpfully warns that, although running with the wind makes sense, there are many examples in the history of maritime exploration in which the voyagers headed *into* the wind because returning was as important as going. Felipe Fernández-Armesto, "Portuguese Expansion in Global Context," in *Portuguese Oceanic Expansion, 1400–1800,* ed. Francisco Bethencourt and Diogo Ramada Curto (New York: Cambridge University Press, 2007), 496–97. Unlike the other gyres, the Indian Ocean gyre reverses direction during the year. It normally moves counterclockwise, but in the winter months it changes course as a result of a complicated mechanism involving heat changes on the Asian mainland. Even before the Christian era, navigators of the Indian Ocean began using these seasonal winds for trade. The monsoon winds were decisive for a successful return from Asia to the Americas, as we shall see. For a general discussion, see Greg Bankoff, "Aeolian Empires: The Influence of Winds and Currents on European Maritime Expansion in the Days of Sail," *Environment and History* 23 (2017): 163–96.

4. Admiral Coutinho discusses this case at length in *A náutica dos descobrimentos,* 1:268–71. See also Maria Armanda de Mira Ribeiro F. Ramos Taveira, "Os roteiros portugueses do Atlântico de finais do século XV à primeira década do século XVII" (MA thesis, Universidade Nova de Lisboa, 1994), 190–200.

5. On the Sargasso Sea, see Gago Coutinho, *A náutica dos descobrimentos,* 1:271. The quote about the "seagull with red legs and other small birds" comes from Vicente Rodrigues, cited in Ramos Taveira, "Os roteiros portugueses do Atlântico de finais do século XV à primeira década do século XVII," 190–91. A debate exists about when the Azores were sighted for the first time, with possibilities going back to the Middle Ages. Whether the Portuguese discovered or merely rediscovered this archipelago, what matters for our purposes is the timing of their definitive exploration and settlement. Various "signs" or *señas* like *Sargassum,* birds, and

later kelp and marine mammals in the Pacific are expertly discussed in Salvador Bernabéu Albert, "La 'audiencia de las señas': Los significados de una ceremonia jocose en la nao de China," in Albert, *La nao de China, 1565–1815*, 91–117.

6. Portuguese navigators used variants of this basic route to India until the nineteenth century. See the discussion in Domingues and Guerreiro, *A vida a bordo na carreira da Índia*, 192–95; Diffie and Winius, *Foundations of the Portuguese Empire*, 175–91; Rossfelder, *In Pursuit of Longitude*, 55–56; Gago Coutinho, *A náutica dos descobrimentos*, 1:271–314; and Ramos Taveira, "Os roteiros portugueses do Atlântico de finais do século XV à primeira década do século XVII," 190–200.

7. The quote is from Vasco da Gama; see the lecture by António Baião, "Borrão original da primeira folha das instruções de Vasco da Gama para a viagem de Cabral," n.p., n.d., in Max Justo Guedes, *O descobrimento do Brasil* (Lisbon: Vega, 1966), document b, 115. In turn, Vasco da Gama learned about the difficulties of a coastal route and the possibilities of a second *volta* from Bartolomeu Dias, who first reached the tip of Africa. My discussion is based on Gago Coutinho, *A náutica dos descobrimentos*, 1:271–314; and Ramos Taveira, "Os roteiros portugueses do Atlântico de finais do século XV à primeira década do século XVII," 190–200.

8. The quote by Bernardo Fernandes appears in Avelino Teixeira da Mota, "Atlantic Winds and Ocean Currents in Portuguese Documents," *Proceedings of the Royal Society of Edinburgh* 73, no. 1 (1972): 63. Teixeira da Mota offers other examples of the term *ventos gerais* being used from 1535 onward.

9. Gago Coutinho, *A náutica dos descobrimentos*, 2:334. The historiography on Magellan is vast, but some of the most useful works include Amândio Barros, *O homem que navegou o mundo: Em busca das origens de Magalhães* (Braga: Publicações de Bruno Daniel Barbosa Antunes, 2015); and Avelino Teixeira da Mota, ed., *A viagem de Fernão de Magalhães e a questão das Molucas* (Lisbon: Junta de Investigações Científicas do Ultramar, 1975). Valuable biographical information can still be found in Visconde de Lagôa, *Fernão de Magalhãis* (Lisbon: Seara Nova, 1938); Joyner, *Magellan;* and José Manuel Garcia, *A viagem de Fernão de Magalhães e os Portugueses* (Lisbon: Editorial Presença, 2007).

10. Prior to 1520, the Pacific Ocean was known as the South Sea, and it would continue to be known as such for a long time. See O.H.K. Spate, "'South Sea to 'Pacific Ocean': A Note on Nomenclature," *Journal of Pacific History* 12, no. 4 (1977): 205–11. The Pacific Ocean is often quite challenging to navigate in the area close to the Strait of Magellan. An example of more typical sailing conditions can be found in Joshua Slocum, *Sailing Alone Around the World* (repr., New York: Dover Publications, 1970), chap. 8. It is likely that an ENSO phenomenon occurred during 1519–20 and may well have contributed to the peacefulness of the Pacific

when Magellan first entered it. See Scott M. Fitzpatrick and Richard Callaghan, "Magellan's Crossing of the Pacific: Using Computer Simulations to Examine Oceanographic Effects on One of the World's Greatest Voyages," *Journal of Pacific History* 43, no. 2 (September 2008): 145–65.

11. Magellan's route matches perfectly well with present-day routes. For instance, evaluating the best routes from southern Chile toward the South Pacific islands, the author of *World Cruising Routes* specifically states that "the route will be decided by the position of the South Pacific High [the area of high pressure around which the gyre turns], normally centered on 30°S," precisely where Magellan's fleet turned west. Cornell, *World Cruising Routes,* 383. On the decision to cross the equator, one of Magellan's pilots later commented that the reason was that they believed they would not find enough food in the Spice Islands. See Fitzpatrick and Callaghan, "Magellan's Crossing of the Pacific," 145–65.

12. The quote is from the report written by Urdaneta and probably intended for Viceroy Don Luis de Velasco (although Viceroy Don Antonio de Mendoza is the one whose name appears on the document), n.p., April 1573 (a date that is much too late for either Mendoza or Velasco), AGI, Patronato, 46, R. 10. Pedro de Alvarado's 1533 expedition is the only one that departed from the coast of Guatemala. It sailed some four hundred leagues and eventually drifted toward the coast of Peru. For the other expeditions, see the discussion that follows in the text.

13. The quote is from Hernán Cortés to Emperor Charles V, Coyoacán, May 15, 1522, in *Documentos cortesianos,* ed. José Luis Martínez, 4 vols. (Mexico City: UNAM-FCE, 1990), 1:231. Detailed information about the outfitting of this expedition as well as one of the main narratives can be found in "Relación de cuentas de los gastos que hizo Cortés en ese viaje en 1529" and "Relación de Vicencio de Nápoles que fue con Saavedra el descubrimiento del Maluco," both in AGN, Hospital de Jesús 53, vol. 438, file 1. According to Nápoles, the daily distances covered by *La Florida* — between twenty-five and forty leagues, and up to seventy — are extraordinary to the point of being difficult to believe. The main point, however, is that the ship benefited immensely from favorable winds and currents. For brief treatments of the Saavedra expedition, see Basil Thomson, "Lost Explorers of the Pacific," *Geographical Journal* 44, no. 1 (July 1914): 12–29; Harry Kelsey, *The First Circumnavigators: Unsung Heroes of the Age of Discovery* (New Haven: Yale University Press, 2016); Wagner, "Spanish Voyages to the Northwest Coast in the Sixteenth Century"; and above all Juan Génova Sotil and Fernando Guillén Salvetti, "Viaje de Saavedra desde Nueva España," in Landín Carrasco, *Descubrimientos españoles en el Mar del Sur,* 1:238.

14. Varela, *El viaje de don Ruy López de Villalobos,* passim; and Barreiro-Meiro Fernández and Landín Carrasco, "La expedición de Ruy López de Villalobos."

15. My calculations assume that the Micronesian islands are scattered over 2,900,000 square miles of ocean (versus 3,120,000 for the lower forty-eight states) while occupying a mere 271 square miles (versus 1,034 for Rhode Island). Many scholars object to the use of Micronesia as a geohistorical category. For a brief discussion, see Paul Rainbird, *The Archaeology of Micronesia* (New York: Cambridge University Press, 2004), chap. 3. For the identification of Islas de los Reyes with Faraulep, I follow Génova Sotil and Guillén Salvetti, "Viaje de Saavedra desde Nueva España," 1:238–45. For the identification of Matalotes, see Barreiro-Meiro Fernández and Landín Carrasco, "La expedición de Ruy López de Villalobos," 334–37. The term *matalote* comes from the French *matelot,* or sailor. It is doubtful that earlier Spaniards had visited the island. More likely the locals had traveled to other islands where they had come in contact with Spaniards (or with other islanders who had) and thus learned the Spanish words.

16. For a discussion of the pilots' latitude estimates at Navidad, see Landín Carrasco and Sánchez Masiá, "El viaje de Legazpi a Filipinas," 446–47. The logbook entry is by Esteban Rodríguez, the *piloto mayor,* "Relación y derrotero," December 6, 1565, in *CDIU* 2, document 33.

17. The quote and information are from the orders given by Commander Legazpi to the captains and pilots about the route that they should follow, Pacific Ocean, November 25, 1564, in *CDIU* 2, document 26.

18. The quotes are from Legazpi, "Relación circunstanciada." On the origins of parallel sailing harking back to the Azores, see Alves Gaspar, "From the Portolan Chart of the Mediterranean to the Latitude Chart of the Atlantic," 13–14.

6. The Tiny Islands

1. Frank L. Peterson, "Hydrogeology of the Marshall Islands," in *Geology and Hydrogeology of Carbonate Islands,* ed. H. L. Vacher and T. M. Quinn (Amsterdam: Elsevier, 1997), 613.

2. The quotes are from the entry for January 9, 1565, in Legazpi, "Relación circunstanciada." Mejit Island is actually at ten degrees and seventeen minutes of northern latitude. On the identification of the island encountered by Legazpi on January 9, 1565, as Mejit, I follow Landín Carrasco and Sánchez Masiá, "El viaje de Legazpi a Filipinas," 451–52.

3. The quotes are from the entry for January 9, 1565, in Legazpi, "Relación circunstanciada."

4. The quotes are from the logbook entry for January 10, 1565, Rodríguez, "Derroteros y relaciones de los pilotos del viaje a Filipinas"; and the entry for January 12, 1565, in Legazpi, "Relación circunstanciada." Esteban Rodríguez actually gave the name *corrales* to some of the islands. See his entry for January 12.

5. The quotes are from Arellano, "Relación mui circunstanciada." For the identification of this place as Likiep Atoll, see Landín Carrasco and Sánchez Masiá, "El viaje redondo de Alonso de Arellano," 477.

6. Quotes from Arellano, "Relación mui circunstanciada." The identification of this island as Kwajalein Atoll is from Landín Carrasco and Sánchez Masiá, "El viaje redondo de Alonso de Arellano," 478.

7. The first quote is from Arellano, "Relación mui circunstanciada." The second quote is from Friar Antonio Vázquez de Espinosa, *Compendium and Description of the West Indies* (Washington, DC: Smithsonian Institution, 1942), 272. Vázquez de Espinosa traveled to the Philippines in the 1620s. His botanical observations are invaluable. For an overview of Micronesians, see Glenn Petersen, *Traditional Micronesian Societies: Adaptation, Integration, and Political Organization* (Honolulu: University of Hawaiʻi Press, 2009), passim. On the strategy for surviving storms, see Rainbird, *The Archaeology of Micronesia,* 52. For an example of the transformative role of new crops, see Glenn Petersen, "Micronesia's Breadfruit Revolution and the Evolution of a Culture Area," *Archaeology in Oceania* 41, no. 2 (July 2006): 82–92.

8. On the naming of "the Island of the Bearded Ones," see the entry for January 9, 1565, in Legazpi, "Relación circunstanciada"; entry for January 9, 1565, in Rodríguez, "Derroteros y relaciones de los pilotos del viaje a Filipinas"; and entry for January 9, 1565, in Pierres Plín, "Derroteros y relaciones de los pilotos del viaje a Filipinas," AGI, Patronato, 23, R. 16. On beard and hairstyles and the character of the islanders, see entry for January 8, 1565, in Arellano, "Relación mui circunstanciada." For women's clothes and objects at the village, see the entry for January 9, 1565, in Legazpi, "Relación circunstanciada"; and entry for January 8, 1565, in Arellano, "Relación mui circunstanciada."

9. Entry for January 8, 1565, in Arellano, "Relación mui circunstanciada." One possibility is that this island may have been Lib. See the discussion in Landín Carrasco and Sánchez Masiá, "El viaje redondo de Alonso de Arellano," 478. Given the previous trajectory of the *San Lucas,* however, it seems too far south to me.

10. The quote about the contingency plan is from the orders issued by Commander Miguel López de Legazpi, Pacific Ocean, November 25, 1564, AGI, Patronato, 23, R. 16. The last quote is from Arellano, "Relación mui circunstanciada."

11. The quotes are all from Legazpi, "Relación circunstanciada." On the inability of

the Villalobos expedition to turn north from Mindanao, see the letter from Friar Gerónimo de Santisteban to Viceroy Don Antonio de Mendoza, Cochin, India, January 22, 1547, in Varela, *El viaje de don Ruy López de Villalobos,* 25. On Urdaneta's earlier experience with the same contrary winds in Mindanao, see Rodríguez, "Andrés de Urdaneta, agustino, 500 años del descubridor del tornaviaje," 180.

7. "The Island of the Thieves"

1. The quotes about bananas and thieves are from Pigafetta, *Magellan's Voyage Around the World,* 1:95. Nonetheless, bananas were known in Iberia at least since the thirteenth century, but they may have been somewhat exotic. For additional context on the Chamorros' trading practices and their first encounters with Europeans, see Frank Quimby, "The Hierro Commerce: Culture Contact, Appropriation and Colonial Entanglement in the Marianas, 1521–1668," *Journal of Pacific History* 46, no. 1 (June 2011): 1–26. Strictly speaking, the Mariana Islands arose out of the plunging of the Pacific Plate underneath the Mariana Plate, which is itself a "micro tectonic plate," in other words, possibly a piece of the Philippine Sea Plate. Sometimes the term Micronesia is restricted to mean the Federated States of Micronesia (FSM), but here I use the term in its broader historical sense to encompass Palau, the Marianas, the Marshalls, Kiribati, and Nauru, as well as the FSM.

2. On Legazpi's arrival at Guam, see entry for January 22, 1565, in Legazpi, "Relación circunstanciada."

3. The quote is from Pierres Plín's logbook, Navidad, entry for November 20, "Derrotero de Pierres Plín," in "Derroteros y relaciones de los pilotos del viaje a Filipinas," AGI, Patronato, 23, R. 16. For the east-west distance between Hierro and Navidad, see Landín Carrasco and Sánchez Masiá, "El viaje de Legazpi a Filipinas," 447. The quote about Rada is from Friar Andrés de Urdaneta in his "Parecer sobre si el Maluco y las Filipinas pertenecen al rey de Castilla y si las Filipinas caen dentro del empeño," Madrid, October 8, 1566, AGI, Patronato, 49, R. 12. See also Uncilla, *Urdaneta y la conquista de Filipinas,* 264.

4. Logbook entries are from the "Derroteros y relaciones de los pilotos del viaje a Filipinas," AGI, Patronato, 23, R.16. Legazpi's quote is from the entry for December 18, 1564, in Legazpi, "Relación circunstanciada."

5. Rui Faleiro's story is well known. For specific citations about him and the text that he submitted to the Spanish crown, see chapter 1. On his mental problems, see Gil, *El exilio portugués en Sevilla,* 350–54. On Francisco Faleiro, see Collins,

"Francisco Faleiro and Scientific Methodology at the Casa de la Contratación in the Sixteenth Century"; and Teixeira da Mota, "A contribuição dos irmãos Rui e Francisco Faleiro no campo da náutica em Espanha." The "Tratado da Agulha de Marear" of João de Lisboa (1515) is the first known source to propose a linear relation between longitude and magnetic declination. Francisco Faleiro wrote down much of what he knew about navigation in his 1535 *Treatise on the Sphere and the Art of Navigating* and broke new ground in chapter 8 by offering the first published treatment of magnetic variation or declination as it is now called. See Faleiro, *Tratado del esphera y del arte del marear,* passim. For appraisals of Faleiro's work and his instrument, see Pereira da Silva, "A arte de navegar dos portugueses desde o Infante a D. João de Castro," 2:361–63; A. Fontoura da Costa, *A marinharia dos descobrimentos* (Lisbon: Imprensa da Armada, 1939), 171–72 and 188–89; and Luís de Albuquerque, "Contribuição das navegações do século XVI para o conhecimento do magnetismo terrestre," *Revista da Universidade de Coimbra* 24 (1921): 14–19. We have news of an even earlier instrument constructed by an apothecary from Seville named Felipe Guillén, who, according to the Portuguese cosmographer Alonso de Santa Cruz, presented his invention to the king of Portugal in 1525. It likely that Guillén and Faleiro knew each other, as they lived in the same town. For what little we know about Guillén and several other early magnetic observations, see G. Hellmann, "The Beginnings of Magnetic Observations," *Terrestrial Magnetism and Atmospheric Electricity* 4, no. 2 (June 1899): 2–86. Alonso de Santa Cruz was also involved in this effort. See Mariano Cuesta Domingo, "Alonso de Santa Cruz, cartógrafo y fabricante de instrumentos náuticos de la Casa de Contratación," *Revista Complutense de Historia de América* 30 (2004): 7–40. Martín Cortés also contributed to the magnetic variation discussion some years later by correctly advancing the idea that it was caused by what he called a "punto atractivo" or "attractive point" on Earth, that is, a magnetic pole as we now call it. See Martín Cortés, *Breve compendio de la sphera* (Seville, 1545), passim; Francisco José González González, *Astronomía y navegación en España: Siglos XVI–XVIII* (Madrid: Editorial Mapfre, 1992), 76; and López Piñero, *El arte de navegar en la España del Renacimiento,* chap. 5. The first report of a voyage making systematic observations of magnetic declination is D. João de Castro's "Roteiro de Lisboa a Goa" (1538). Joaquim Alves Gaspar discusses this *roteiro* and compares it to estimations of magnetic declination in "From the Portolan Chart of the Mediterranean to the Latitude Chart of the Atlantic," chap. 2. I thank Joaquim Alves Gaspar for going over some of this material. Needless to say, I am responsible for any lingering mistakes or inaccuracies.

6. The logbook entries are all from Jaymes Martínez Fortún and Diego Martín, pilots of the *San Pablo,* "Derrotero del viaje a las islas del poniente," Philippines, April 9, 1565, AGI, MP-Filipinas, 2. All of my sixteenth-century estimations of magnetic declination in the text and the maps were done with the National Centers for Environmental Information calculator based on the International Geomagnetic Reference Field using the date of January 1, 1590. See https://www.ngdc.noaa.gov/geomag/calculators/magcalc.shtml. Although twenty-five years may seem like a long time, the difference in magnetic variation is not that significant. The estimation of the line of zero magnetic declination 1,500 miles west of Navidad assumes a latitude of nine degrees.

7. In the absence of a better method, pilots continued to use magnetic declination as a proxy for longitude for many years. In 1585, two decades after Legazpi's expedition, a Portuguese cosmographer elaborated a map of the western Pacific with isogonic lines, the first isogonic chart that we know of in the history of humankind; and more than a century later, in 1702, English astronomer Edmond Halley published an isogonic chart of the Atlantic as an aid to navigation. See Alves Gaspar and Leitão, "Luís Teixeira, c. 1585."

8. All quotes are from Legazpi, "Relación circunstanciada." See also Quimby, "The Hierro Commerce," 6–8.

9. See W. H. Easton and T. L. Ku, "Recent Reefs and Shore Lines of Guam," *Micronesica* 14, no. 1 (June 1979): 1–11. The shore bench is widest by Cocos Lagoon and Achang Reef, reaching 850 meters. On the Battle of Guam, see Gordon L. Rottman, *Guam 1941 & 1944: Loss and Reconquest* (Oxford: Osprey Publishing, 2004), 43.

10. Magellan's landfall in Guam probably occurred somewhere along the northwest coast, even though today a marker commemorating Magellan's landing site exists at Umatac Bay on the southwest coast. See Robert F. Rogers and Dirk Anthony Ballendorf, "Magellan's Landfall in the Mariana Islands," *Journal of Pacific History* 24 (1989): 193–99. I thank Omaira Brunal-Perry for bringing this article to my attention. On Loaísa's brief stay in Guam, see Fernando Guillén Salvetti and Carlos Vila Miranda, "La desdichada expedición de García Jofre de Loaísa," in Landín Carrasco, *Descubrimientos españoles en el Mar del Sur,* 207–8. It is possible that Saavedra too may have seen Guam on December 29, 1527, but could not make landfall in any case. See the discussion in Génova Sotil and Guillén Salvetti, "Viaje de Saavedra desde Nueva España," 241–44.

11. The quote is from George Bryan Souza and Jeffrey S. Turley, eds., *The Boxer Codex: Transcription and Translation of an Illustrated Late Sixteenth-Century Spanish Manuscript Concerning the Geography, Ethnography and History of the Pacific, South-*

East Asia and East Asia (Leiden: Brill, 2016), 40. Quimby, "The Hierro Commerce," 3–4.

12. All the quotes are from Legazpi, "Relación circunstanciada." Population estimates for Guam prior to the 1660s are highly speculative, and the figure of thirty thousand is little more than a rough guess. See the discussion in Jane H. Underwood, "Population History of Guam: Context of Microevolution," *Micronesica* 9, no. 1 (July 1973): 11–44. The full name of the Magellan castaway is Gonzalo de Vigo. As his name indicates, he hailed from Vigo in northwestern Spain and had joined Magellan's expedition as a cabin boy aboard the *Concepción*. He had then deserted along with two Portuguese men and survived in the Marianas for five years until the Loaísa expedition found him. Father Urdaneta would have remembered him very well.

13. Legazpi, "Relación circunstanciada." The bundles of rice brought by the Chamorro merchants were reportedly "three or four *almudes*." An *almud* is an old Spanish measurement of volume rather than weight equivalent to 4.635 liters. My conversion assumes that a liter of rice weighs 782 grams. The actual results would be 23.9 for three *almudes* and 31.9 for four *almudes,* which I took the liberty of rounding off in the text, given that the original source offered merely an approximation.

14. All the quotes are from Legazpi, "Relación circunstanciada."

15. See ceremony of possession of Guam, Umatac Bay, January 26, 1565, AGI, transcribed for the Micronesian Area Research Center, University of Guam; and Legazpi, "Relación circunstanciada."

16. Legazpi, "Relación circunstanciada." Even so, Legazpi recognized the strategic value of Guam. For the identity of the unfortunate youngster, see García-Abásolo, "Compañeros y continuadores de Urdaneta," 451–52. In 1569 the Spanish commander petitioned and obtained from the Spanish king the right to "discover and people the said Islands of the Thieves." For Legazpi's later designs on Guam, see Legazpi's title of governor of the Islands of the Thieves, Madrid, August 14, 1569, AGI; and instructions given to Legazpi about what to do in the Islands of the Thieves, Madrid, August 28, 1569, AGI, both documents transcribed for the Micronesian Area Research Center, University of Guam. It took time for Spaniards to colonize Guam. They did not build the San Dionisio church at the bottom of the bay until 1681, as well as a two-story governor's palace also dating to the 1680s. The impact of the Spanish language on the Indigenous Chamorro is difficult to exaggerate. See Donal M. Topping, Pedro M. Ogo, and Bernadita C. Dungca, *Chamorro-English Dictionary* (Honolulu: University of Hawai'i Press, 1975), passim.

8. The Far Side of the World

1. Arellano, "Relación mui circunstanciada." See also Landín Carrasco and Sánchez Masiá, "El viaje redondo de Alonso de Arellano," 483–84.

2. Arellano, "Relación mui circunstanciada." Don Alonso de Arellano writes that the *San Lucas* reached Mindanao at a latitude of nine degrees, which seems unlikely; it may have been seven degrees or even six. From that point, the vessel followed the coast toward the south until reaching what Don Alonso described as "el remate de la tierra donde fenece la costa norte-sur," or "the very end of the north-south coast," a description that fits perfectly with Cape San Agustin. After that, the *San Lucas* entered the Davao Gulf and found shelter in one of the coves. In all of this, I am in perfect agreement with the discussion in Landín Carrasco and Sánchez Masiá, "El viaje redondo de Alonso de Arellano," 483. For an excellent geographic introduction to the Philippines, see Frederick L. Wernsted and J. E. Spencer, *The Philippine Island World: A Physical, Cultural, and Regional Geography* (Berkeley: University of California Press, 1967), passim. The conversion of some communities in Mindanao to Islam set the stage for a multi-secular religious, ethnic, and racial showdown with the Spanish that continued after the US takeover in 1898. On Mindanao and its history, see F. Delor Angeles, *Mindanao: The Story of an Island* (Davao City: San Pedro Press, 1964); and above all William Henry Scott, *Barangay: Sixteenth-Century Philippine Culture and Society* (Manila: Ateneo de Manila University Press, 1994), passim.

3. The quotes are from Arellano, "Relación mui circunstanciada." See also Landín Carrasco and Sánchez Masiá, "El viaje redondo de Alonso de Arellano," 483–84.

4. The quote is from Arellano, "Relación mui circunstanciada." The Cortés-Moctezuma encounter shows different cultural practices with respect to hugging. When Hernán Cortés approached the Aztec leader with the intention of wrapping his arms around Moctezuma, two attendant lords restrained the Spanish conquistador and admonished him that their *tlatoani* could not be touched. This is well known and narrated by Cortés himself in his second letter to Emperor Charles V, October 30, 1520. The dagger may have been a barong knife or a kris. Among prior commanders who had gone through the bloodletting ritual was Álvaro de Saavedra. See Vicencia de Nápoles, "Relación de la navegación de Álvaro de Saavedra desde la Nueva España en descubrimiento de los malucos . . . ," n.p., n.d., AGN, Instituciones Coloniales, Hospital de Jesus 53, vol. 438, expediente 1. The rest of Legazpi's fleet also performed the same blood ritual on the island of Leyte around February 20, 1565. On the Spanish side, Andrés de Ibarra cut himself.

5. Arellano, "Relación mui circunstanciada."

6. All the quotes are from Arellano, "Relación mui circunstanciada." This is the only source describing these events that we know of.

7. Arellano, "Relación mui circunstanciada."

8. On the division of labor on a sixteenth-century vessel, see Contente Domingues and Guerreiro, *A vida a bordo na carreira da Índia*, 198–99.

9. Arellano, "Relación mui circunstanciada."

10. The quotes are from Arellano, "Relación mui circunstanciada."

11. Arellano, "Relación mui circunstanciada."

12. The quotes are from Arellano, "Relación mui circunstanciada." The list of products is derived from the "Copia de una carta venida de Sevilla a Miguel Salvador de Valencia, la cual narra el venturoso descubrimiento . . . ," Barcelona, 1566, facsimile version in *Viaje y tornaviaje a Filipinas, 1564,* ed. Andrés Henestrosa (Mexico City: Fondo Pagliai, 1975), 5.

13. San Agustín, *Conquistas de las Islas Filipinas, 1565–1615,* 236–37. Amancio Landín Carrasco and Luis Sánchez Masiá speculate that a Greek crew member of the *San Lucas* named Nicolao may have been Friar Gaspar's additional source, as he subsequently joined the Augustinian order. Landín Carrasco and Sánchez Masiá, "El viaje redondo de Alonso de Arellano," 485–86.

14. The quote is from the entry beginning on March 19, 1565, in Legazpi, "Relación circunstanciada." There may have been a second source of local knowledge: a survivor of the Villalobos expedition held captive for more than twenty years in the Philippines. This Spaniard (whose name has also disappeared in the mists of time) had gone completely native: "married and with children, and his body was tattooed in the fashion of these Indians." The people of Samar had been careful not to bring this man near the visiting Spaniards. Yet the captive was resourceful and made his presence known by writing a message with charcoal on a piece of wood "to please ransom him, for the love of God." Commander Legazpi reportedly demanded the captive's release and offered some trade goods for him. The castaway promised to lead the expeditionaries "to where they had killed Ferdinand Magellan, because in that island there was only one main port that had a great population and wooden houses with thatched roofs, and soldiers who slept at the top of these houses." Juan de Borja, Spanish ambassador in Portugal, n.p., 1565, "Cartas de Juan de Borja," AGI, Patronato, 46, R. 8. Borja's letters provide information conveyed through Portuguese channels, often adding unique details. The information is usually in agreement with other accounts, but in this case, the existence of this Spanish survivor in Samar cannot be corroborated through other sources. See also Scott, *Barangay,* 74–75. The junk was carrying merchandise from

the sultan of Brunei, but the vessel reportedly belonged to a Portuguese resident of Borneo named Antón Maletis.

15. All quotes are from Legazpi, "Relación circunstanciada."

16. All quotes are from Legazpi, "Relación circunstanciada." Tuasan's explanation was entirely correct, as Legazpi and other fleet officials were able to corroborate. See Commander Miguel López de Legazpi, "Información sobre el daño que los Portugueses del Maluco hicieron en las Filipinas," island of Bohol, March 25, 1565, in *CDIU* 3, document 43; and Guido de Lavezaris, Andrés Cauchela, and Andrés de Mirandaola to the Audiencia of Mexico, Cebu, May 28, 1565, in *CDIU* 3, document 31.

17. The first quote is from Commander Miguel López de Legazpi, "Relación circunstanciada . . . ," Philippines, May 27, 1565, *CDIU* II, document 27. The second quote is from "Auto para poblar a Cebú," Bohol, April 21, 1565, AGI, transcription made for the Micronesian Area Research Center, University of Guam. On the choice of Cebu, see also the introductory essay by Patricio Hidalgo Nuchera in *Los primeros de Filipinas: Crónicas de la conquista del archipiélago de San Lázaro,* ed. Patricio Hidalgo Nuchera (Madrid: Ediciones Polifemo, 1995), 43. Cebu, however, was not ideal for international trade. For instance, Chinese sailing guides published in 1617 clearly avoided inland Visayan waters. See Scott, *Barangay,* 75; and Chen Ching-Ho, *The Chinese Community in the Sixteenth-Century Philippines* (Tokyo: Centre for East Asian Cultural Studies, 1968), chaps. 1 and 2.

18. "Requerimientos y apercibimientos que se hicieron a los indios y nunca quisieron venir de paz," Cebu, April 28, 1565, AGI, transcription for the Micronesian Area Research Center, University of Guam.

19. "Requerimientos y apercibimientos que se hicieron a los indios y nunca quisieron venir de paz," Cebu, April 28, 1565, AGI, transcription for the Micronesian Area Research Center, University of Guam.

20. The first quote is from Legazpi, "Relación circunstanciada." For the quote from Juan de Camuz, see "Testimony about the Christ Child found in the Philippines," Cebu, May 16, 1565, in *CDIU* 3, document 42.

21. The quote is from Legazpi, "Relación circunstanciada." See also "Testimony about the Christ Child found in the Philippines."

9. Vuelta

1. On the return attempt of the *Trinidad,* see Landín Carrasco and Romero de Pazos, "Gómez de Espinosa y su intento de regreso por el Pacífico," 163–86.

2. On the first attempt of the Villalobos expedition, see Barreiro-Meiro Fernández,

"Bernardo de la Torre y su intento de tornaviaje." For Villalobos's second return attempt, see Génova Sotil, "Ortiz de Retes, por aguas australes."

3. It is possible that castaways from Japan may have drifted to the coast of North America before 1565, but no clear evidence of any such event has reached us, at least not to my knowledge. For some context, see Frederik L. Schodt, *Native American in the Land of the Shogun: Ranald MacDonald and the Opening of Japan* (Berkeley: Stone Bridge Press, 2003), 57–60.

4. We know that Legazpi's fleet was in Bohol on April 21, 1565, and arrived in Cebu six days later, on April 27 (see the previous chapter), where it remained. Don Alonso's account is less precise as to the timing and ports visited, but we know that the *San Lucas* left from a cove in southeastern Mindanao on March 4, 1565, passed through "Magellan's Island," or Cebu, and reached what the expeditionaries called the "Islas del Cabo" somewhere on the San Bernardino Strait on April 21–22, 1565. The distance between Cebu and the San Bernardino Strait is 165 miles as the crow flies. On a sailing ship, this would have taken at least three days, and therefore we can be certain that the *San Lucas* could not have been in Cebu any later than April 18, 1565, ahead of the rest of the fleet by at least nine days. Arellano, "Relación mui circunstanciada." For the mistaken assertion, see San Agustín, *Conquistas de las Islas Filipinas, 1565–1615*, 236–37.

5. All the quotes are from Arellano, "Relación mui circunstanciada."

6. For an introduction to wind circulation, see Pinet, *Invitation to Oceanography*, chap. 6; and for cruising routes out of the Philippines, see Cornell, *World Cruising Routes*, 265–313.

7. On Urdaneta's obvious knowledge of the monsoon and the general circulation of currents and winds in the Pacific, see Miguel Bosch, "Las dificultades náuticas del tornaviaje," 495–98.

8. Of the previous return attempts across the Pacific, the one aboard the *Trinidad* during the Magellan expedition began on April 6, 1522. The first return attempt of the Saavedra expedition did not start until June 12, 1528, its progress by way of the coast of New Guinea was extremely slow, and thus by early September it had only reached the Caroline Islands. The following year the Saavedra expedition tried again, starting more than a month earlier, on May 3, 1529, but progress was even slower this time (also by way of New Guinea), reaching the Carolines only in late September or early October. The first return attempt of the Villalobos expedition did not depart until August 4, 1543, and made good progress, but because of the late start and lack of water had to turn back on October 18, 1543. The second return attempt of the Villalobos expedition started on the island of Ti-

dore on May 16, 1545, once again by way of the coast of New Guinea, resulting in a very slow and meandering trajectory. For all of the return attempt reconstructions, I rely on Landín Carrasco, *Descubrimientos españoles en el Mar del Sur,* passim. Other navigators also agreed that the best time to return began in late April. Juan de la Isla, for instance, wrote in 1565 that "from the end of April to the end of October was a time of vendavales [storms] that were nonetheless useful for the return voyage." Possibly Juan de la Isla, "Relación de las Islas del Poniente y del camino que a ella se hizo desde la Nueva España."

9. The quote is from Gemelli Careri, *Giro del Mondo,* bk. 3, chap. 1. The information about the storms endured by Spanish navigators in the seventeenth century comes from Schurz, *The Manila Galleon,* 253–55. On the galleons lost, see James Francis Warren, "Weather, History, and Empire: The Typhoon Factor and the Manila Galleon Trade, 1565–1815," in *Anthony Reid and the Study of the Southeast Asian Past,* ed. Geoff Wade and Li Tana (Singapore: Institute of Southeast Asian Studies, 2012), 183. For present-day sailing recommendations and typhoons, see Cornell, *World Cruising Routes,* 308–9. The year 2015 alone witnessed a staggering twenty-seven tropical storms—eighteen typhoons, and nine super-typhoons—and a total of fifty-four meteorological events for an average of about one per week. Although in North America we tend to hear more about the hurricanes in the Caribbean and the Gulf of Mexico, the western North Pacific is more active still.

10. The first quote comes from Arellano, "Relación mui circunstanciada." The second quote appears in the "Parecer dado a Antonio de Mendoza: Viaje al Maluco," n.p., April 1573, AGI, Patronato, 46, R. 10. In spite of its present classification and dating, this *parecer* was written by Urdaneta for Viceroy Don Luis de Velasco sometime before November 1564. See also Miguel Bosch, "Las dificultades náuticas del tornaviaje," 489–90. The sources indicate that Magellan's *Trinidad* weighed between 110 and 120 tons. Interestingly, Villalobos's orders were to attempt the return not with the sixty-ton *San Juan de Letrán* but with the bigger and sturdier galleon *San Jorge,* which weighed 120 tons. The crew was of the same opinion, evidently believing that a larger ship would have a better chance of succeeding. The commander's determination, however, was to try the return with the lighter *San Juan de Letrán,* probably motivated by vested interests. See Barreiro-Meiro Fernández, "Bernardo de la Torre y su intento de tornaviaje," 362.

11. The quote comes from Arellano, "Relación mui circunstanciada." Instead of seventy days, the return voyage lasted 109 days: 1.56 times longer. This would bring down the daily water ration to a disquieting 5.6 cups. For an excellent discussion of *pipas, arrobas,* and measurements of volume in sixteenth-century ships, see Dueñas Fontán, "Medidas de los navíos de la jornada de Inglaterra," 11–12.

On life aboard the ships, see Pérez-Mallaína, *Spain's Men of the Sea,* 144. My calculation of the total amount of water aboard the *San Lucas* assumes that four of the *pipas* were missing four *arrobas* of water each and the other four lacked five *arrobas*. It also assumes that a cup of water contains eight ounces, or sixteen cups per gallon. For some present-day ideas about hydration, see Jessica Brown, "How Much Water Should You Drink a Day?," BBC, April 5, 2019.

12. Arellano, "Relación mui circunstanciada." My calculation of the amount of food assumes that a *quintal* is equivalent to one hundred Castilian pounds, about forty-six kilograms, or 101.4 modern pounds, and further assumes a return voyage lasting 109 days.

13. The quote is from Arellano, "Relación mui circunstanciada."

14. Arellano, "Relación mui circunstanciada." The identification of "Pago Mayor" as Japan was discussed in Landín Carrasco and Sánchez Masiá, "El viaje redondo de Alonso de Arellano," 486–87. For an excellent study of early European contact with Japan and the evolving cartography, see the preface by Rui Loureiro in *La découverte du Japon par les Européens (1543–1551),* ed. Xavier de Castro (Paris: Éditions Chandeigne, 2013), 7–91. See also Ainhoa Reyes Manzano, "La cruz y la catana: Relaciones entre España y Japón (siglos XVI–XVII)" (PhD diss., Universidad de la Rioja, 2014).

15. For mentions of the chart of the North Pacific aboard the *San Lucas,* see Arellano, "Relación mui circunstanciada." For a close analysis of Gastaldi's map, see Thomas Suárez, *Early Mapping of Southeast Asia: The Epic Story of Seafarers, Adventurers, and Cartographers Who First Mapped the Regions Between China and India* (Singapore: Periplus Editions, 1999), chap. 11. Although Gastaldi's map is among the most relevant, it is possible to consider other maps, like Sebastian Cabot's map of 1544. I thank Ricardo Padrón for his cartographic advice and appreciate his admonition that humanistic maps such as Gastaldi's cannot substitute for the charts used by working pilots. For the broader context, see Suárez, *Early Mapping of Southeast Asia,* chaps. 2–3; and Loureiro, *La découverte du Japon,* preface, 55–96.

16. Another map, also elaborated in the 1550s but in China and no less remarkable, would have offered an excellent corrective, making clear Japan's proximity to the Asian landmass. Yet the Spanish didn't know about this remarkable map until 1574, when a group of Chinese merchants took a copy of it to Manila. The map in question is at the Archivo General de Indias in Seville: "Mapa de China," MP-Filipinas, 5. A report from Philippines governor Guido de Lavezaris explained the map's provenance. Guido de Lavezaris, Manila, July 30, 1574, AGI, Filipinas, 6, R. 2, N. 21. For the trajectories of later Spanish ships with respect to Japan, see Schurz, *The Manila Galleon,* 230.

17. The quote is from Arellano, "Relación mui circunstanciada." Sōfu Gan's exact latitude is 29°47'39"N, so Lope Martín's estimates were off by more than one degree in this case. Only in 2017 did a team of scientists conduct a detailed survey of this very remote ecosystem. Much information from the 2017 survey was featured in the NHK documentary *Tokyo's Lost Islands: Sofugan,* which aired on February 23, 2019. Some authors speculate that the rock formation visited by the *San Lucas* may have been Sumisu-tō, also known as Smith Island or Smith Rock. Its latitude of 31°26'13"N corresponds more closely to what Lope Martín recorded, although Arellano's description "very narrow, no more than a small house" does not fit Sumisu-tō so well. See the discussion in Landín Carrasco and Sánchez Masiá, "El viaje redondo de Alonso de Arellano," 487. In any case, these two rock formations are relatively close to each other and presented the same conditions to the men of the *San Lucas,* so the precise identity is not particularly relevant.

18. On the Kuroshio Current, see Ken Sawada and Nobuhiko Handa, "Variability of the Path of the Kuroshio Ocean Current over the Past 25,000 Years," *Nature* 392 (1998): 592–95. The Japanese refer to these castaways or drifters as *hyoryusha.* Some of them were carried by the currents and winds to the Kuril Islands, the Kamchatka Peninsula, the Aleutian Islands, or even Hawai'i, in addition to the few who reached North America. See Schodt, *Native American in the Land of the Shogun,* 57–60. Japanese sources may turn up more than a handful of drifters reaching the coast of North America.

19. All quotes are from Arellano, "Relación mui circunstanciada." Sooty shearwaters cover more than 34,000 miles, the longest animal migration ever recorded, as electronic trackers have revealed. See Scott A. Shaffer et al., "Migratory Shearwaters Integrate Oceanic Resources Across the Pacific Ocean in an Endless Summer," *Proceedings of the National Academy of Sciences* 103, no. 34 (August 2006): 12799–802.

20. Arellano, "Relación mui circunstanciada."

21. Arellano, "Relación mui circunstanciada." Low-pressure systems developing in the Sea of Japan or off the Kamchatka Peninsula and then barreling east across the Aleutian Islands are common in the summer, bringing unsettled and very cold weather to the region. The skeptical scholar is O.H.K. Spate, *The Spanish Lake* (Canberra: Australian National University Press, 1979), 105.

22. The quote is from Arellano, "Relación mui circunstanciada." On the attempt to reach Asia by land in 1539–1542, see Flint and Flint, *A Most Splendid Company,* 71–74. Twenty-five years after the *San Lucas* voyage, a Jesuit polymath named Joseph de Acosta similarly advanced "a great conjecture that the New World is not completely separated from the other world [Eurasia], but that one part of the earth and the other must join and continue, or at least they come very close." See

Joseph de Acosta, *Natural and Moral History of the Indies* (Durham: Duke University Press, 2002), 63. Acosta's book was first published in 1590. He also provided a succinct explanation of the circular winds and currents in both the Atlantic and the Pacific. Acosta, *Natural and Moral History of the Indies,* 106–8.

23. The quote is from Arellano, "Relación mui circunstanciada."

24. Arellano, "Relación mui circunstanciada."

25. The quotes are from Arellano, "Relación mui circunstanciada." The calculation of 294 gallons still assumes that a *pipa* contains 27.5 *arrobas* and each *arroba* is equivalent to 4.36 gallons.

26. Arellano, "Relación mui circunstanciada." Later Spanish pilots returning to America from the Philippines learned to look for kelp as a sign of the proximity of North America. They described this characteristic seaweed as "like the onions from Europe with stems that are three or four fathoms in length, and are green or red in color." José González Cabrera Bueno, *Navegación especulativa y práctica* (Manila: Convento de Nuestra Señora de Los Ángeles, 1734), 294. At greater length, the Italian traveler Giovanni Francesco Gemelli Careri explained how pilots involved in the return voyage, after reaching a latitude of forty degrees, "afterward fall until they meet the signs—being weeds that the Sea of California carries for hundreds of leagues—and thus continue with favorable winds." Gemelli Careri, *Giro del Mondo,* bk. 3, chap. 3.

27. The quote is from Arellano, "Relación mui circunstanciada." Working out the exact location of the *San Lucas* in the weeks immediately before landfall is impossible. As noted earlier, there are at least two different ways to interpret the captain's offhand statement. One is that the "certain variation of the compass needle"—never quantified in the narrative—caused the pilot to adjust the course of the *San Lucas* by "one-quarter" of "northeasting." In practice, this would have made no sense, as the pilot would have had to correct to the *southeast,* given the declination. Still, this interpretation cannot be entirely ruled out. Second, if Lope Martín had actually estimated the magnetic variation to be "one-quarter" of "northeasting," or 11.25 degrees east of true north, then it is possible to do this calculation. First, we need to assume a certain latitude, and unfortunately, one paragraph earlier, Don Alonso merely notes that in the final stretch of the voyage, the *San Lucas* ranged between thirty-eight and twenty-seven degrees of northern latitude without giving any specific dates. For the purposes of this calculation, I assume a latitude of thirty-eight degrees. Then, if we rely on the most accepted geomagnetic model at our disposal going back to the sixteenth century, this would result in 142 degrees of western longitude, or 1,033 miles due west of Point Reyes. The distance of the *San Lucas* from the coast of North America

would have been greater, assuming that the latitude was less than thirty-eight degrees. Later Spanish navigators approaching North America used magnetic declination to estimate longitude as a matter of course. In the eighteenth century, the *piloto mayor* of the Carrera de Filipinas (the route to the Philippines) wrote, "You will be careful to ascertain the variation of the needle which will be between nine and ten degrees, and from there you will steer due east until sixty-four degrees of longitude, and at that meridian, you will find that the variation will have increased to fourteen degrees, which is the greatest that the modern navigators have found, and from there it begins to diminish." González Cabrera Bueno, *Navegación especulativa y práctica*, 294.

28. Arellano, "Relación mui circunstanciada"; Landín Carrasco and Sánchez Masiá, "El viaje redondo de Alonso de Arellano," 490.

29. The quote is from Arellano, "Relación mui circunstanciada."

30. Arellano, "Relación mui circunstanciada."

31. Quote from Arellano, "Relación mui circunstanciada."

10. Fall from Glory

1. The quote is from Acosta, *Natural and Moral History of the Indies*, 108. Economic historians Dennis O. Flynn and Arturo Giráldez have rightfully dated the start of the much-debated process of globalization precisely to 1571, when the Spanish established Manila as an entrepôt, and the five continents finally came to be connected. Dennis O. Flynn and Arturo Giráldez, "Cycles of Silver: Globalization as Historical Process," *World Economics* 3, no. 2 (April–June 2002): 1–2. On the Anglo-American takeover, see Benito Legarda Jr., *After the Galleons: Foreign Trade, Economic Change and Entrepreneurship in the Nineteenth-Century Philippines* (Quezon City: Ateneo de Manila University Press, 1999), esp. chaps. 5, 8, and 9; John Mayo, *Commerce and Contraband on Mexico's West Coast in the Era of Barron, Forbes & Co., 1821–1859* (New York: Peter Lang, 2006); and Vera Valdés Lakowsky, *De las minas al mar: Historia de la plata mexicana en Asia, 1565–1834* (Mexico City: Fondo de Cultura Económica, 1987), 138–48.

2. The quote is from Juan de Borja, Spanish ambassador in Portugal, n.p., 1565, "Cartas de Juan de Borja," AGI, Patronato, 46, R. 8. As mentioned earlier, Borja's letters provide information conveyed through Portuguese channels, often adding unique details. The first published account referred excitedly to the "venturous discovery and marvelous things that have happened" and predicted "a great benefit to the whole of Christendom." "Copia de una carta venida de Sevilla a Miguel Salvador de Valencia, la cual narra el venturoso descubrimiento," passim.

By 1566, when the letter was published in Barcelona, Urdaneta's return was also known, so the letter writer refers to both. In his *Sucesos de las Islas Filipinas* published in 1609, Antonio de Morga raises the possibility that Don Alonso and Lope Martín may have attempted to claim the reward. Antonio de Morga, *Sucesos de las Islas Filipinas* (Mexico City: Fondo de Cultura Económica, 2007), 17.

3. On the provisions of the *San Pedro,* see logbook of Esteban Rodríguez, in *CDIU* 2, document 34; and above all the "Registro de la nao *San Pedro,*" transcribed in its entirely in García-Abásolo, "Compañeros y continuadores de Urdaneta," 455–58. See also Amancio Landín Carrasco and Luis Sánchez Masiá, "Urdaneta y la vuelta de poniente," in Landín Carrasco, *Descubrimientos españoles en el Mar del Sur,* 495. On the numbers of deaths and men still able to help, see the logbook of pilot Rodrigo de Espinosa, entry for October 1, 1565, in *CDIU* 2, document 34.

4. The first quote is from Esteban de Salazar (1532–1596), who was Urdaneta's contemporary and knew him well. Esteban de Salazar, *Veinte discursos sobre el Credo en declaración de nuestra Sancta Fe Catholica y Doctrina Christiana* (Seville: Imprenta de Andrea Pescioni y Juan de León, 1586), 61. The same fragment of Salazar's work is quoted by Friar Gaspar de San Agustín in *Conquistas de las Islas Filipinas, 1565–1615,* 374–75. The last two quotes are from Friar Juan de Grijalva, *Crónica de la Orden de N.P.S. Agustín en las provincias de la Nueva España,* 264.

5. Quotes from Gabriel Díaz, treasurer of the Casa de Moneda in Mexico City and legal representative of Commander Legazpi, accusation against Don Alonso de Arellano, Mexico City, November 7, 1565, in *CDIU* 2, document 37.

6. Gabriel Díaz, legal representative of Commander Legazpi, second accusation against Don Alonso de Arellano and others, Mexico City, November 11, 1565, in *CDIU* 2, document 37.

7. Quote from Gabriel Díaz, second accusation against Don Alonso de Arellano and others.

8. Reference to the Villalobos incident and commentary by editor Martín Fernández de Navarrete in *CDIU* 3:15–16. For a broader perspective on methods used to discipline the crew, see Pérez-Mallaína, *Spain's Men of the Sea,* chap. 5.

9. The quotes are from *piloto mayor* Esteban Rodríguez's logbook, entry for December 1–3, 1564, in *CDIU* 2, document 33; pilot Pierres Plín's logbook, same dates, "Derroteros y relaciones de los pilotos del viaje a Filipinas," AGI, Patronato, 23, R. 16; and pilots Jaymes Martínez Fortún and Diego Martín's logbook, same dates, AGI, MP-Filipinas, 2. See also the very reasonable analysis in https://ilustresmarinos.wordpress.com/2014/01/10/el-pleito-que-perdio-arellano-i-los-derroteros-que-exoneran-al-san-lucas/#sdendnote14sym. The final quote is from Arellano, "Relación mui circunstanciada." Throughout this book I have

identified this last document as Don Alonso's account. Strictly speaking, the signatories of this account included pilot Lope Martín, boatswain Juan Yáñez, and sailor Juan de Bayona as well as Don Alonso. Even a cursory reading of this account, however, makes clear that it was written from Don Alonso's perspective and always refers to the pilot and the others in the third person.

10. The contingency plan appears in Commander Miguel López de Legazpi, Pacific Ocean, November 25, 1564, AGI, Patronato, 23, R. 16. For a full transcription, see document 20 in Hidalgo Nuchera, *Los primeros de Filipinas,* 138–39. See chapter 4 for more details about this part of the voyage. It is possible to make the argument that by going to between eight and nine degrees of latitude, the *San Lucas* remained a tad too far south of the agreed route. It probably never climbed to ten degrees, as Don Alonso and Lope Martín themselves declared that they had struck Mindanao at nine degrees. In my view, if they had truly wished to abscond, they would have steered either farther north or farther south and never have remained within a range where they could actually have been found.

11. The quote is from Arellano, "Relación mui circunstanciada." Mariano Cuevas arrives at the same conclusion. "In truth, we do not find any fault in Arellano's conduct," he writes, later adding that the men's actions reveal a sincere desire to rejoin the fleet, "and it could not have been any other way because the hunger, thirst, the sick men, and the lack of arms forced them to such a course." Cuevas, *Monje y marino,* 235–37.

12. "Relación muy circunstanciada de lo ocurrido en el Real y Campo de la Isla de Zubu de las Islas Philipinas desde el 1 de junio de 1565 . . . hasta el mes de julio de 1567," Cebu, Philippines, 1567, transcribed in *CDIU* 3, document 38. In all likelihood, the very capable French pilot Pierres Plín suggested such a destination, as he was one of the ringleaders, along with a Venetian corporal named Pablo Hernández and another man simply identified as Jorge the Greek.

13. The quote is from "Relación muy circunstanciada de lo ocurrido en el Real y Campo de la Isla de Zubu de las Islas Philipinas desde el 1 de junio de 1565." From this scant evidence, later historians have affirmed the existence of a cabal of conspirators, including Lope Martín, bent on "carrying out their piratical design before the sailing of the expedition." Sharp, *Adventurous Armada,* 20.

14. Although no document has surfaced clearing Don Alonso and Lope Martín of all charges, such an outcome can be inferred from the subsequent actions of the two men. Don Alonso was allowed to go to Spain, and Lope Martín was advanced an enormous sum of money. Mariano Cuevas also raises the possibility that Don Alonso's high social standing may have swayed the Audiencia but concludes that its members were "honorable and just men," adding, "To assume that

they were closing their eyes to reality and shirking their duty is to give them too little credit." Cuevas, *Monje y marino,* 236. I do not share Cuevas's confidence in the Audiencia members, especially given earlier accusations of corruption as well as their secretive and deceptive proceedings at the start of the voyage.

15. This part of the story is very difficult to piece together and is based on a few but very telling sources. The first quote is from Juan Martínez, a soldier aboard that follow-up expedition, "Relación detallada de los sucesos ocurridos . . . ," Cebu, July 25, 1567, in *CDIU* 3, document 47. The second quote is from Juan de Borja, Spanish ambassador to Portugal, n.p., 1565, "Cartas de Juan de Borja," AGI, Patronato, 46, R. 8. The initial plan of the Audiencia members was to repair the *San Lucas* and the *San Pedro,* recently arrived from the Philippines. The vessels were in such a state of disrepair, however, that by early November 1565, the Audiencia countermanded their previous order and decided to look for another vessel. See José Ignacio Rubio Mañé, "Más documentos relativos a la expedición de Miguel López de Legazpi a Filipinas," and Rubio Mañé, "Más documentos relativos a la expedición de Miguel López de Legazpi a Filipinas, II (Concluye)," *Boletín del Archivo General de la Nación* 11, 2nd ser. (Mexico City, 1970): 83–156 and 453–556, respectively; and Salvador Bernabéu Albert, "Descubrimientos y desventuras del primer galeón del Pacífico: El *San Jerónimo* (1566)," in *Filipinas y el Pacífico: Nuevas miradas, nuevas reflexiones,* ed. Salvador Bernabéu Albert, Carmen Mena García, and Emilio José Luque Azcona (Seville: Editorial Universidad de Sevilla, 2016), 98–99.

16. Pericón's characterization is from Martínez, "Relación detallada de los sucesos ocurridos." The second quote is from Juan de Borja, n.p., 1565, "Cartas de Juan de Borja," AGI, Patronato, 46, R. 8.

11. Survival and Revenge

1. Juan Martínez, soldier aboard the *San Jerónimo,* Cebu, July 25, 1567, "Relación detallada de los sucesos ocurridos durante el viaje de la nao San Jerónimo que salió de Acapulco . . . ," transcribed in *CDIU* 3, document 47. The original is at AGI, Patronato, 24, R. 2. For the likelihood of an El Niño event in 1565, see Ross Couper-Johnston, *El Niño: The Weather Phenomenon That Changed the World* (London: Hodder and Stoughton, 2000), xiii. The ship's name is sometimes spelled *San Gerónimo,* a vessel of between 100 and 150 tons that had been in the water for about sixteen years—very old for ocean passages. Previously the *San Jerónimo* had been plying the Mexico–Peru route. See the discussion in Bernabéu Albert, "Descubrimientos y desventuras del primer galeón del Pacífico," 100. It

was sometimes referred to as a "galleon." See Luis Sánchez Masiá, "La dramática
aventura del 'San Jerónimo,'" in Landín Carrasco, *Descubrimientos españoles en el
Mar del Sur*, 519. For the number of travelers aboard the *San Jerónimo*, see the
discussion in the text.

2. All the quotes are from Martínez, "Relación detallada de los sucesos ocurridos
durante el viaje de la nao San Jerónimo que salió de Acapulco." On some of Captain's Pericón's antecedents in Málaga, see Bernabéu Albert, "Descubrimientos
y desventuras del primer galeón del Pacífico," 102. According to Martínez, the
rumor was that Captain Pericón initially intended to go along with Lope Martín.

3. All references are from Martínez, "Relación detallada de los sucesos ocurridos
durante el viaje de la nao San Jerónimo que salió de Acapulco." Martínez observes
that Lope Martín may have been hurrying Captain Pericón because he feared that
new orders from Mexico City would remove him as pilot of the *San Jerónimo*.
This seems unlikely. On the preparations, see Rubio Mañé, "Más documentos
relativos a la expedición de Miguel López de Legazpi a Filipinas, II (Concluye),"
540–43. On the sailing routes out of Acapulco and optimal timing, see Cornell,
World Cruising Routes, 286.

4. There is no consensus about the number of travelers aboard the *San Jerónimo*.
Reporting on the voyage a few months after the fact, the Spanish ambassador to
Portugal put the number at one hundred, split between sixty soldiers and forty
sailors. Juan de Borja, n.p., n.d., "Cartas de Juan de Borja," AGI, Patronato, 46,
R. 8. By contrast, the soldier Martínez's narrative, the main source for this voy-
age, implies that there may have been as many as 170, of whom 136 arrived in the
Philippines, twenty-seven were marooned in the Marshall Islands, and at least
five died along the way, although the author never provides an overall number.
Martínez, "Relación detallada de los sucesos ocurridos durante el viaje de la nao
San Jerónimo que salió de Acapulco." Of the same opinion are Andrew Sharp in
Adventurous Armada, 115, and Bernabéu Albert, "Descubrimientos y desventuras
del primer galeón del Pacífico," 104. The documentation regarding the provisioning of the *San Jerónimo* in Acapulco mentions seventy soldiers and fifteen additional travelers. Adding the crew, we would get to about 130. See José Ignacio
Rubio Mañé, "La expedición de Miguel López de Legazpi a Filipinas," *Boletín
del Archivo General de la Nación* 5, nos. 3–4, 2nd ser. (Mexico City, 1964), documents 36 and 37. Given the overall dimensions of the *San Jerónimo* and the fact
that Martínez never specifies the total number of men traveling aboard, I believe
that 130 is the most reasonable figure. See also the discussion in Sánchez Masiá,
"La dramática aventura del 'San Jerónimo,'" 519.

5. Martínez, "Relación detallada de los sucesos ocurridos durante el viaje de la nao San Jerónimo que salió de Acapulco."

6. The first quote is from Martínez, "Relación detallada de los sucesos ocurridos durante el viaje de la nao San Jerónimo que salió de Acapulco." The other quotes are from Commander Miguel López de Legazpi, "Relación muy circunstanciada de lo ocurrido en el real . . . ," Cebu, July 10, 1567, in *CDIU* 3, document 52. Eventually when the *San Jerónimo* made it to Cebu, Legazpi was able to interview some of the survivors about what had happened. On Captain Pericón's greed, see Bernabéu Albert, "Descubrimientos y desventuras del primer galeón del Pacífico," 103.

7. All the quotes are from Martínez, "Relación detallada de los sucesos ocurridos durante el viaje de la nao San Jerónimo que salió de Acapulco."

8. Martínez, "Relación detallada de los sucesos ocurridos durante el viaje de la nao San Jerónimo que salió de Acapulco."

9. The first two quotes are from Legazpi, "Relación muy circunstanciada de lo ocurrido en el real." The remaining quotes are from Martínez, "Relación detallada de los sucesos ocurridos durante el viaje de la nao San Jerónimo que salió de Acapulco."

10. Martínez, "Relación detallada de los sucesos ocurridos durante el viaje de la nao San Jerónimo que salió de Acapulco."

11. Martínez, "Relación detallada de los sucesos ocurridos durante el viaje de la nao San Jerónimo que salió de Acapulco." Pentecost marks fifty days after the resurrection of Jesus Christ, when, according to the Bible, the Holy Spirit descended on his disciples and urged them to evangelize.

12. Quotes from Martínez, "Relación detallada de los sucesos ocurridos durante el viaje de la nao San Jerónimo que salió de Acapulco."

13. Martínez, "Relación detallada de los sucesos ocurridos durante el viaje de la nao San Jerónimo que salió de Acapulco."

14. The quotes are from Martínez, "Relación detallada de los sucesos ocurridos durante el viaje de la nao San Jerónimo que salió de Acapulco." Rodrigo del Angle is sometimes rendered as Rodrigo del Langle. See also Bernabéu Albert, "Descubrimientos y desventuras del primer galeón del Pacífico," 103.

15. Martínez, "Relación detallada de los sucesos ocurridos durante el viaje de la nao San Jerónimo que salió de Acapulco."

16. Martínez, "Relación detallada de los sucesos ocurridos durante el viaje de la nao San Jerónimo que salió de Acapulco." See also Sharp, *Adventurous Armada*, 123–24.

17. The quotes are from Martínez, "Relación detallada de los sucesos ocurridos du-

rante el viaje de la nao San Jerónimo que salió de Acapulco." Pablo Pérez-Mal-laína was the first to call Lope Martín a "true 'Lope de Aguirre' of the Pacific." Pérez-Mallaína, *Spain's Men of the Sea,* 41.

18. Martínez, "Relación detallada de los sucesos ocurridos durante el viaje de la nao San Jerónimo que salió de Acapulco." The *San Jerónimo* had remained at nine or ten degrees of latitude. Earlier in the voyage it had passed very close to Clipperton Island. See the discussion in Sánchez Masiá, "La dramática aventura del 'San Jerónimo,'" 524–26; and Bernabéu Albert, "Descubrimientos y desventuras del primer galeón del Pacífico," 108.

19. Martínez, "Relación detallada de los sucesos ocurridos durante el viaje de la nao San Jerónimo que salió de Acapulco." See also Sharp, *Adventurous Armada,* 123–24.

20. Martínez, "Relación detallada de los sucesos ocurridos durante el viaje de la nao San Jerónimo que salió de Acapulco." The identification of Ujelang Atoll as the place where the *San Jerónimo* came to rest is the most standard interpretation. For example, see Sharp, *Adventurous Armada,* 127–28; Sánchez Masiá, "La dramática aventura del 'San Jerónimo,'" 528; and Richard V. Williamson and Donna K. Stone, *Archaeological Survey of Rongelap Atoll* (Majuro Atoll: Republic of the Marshall Islands Historic Preservation Office, 2001), 5.

21. All quotes are from Martínez, "Relación detallada de los sucesos ocurridos durante el viaje de la nao San Jerónimo que salió de Acapulco." See also Legazpi, "Relación muy circunstanciada de lo ocurrido en el real"; and Sharp, *Adventurous Armada,* 129–31.

22. Martínez, "Relación detallada de los sucesos ocurridos durante el viaje de la nao San Jerónimo que salió de Acapulco." See also Sharp, *Adventurous Armada,* 128–31. Lope Martín reportedly said that Cortés had "burned" the ships when in fact he had had them sunk; he was already getting some of the details of the story wrong.

23. Martínez, "Relación detallada de los sucesos ocurridos durante el viaje de la nao San Jerónimo que salió de Acapulco." See also Sharp, *Adventurous Armada,* 131–32.

24. Martínez, "Relación detallada de los sucesos ocurridos durante el viaje de la nao San Jerónimo que salió de Acapulco." See also Legazpi, "Relación muy circunstanciada de lo ocurrido en el real"; and Sharp, *Adventurous Armada,* 133–35.

25. All the quotes are from Martínez, "Relación detallada de los sucesos ocurridos durante el viaje de la nao San Jerónimo que salió de Acapulco." See also Legazpi, "Relación muy circunstanciada de lo ocurrido en el real"; and Sharp, *Adventurous Armada,* 134–35. Counter-plotter Marcos de Cubillas left additional records that confirm the overall story but do not add any significant details. See "Memorial de

Marcos de Cubillas," Mexico City, January 13, 1568, AGI, Audiencia de Filipinas 34, N. 10.

26. Martínez, "Relación detallada de los sucesos ocurridos durante el viaje de la nao San Jerónimo que salió de Acapulco"; and Legazpi, "Relación muy circunstanciada de lo ocurrido en el real."

27. All the quotes are from Martínez, "Relación detallada de los sucesos ocurridos durante el viaje de la nao San Jerónimo que salió de Acapulco." See also Legazpi, "Relación muy circunstanciada de lo ocurrido en el real"; and Sharp, *Adventurous Armada,* 136–37.

28. Martínez, "Relación detallada de los sucesos ocurridos durante el viaje de la nao San Jerónimo que salió de Acapulco"; also Legazpi, "Relación muy circunstanciada de lo ocurrido en el real"; and Sharp, *Adventurous Armada,* 136–41.

12. At the Spanish Court

1. The first two quotes are from San Agustín, *Conquistas de las Islas Filipinas, 1565–1615,* 364–65; the last quote is from "Copia de una carta venida de Sevilla a Miguel Salvador de Valencia, la cual narra el venturoso descubrimiento," passim. Legazpi had reportedly sent a gift for the Spanish king consisting of a "painted stick with two ears of gold and two painted textiles." Antonio García-Abasolo, "Compañeros y continuadores de Urdaneta," in Truchuelo García, *Andrés de Urdaneta,* 460.

2. The quote is from Martínez, "Relación detallada de los sucesos ocurridos durante el viaje de la nao San Jerónimo que salió de Acapulco." Urdaneta set out to travel with fellow friar Andrés de Aguirre, who had also returned from the Philippines, and Legazpi's son Melchor de Legazpi, who had stayed in Mexico City to represent his father and was eager to continue to do so in Spain. For Urdaneta's movements during this time, see Cuevas, *Monje y marino,* 278–79; Arteche, *Urdaneta (el dominador de los espacios del Océano Pacífico),* 195; and Uncilla, *Urdaneta y la conquista de Filipinas,* chap. 13. It is unclear when exactly Don Alonso left for Spain. We know that he was already engaged in preparations for his voyage on November 11, 1565. See also San Agustín, *Conquistas de las Islas Filipinas,* 366–67.

3. María del Pilar Cuesta Domingo, *Pedro de Medina en la ciencia y en la historia* (Madrid: Fundación Ignacio Larramendi, 2016), 11–12. For a brief sketch of Alonso de Santa Cruz, see María M. Portuondo, *Secret Science: Spanish Cosmography and the New World* (Chicago: University of Chicago Press, 2009), 68–79.

4. Consultation of the Council of the Indies and Philip II's reply, Madrid, July 5,

1566, AGI, Indiferente, 738, N. 82. See also Geoffrey Parker, "Maps and Ministers: The Spanish Habsburgs," in *Monarchs, Ministers, and Maps: The Emergence of Cartography as a Tool of Government in Early Modern Europe,* ed. David Buisseret (Chicago: University of Chicago Press, 1992), 124–52.

5. The literature on this issue is copious. For a good discussion, see Rossfelder, *In Pursuit of Longitude,* chap. 1. Incidentally, Urdaneta was in the Spice Islands in 1529, when Spain agreed to the Treaty of Zaragoza. See Rodríguez, "Andrés de Urdaneta, agustino, 500 años del descubridor del tornaviaje," 194.

6. "Opinion of Friar Andrés de Urdaneta," Madrid, October 8, 1566, AGI, Patronato, 49, R. 12. See other opinions by Alonso de Santa Cruz, Francisco Faleiro, Jerónimo de Chaves, and Sancho Gutiérrez. These opinions were written around the same time although not necessarily on the same day. See also Rumeu de Armas, *El Tratado de Tordesillas,* 233–36; and Juan Gil, *Mitos y Utopías del descubrimiento,* 3 vols. (Madrid: Alianza Editorial, 1989), 2:90–93. For Urdaneta, the stakes could not have been any higher nor his position any more contradictory. In his youth he had traveled through the Philippines and the Spice Islands. Therefore he was well aware of the relative position of these two archipelagos and knew that the Philippines lay directly north of the Spice Islands, both at roughly the same longitude and therefore both necessarily included in the "pawned territories." This is why, during the run-up to the Navidad expedition of 1564, the friar-mariner had opposed going to the Philippines, proposing New Guinea instead. His position had been so fixed that the expedition planners had secured his participation only by misleading him into believing that the expedition was going to New Guinea, only to change the destination to the Philippines in the middle of the ocean. Nevertheless, Urdaneta had overcome this initial betrayal and gone along with the new plan to establish a Spanish base in the Philippines. In the end, Commander Legazpi had nothing but praise for the friar-mariner. "The merit and service provided by Father Andrés de Urdaneta is very great and worthy of your consideration," he had written from his encampment to the Spanish king. Whether he liked it or not, Urdaneta's lifelong work and legacy were now inextricably tied to the controversial archipelago, where dozens of Spaniards along with Legazpi had remained and now depended on his lobbying at the Spanish court for their continued survival. Legazpi to King Philip II, Cebu, June 1, 1565, transcribed in Rodríguez, "Andrés de Urdaneta, agustino, 500 años del descubridor del tornaviaje," 219–20.

7. "Opinion of Friar Andrés de Urdaneta," Madrid, October 8, 1566. See also José Antonio Cervera Jiménez, "El trabajo científico de Andrés de Urdaneta y el problema de la longitud geográfica," in Truchuelo García, *Andrés de Urdaneta,* 507–53.

Ferdinand Columbus, Christopher's son, offered his opinion about the difficulties of measuring Earth in 1524. He said that there were only two methods available. One was to use "a string" and literally go around the planet to arrive at a final circumference. Ferdinand Columbus stated that this would be "very difficult." The second method was astronomical, but, as he noted, "many wise men have offered a great variety of proofs and demonstrations." At least Ferdinand went on to support his father's assertion that in the parlance of seamen, a *legua* was equivalent to four Roman miles. See "Dictámen de don Fernando Colón," Badajoz, April 13, 1524, in *Colección general de documentos relativos a las Islas Filipinas existentes en el Archivo de Indias de Sevilla,* vol. 4, document 185.

8. As early as 1514, the Nuremberg mathematician and astronomer Johannes Werner proposed such an elegant astronomical solution to the problem of longitude: Given that the Moon is much closer to Earth than the background stars, its movement appears faster to us and can thus be used as an absolute clock of sorts. Every two hours, the Moon moves about one degree with respect to the background stars. The angle formed between the Moon and any given reference star — even the Sun — represents absolute time because it is the same wherever it is visible on Earth. Therefore, by comparing this absolute observation with local time, it is possible to derive longitude. On paper, this solution was impeccable; in practice, however, this was beyond the capabilities of sixteenth-century instrument makers. See the discussion in Costa Canas, "Longitude," 1:653–55. Rada could have also used a lunar eclipse to obtain longitude. Just a few years later, this was exactly the method attempted to measure longitude in different parts of the empire. See Manuel Morato-Moreno, "La medición de un imperio: Reconstrucción de los instrumentos utilizados en el proyecto de López de Velasco para la determinación de la longitud," *Anuario de Estudios Americanos* 73, no. 2 (July–December 2016): 597–621. Regardless of the method used, Urdaneta's report of Rada's measurements is intriguing. "From the meridian line of the said city of Toledo to that of Cebu," the friar-mariner stated, "there are 215 degrees and 15 minutes according to Copernicus's tables." Translating these values to our current system of longitude, we find that Cebu would have been about seven degrees to the east of the antimeridian. Interestingly, Rada also computed the longitude difference between Toledo and Cebu using the tables of King Alfonso el Sabio, a set of medieval astronomical tables made in Toledo in 1263–1272. See "Opinion of Friar Andrés de Urdaneta," Madrid, October 8, 1566. For a discussion of Rada's method, see also Cervera Jiménez, "El trabajo científico de Andrés de Urdaneta y el problema de la longitud geográfica," 545–53. In 1575 Rada would go on to travel to China and write a very insightful chronicle of his experiences there. See

Charles Ralph Boxer, ed., *South China in the Sixteenth Century: Being the Narratives of Galeote Pereira, Fr. Gaspar de Cruz, O.P., and Fr. Martín de Rada, O.E.S.A. (1550–1575)* (Bangkok: Orchid Press, 2004), 243–310.

9. "Opinion of Friar Andrés de Urdaneta," Madrid, October 8, 1566. See also Cervera Jiménez, "El trabajo científico de Andrés de Urdaneta y el problema de la longitud geográfica," 545–53. A navigator who returned from the Philippines with Urdaneta in 1565 was so convinced that the Philippines and the Spice Islands were on the Spanish side of the world according to the original antimeridian that he was of the opinion that it would be well worthwhile for the Spanish king to return the money to Portugal for the "pawned territories." Possibly Juan de la Isla, "Relación de las Islas del Poniente y del camino que a ella se hizo desde la Nueva España."

10. As Cuevas notes, royal audiences are usually grand affairs widely reported, and there is no evidence of such an event in the case of Urdaneta. Cuevas, *Monje y marino,* 280. Similarly, the Council of the Indies gave Urdaneta and his companion Aguirre a stipend of three *reales* per day. Rodríguez, "Andrés de Urdaneta, agustino, 500 años del descubridor del tornaviaje," 224. Urdaneta's opinion was added to those of the other cosmographers to elaborate a *parecer conjunto,* or collective opinion, brought before the king. The collective opinion was that the Philippines were included in the territories pawned to Portugal in 1529 but were nonetheless on the Spanish side with respect to the Tordesillas line. It was therefore up to the lawyers to decide how to proceed. Rumeu de Armas, *El Tratado de Tordesillas,* 133–36; Pedro Insua Rodríguez, "China y la fundación de Manila," *El Catoblepas* 82 (December 2008): 1–27.

11. The quote is from San Agustín, *Conquistas de las Islas Filipinas,* 366–67. Henry Wagner was among the first to note that "there is no record that he [Arellano] received any punishment." Wagner, *Spanish Voyages to the Northwest Coast of America in the Sixteenth Century,* 112.

12. The quote is from the entry for January 8, 1565, Arellano, in "Relación mui circunstanciada." See Charles E. Nowell, "Arellano Versus Urdaneta," *Pacific Historical Review* 31, no. 2 (May 1962): 114; and Erik W. Dahlgren, *Were the Hawaiian Islands Visited by the Spaniards Before Their Discovery by Captain Cook in 1778? A Contribution to the Geographical History of the North Pacific Ocean Especially of the Relations Between America and Asia in the Spanish Period* (Tucson: AMS Press, 1977), 161. Other maps list the same islands visited by the *San Lucas.* A map of the Pacific Ocean drawn by Gabriel Tatton around 1575, engraved by Benjamin Wright, and published in London in 1600, features the "I. de don Alonso de Arellano," "Dos Vezinos," "Nadadores," and "Miracomo Vaz." See "Maris Pacifici quod

vulgo mar del zur," John Carter Brown Map Collection, accession no. 30537a, Providence, RI.

13. Friar Gaspar de San Agustín writes that Don Alonso returned to New Spain and, on hearing about Legazpi's death, went to the Philippines in 1577. San Agustín, *Conquistas de las Islas Filipinas,* 366–67. Once again, this cannot be corroborated. In a brief biographical note about Arellano, Martín Fernández de Navarrete repeats San Agustín's version but also citing a letter that Don Alonso supposedly wrote to Philip II from Mexico City on March 31, 1575. Navarrete, however, provides no concrete citation. Martín Fernández de Navarrete, *Biblioteca marítima española,* 2 vols. (Madrid: Imprenta de la Viuda de Calero, 1851), 1:9–10. Henry Wagner cites the same letter (although in his case addressed to the president of the Council of the Indies rather than to the king), but as Wagner himself notes, there is doubt about this being the same Arellano. Wagner, "Spanish Voyages to the Northwest Coast in the Sixteenth Century," 112. A search of the Spanish archives through PARES reveals that there were indeed multiple individuals named Alonso de Arellano in the 1560s–1570s. I was not able to find the letter cited by Navarrete and Wagner but did find multiple documents of an individual named Alonso de Arellano traveling to Mexico in 1575 but who was clearly a different person.

14. The quotes are from San Agustín, *Conquistas de las Islas Filipinas,* 376–77. See also Cuevas, *Monje y marino,* 280–84; Uncilla, *Urdaneta y la conquista de Filipinas,* 247–48; and Rodríguez, "Andrés de Urdaneta, agustino, 500 años del descubridor del tornaviaje," 224–25.

Epilogue

1. Martínez, "Relación detallada de los sucesos ocurridos durante el viaje de la nao San Jerónimo que salió de Acapulco."

2. Martínez, "Relación detallada de los sucesos ocurridos durante el viaje de la nao San Jerónimo que salió de Acapulco."

3. This episode is reported in the *Historia del descubrimiento de las regiones australes hecho por el general Pedro Fernández de Quirós,* ed. Don Justo Zaragoza, 3 vols. (Madrid: Imprenta de Manuel Hernández, 1876), 1:185. For an English translation, see *The Voyages of Pedro Fernández de Quirós, 1595–1606,* ed. Sir Clements Markham, 2 vols. (London: Hakluyt Society, 1904), 1:138–39. See also Sánchez Masiá, "La dramática aventura del 'San Jerónimo,'" 529; and Francis X. Hezel, SJ, *The First Taint of Civilization: A History of the Caroline and Marshall Islands in Pre-Colonial Days, 1521–1885* (Honolulu: University of Hawai'i Press, 1983), 33.

4. Justo Zaragoza, *Historia del descubrimiento de las regiones australes hecho por el general Pedro Fernández de Quirós,* 1:298. See also Markham, *The Voyages of Pedro Fernández de Quirós, 1595–1606,* 2:237.

5. Father Juan Antonio Cantova, *Lettre édifiantes,* cited in Francis X. Hezel and Maria Teresa del Valle, "Early European Contact with the Western Carolines: 1525–1750," *Journal of Pacific History* 7 (1972): 43.

6. The quotes are from San Agustín, *Conquistas de las Islas Filipinas, 1565–1615,* 364–65; Pierre Chaunu, "Le galion de Manille," *Annales Économies Sociétés Civilisations* 6, no. 4 (October–December 1951): 452; and Landín Carrasco and Sánchez Masiá, "Urdaneta y la vuelta de poniente," 512. José Antonio Cervera Jiménez shares this last opinion. Cervera Jiménez, "El trabajo científico de Andrés de Urdaneta y el problema de la longitud geográfica," 523–25. See also Nowell, "Arellano Versus Urdaneta," 111–20; and Wagner, "Spanish Voyages to the Northwest Coast in the Sixteenth Century," 112. There is even a screenplay based on Urdaneta's life. See José María de Quintana García, "La ruta de Urdaneta: Argumento para guión cinematográfico" (Madrid: Imp. Multihispano, 1949), transcribed in Hidalgo Nuchera, "La figura de Andrés de Urdaneta en la historiografía indiana, conventual, documental y moderna," app. 1, 71–76. As I mentioned earlier, the Australian historian O.H.K. Spate was among the doubters, noting that "porpoises as big as cows present no difficulty, but it is unlikely that cooking oil would freeze in midsummer." Spate, *The Spanish Lake,* 101.

7. Ping-ti Ho, "The Introduction of American Food Plants into China," in *Agriculture and Rural Connections in the Pacific, 1500–1900,* ed. James Gerber and Lei Guang (Aldershot, UK: Ashgate, 2006), 1–11; and Sucheta Mazumdar, "The Impact of New World Food Crops on the Diet and Economy of China and India, 1600–1900," in *Food in History,* ed. Raymond Grew (Boulder: Westview Press, 1999), 58–78.

8. Dennis O. Flynn and Arturo Giráldez, "Arbitrage, China, and World Trade in the Early Modern Period," in *European Entry into the Pacific: Spain and the Acapulco-Manila Galleons,* ed. Dennis O. Flynn and Arturo Giráldez (Aldershot: Ashgate, 2001), 261–80; Andre Gunder Frank, *ReOrient: Global Economy in the Asian Age* (Berkeley: University of California Press, 1998), passim; Arturo Giráldez, *The Age of Trade: The Manila Galleons and the Dawn of the Global Economy* (Lanham, MD: Rowman & Littlefield, 2015), passim; and Kris Lane, *Potosí: The Silver City That Changed the World* (Berkeley: University of California Press, 2019), xiv–xv, among others.

Analytical Index

Page numbers in *italics* refer to figures.